UFOs: INTERPLANETARY VISITORS

UFOs:
Interplanetary
Visitors

A UFO Investigator Reports
on the Facts, Fables, and Fantasies
of the Flying Saucer Conspiracy

Raymond E. Fowler

Foreword by
J. ALLEN HYNEK
Northwestern University

Authors Choice Press

San Jose New York Lincoln Shanghai

UFOs: Interplanetary Visitors

Authors Choice Press
an imprint of iUniverse.com, Inc.

For information address:
iUniverse.com, Inc.
5220 S 16th, Ste. 200
Lincoln, NE 68512
www.iuniverse.com

Originally published by Exposition Press

ISBN: 0-595-18694-7

Printed in the United States of America

To my father, whose lifelong interest and experience with extraordinary phenomena has taught me over the years that understanding and progress do not come by ignoring or ridiculing the inexplicable. Rather, they come by facing the problem squarely through investigation, acknowledgment and study.

ACKNOWLEDGMENTS

J. ALLEN HYNEK and JOHN G. FULLER for reviewing and commenting upon my manuscript for this book. Their interest and encouragement provided motivation when needed most.

JOHN ACUFF and STUART NIXON of the National Investigations Committee on Aerial Phenomena (NICAP) for giving me permission to quote from NICAP publications.

DARREL BATES, JOSEPH SANTANGELO and ALBERT D. SIKES for their many hours of proofreading.

WALTER COOK and MERLYN SHEEHAN for assisting me in a number of ways.

JOHN P. OSWALD and JOHN REYNOLDS for providing documented UFO reports originating in New Hampshire.

WALTER N. WEBB for helping me get started as a NICAP investigator and for supplying UFO reports from his personal files for use in this book.

DR. PAUL SANTORINI for his contribution to the chapter on the Northeast Blackout.

Special acknowledgments to RUBIN SILVER, who provided the illustrations for the book, to my mother for her encouraging remarks, and especially to my wife, who spent many hours proofreading and spurring me on. My appreciation to all those assistant investigators who served me well on the NICAP Investigating Subcommittee.

CONTENTS

Part III
AN ESTIMATE OF THE SITUATION

FOREWORD

Getting the facts—and getting them straight—is all too often an unsung task. Especially is this so in controversial fields of human thought, and certainly unidentified flying objects, the mystery objects that have been reported in the skies of many countries, and on or near the ground, represent such a field. There is scarcely a country in which the concept of UFO is not well known, and "flying saucer" appears in the dictionaries of many languages. Gathering facts should always come before spinning theories. But what are the facts in the matter of UFOs?

This foreword is primarily a tribute to an outstanding UFO investigator and fact-finder. I know of none who is more dedicated, trustworthy or persevering than Ray Fowler. He is no armchair investigator or spinner of tales. For years he, and associates closely guided by him, have tracked down UFO reports in his New England area, locating original witnesses, visiting the sites of the UFO sightings as soon after the event as possible and meticulously collecting the evidence, cross-checking witnesses and probing for inconsistencies as well as for corroborations. Throughout, getting the facts straight has been his objective.

The UFO phenomenon is coming increasingly to the attention of scientists, engineers, and other technically trained people. As Fowler points out in his introduction, it appears inconceivable to him that since the number of established scientists in this and other countries (France, England, and Australia, for example) have come to the conclusion—although generally reluctantly—that the UFO phenomenon is worthy of serious scientific attention, the U.S. Air Force, the military establishment in general, and higher governmental circles would be unaware of this and not show some covert concern. Indeed, Fowler feels that the inner establishment may well have arrived at this conclusion independently, and even

considerably earlier. Their overt cavalier public attitude toward
the subject, Fowler holds, is probably a calculated posture, aimed
at "protecting" the public from matters which, because they are
both misunderstood and not understood, are potential sources of
unrest and even of panic.

Fowler has made it a practice, because of this belief, of regularly sending the Air Force a copy of each of his excellent reports;
where they are stored and by whom they are seen and possibly
even studied, he does not know. Nor does he know whether they
are consigned to the "circular file." He feels, however, that somewhere up the line they are not only noticed but even appreciated.

In this book, Fowler tells the story—in an easy and open
style—of his adventures as a UFO investigator. It is in every
sense a firsthand story. The UFOs he writes about are New England UFOs, not those in faraway places, for which documentation is difficult, if not almost impossible. And the UFO witnesses
are real, essentially neighborhood, people—people in his own ter-
ritory—who were just as puzzled by the strange events they described to him as you who read about these same events must
surely be.

A quarter of a century has passed since unidentified flying
objects first claimed the wide attention of people in this and many
other countries. However, since it is always easier to laugh and
scoff than to think, especially about things that seem to affront
our "common sense," UFOs have never been admitted to the pre-
cincts of serious science during this long period. But during that
quarter century, certain things became amply clear to those who
took the trouble to inquire seriously into the matter. First, it became emphatically clear that UFO reports are not generated by
the mentally unstable. To hold that view is to cast serious doubt
upon the sanity of people we otherwise implicitly trust and respect—airline pilots, air traffic control operators, public officers,
astronauts, skilled technicians, and, yes, even some scientists who
have the courage to own up to having had a UFO experience.

Secondly, it became clear that UFO reports do not cover a
wide spectrum of strangeness but rather describe a relatively restricted pattern of events. I, for instance, have never had a UFO

report concerned with a flying pink elephant or of an angel astride an octopus! And, thirdly, it also became apparent that, apart from the many reports that admittedly do arise from misperceptions of natural and man-made objects and phenomena and that can easily be identified as such by the mature and practiced investigator, there remain events that truly "stump the experts" and defy conventional explanations. Only these latter phenomena can properly be termed unidentified flying objects. Unless, however, such UFO reports are properly investigated and the caliber of the witnesses firmly established, many will still succumb to the easy temptation of dismissing such reports, and hence no proper investigation will result. It is indeed a vicious circle. The thinking about UFOs, particularly on the part of many scientists who are "not familiar with the literature," goes something like this: UFO reports are unworthy of attention because of their very nature; no valuable scientific time or thought should be spent on them. Scientific resources should be spent on more worthwhile things. But how, one may well ask, can one expect the worthiness of giving attention to UFOs ever to be established—or rejected—without giving them serious attention in the first place?

Ray Fowler sets forth and demonstrates, from long personal experience as a UFO investigator, the extreme worthiness of paying attention to many truly puzzling UFO reports. He feels that this worthiness has undoubtedly been recognized in some high places in our government, but certainly not publicly. The reader is left to ponder this issue. But about the existence of the UFO phenomenon itself there seems to be little question. It is an incontrovertible fact that UFO reports, from all over the world, exist.

It is my feeling that the work of Ray Fowler, and that of his colleagues in other parts of the country and the world, will come to be recognized as a solid contribution to our knowledge and as a clear call for recognizing publicly the scope of the UFO problem and the challenge it represents.

J. ALLEN HYNEK
Northwestern University
Evanston, Illinois

INTRODUCTION

After years of study, I am certain that there is more than ample high quality observational evidence from highly trained reliable witnesses to indicate that there are machine-like solid objects under intelligent control operating in our atmosphere. The aerodynamic performance and characteristics of the true UFO rule out man-made or natural phenomena. Such observational evidence has been well supported in many instances by reliable instruments such as cameras, radar, Geiger counters, electrical interference, physical indentations in soil and scorching at landing sites.

I am reasonably sure that if qualified civilian scientists and investigators are able to come to this conclusion, the United States Air Force, supported by the tremendous facilities at its disposal, has come to the same conclusion long ago. However, present official policy deliberately attempts to discredit the validity of UFOs and a wealth of data and facts are not being released to the public. It is high time that the real facts about UFOs are released. A public information program should be inaugurated that presents facts.[1]

> *Personal testimony*
> ARMED SERVICES COMMITTEE
> *UFO Hearings*

The above statement and my complete report on the classical Exeter, New Hampshire, UFO sightings were unanimously voted into the *Congressional Record* during the first *open* congressional hearings on UFOs. Prior to these hearings, all such sessions had been closed and classified.[2] Why?

I, like most of the public at large, had been both puzzled and frustrated over the controversy surrounding UFOs. Years of study had convinced me that UFOs were real and that a definite need existed for thorough documentation of UFO events. It became apparent to me that the United States Air Force was not conducting serious investigations into civilian UFO sightings unless public pressure demanded it. This procedure may have aided Pentagon policy, but it certainly was not contributing to realistic public information on UFOs nor to a thorough civilian scientific study of the problem. It was with this in mind that I decided to become a UFO investigator in order that some of the data being overlooked might be recorded properly for present and future UFO research.

I was barely a teenager when Kenneth Arnold, an experienced mountain pilot, sighted nine large, flat, shiny objects flying in line over Mount Rainier, Washington, on June 24, 1947. During the months that followed, flying silvery discs were being reported from all over the world. At that time, I believed that either people were imagining things or else the United States was testing a new weapon. However, the phenomena continued year after year. Intrigued, I collected and read everything that I could find on the subject. This interest continued through high school and college, as well as during an overseas tour with the *top secret* United States Air Force Security Service. Later, I became a member of a civilian UFO research group based in Washington, D.C., called the National Investigations Committee on Aerial Phenomena (NICAP). In 1964, I was appointed to head a technical investigating team for NICAP. This, in turn, led to my being selected to serve as an "early warning coordinator" for the U.S. Air Force Colorado University UFO Project.

Now it is the summer of 1973. It is incredible to look back over the past decade and recall what has happened since I became involved in UFO investigation. Personal on-site investigations have documented well over a hundred inexplicable UFO events originating in the New England area. The reports resulting from some of these investigations have appeared all over the world in both official and nonofficial documents.

This book is a record of these investigations. It is not just another book on UFOs written by a professional journalist or scientist. It is written by a private citizen who decided to conduct his own detailed enquiry into the UFO mystery. Within these covers you will read the inside story behind both well-known and never-before published UFO sightings. You will meet and work with both civilian and government scientists connected with UFO investigation. Together we shall see patterns and consistent characteristics emerge that are compatible with those extracted from international studies of the UFO phenomena. By the time you finish reading this book, you will have come as close to the UFO problem as most civilians have ever been, because you will be reliving the last ten years through the eyes of a *flying saucer investigator!*

NOTES

1. U.S. Congress, House Document No. 55, *UFO Hearing by Committee on Armed Services,* 89th Congress, 2nd Session, April 5, 1966.

2. "Congressional investigations are being held on the problem of Unidentified Flying Objects. Since most of the material is classified, the hearings are never printed." (Letter on file at NICAP from Congressman W. Ayres, Ohio, January 28, 1958.)

PART I

INCREDIBLE REPORTS
BY CREDIBLE PEOPLE

There has remained a percentage of the total, in the order of twenty percent of the reports, that have come from credible observers of relatively incredible things.

MAJOR GENERAL JOHN A. SAMFORD, USAF,
Director of Intelligence, in a press conference held in Washington, D.C., July 29, 1952

1

IT STARTED
WITH A HAMBURGER

It was like two hamburger buns, one on top of the other,
with a sandwiched piece of meat sticking out all around.

ENRICO GILBERTI
June 26, 1963

It was a hot, sultry night. The cool sea breezes that usually
graced the coastal town of East Weymouth, Massachusetts, were
conspicuously absent. The whole area lay in the grip of an early
summer heat wave. Enrico and Janet Gilberti tossed and turned
sleeplessly. They finally found some relief by moving the bed up
to an open window and dropped off to sleep around midnight.
Scarcely an hour had passed when the early morning solitude was
abruptly shattered by an ear-piercing vibrating roar that jolted
the Gilbertis out of a sound sleep. Quickly leaning over and looking out the window, they saw an incredible sight.

"Enrico! Enrico! Get away from the window!" shrieked Janet
as she plunged under the bedcovers in fright.

Enrico did not move a muscle. Spellbound and only half be-
lieving what his eyes and ears told him was plainly there, he just
stared. Suspended about one hundred feet above the ground and
only three hundred feet away from the window was a lighted
object fully as large as a ten-wheel truck! Two softly glowing
orange lights affixed to its top and bottom midsection unmistakably
outlined an unworldly structure. It was shaped like two grayish
bowls, one inverted upon another and connected by a darker rim.
Enrico leaned transfixed against the open screened window for a
full minute before the object smoothly tilted upwards and moved
slowly away into the early morning darkness.

I sat across the table from the Gilbertis and took notes as they related their bizarre experience to me. They were a striking young couple in their early twenties. Enrico looked in every way like the typical handsome football player, and his wife Janet could very well have been a model. They had just returned home from the beach with their little girl and were so caught up in family pleasures that they had almost forgotten my appointment with them.

A newsclip from a local paper had alerted me to the incident, and the desire to examine a close-encounter UFO sighting first-hand had prompted me to arrange this visit to their home. I was soon convinced that this pleasant young couple were neither psychotics nor publicity seekers. They were sincerely and uninhibitedly reliving a real experience.

"We stayed awake until 4:30 just talking about it," said Janet. "I couldn't get to sleep thinking about what we had just seen!"

"What did you do the next morning?" I asked.

"Well," said Janet, "after Enrico left for work, I called the South Weymouth Naval Air Station to see if they knew what it could have been. They told me that there were no aircraft in the area at that time. The man said that I would be called back for more information, but no one ever called."

"Did your neighbors say anything about seeing or hearing anything strange?" I asked.

Enrico looked at me sheepishly and remarked, "Both of us felt sort of funny about telling the neighbors about this, so we just casually asked them if they had heard anything strange during the night. Three different families told us that they were awakened by what they assumed was a low-flying jet."

I then confessed to them that I had already interviewed their next-door neighbors. They told me that a loud humming sound had awakened them about 1:00 A.M. The husband had just returned home from working a night shift. He told me that no sooner had he dropped off into a sound sleep when a "loud vibrating sound" filled the house.

"My wife kept telling me to get up to see what it was. I was too tired to get right up and was trying to figure out what it could be. Before I could collect my senses, the noise went away so I went back to sleep."

"What did it sound like?" I asked. He told me that he had flown in B-17s during World War II and had been reactivated during the Korean conflict.

"I thought I was familiar with aircraft sounds, but this sound was different. It seemed to go right through you!"

Enrico and Janet related to me how greatly relieved they both had been to find out that others had at least heard the object. Later, after the local paper had published other accounts of objects seen that night, Janet called the paper and reported what they had seen.

"I thought it would help other people who had seen something strange if they realized that they were not alone in their experience," she explained.

I left the Gilberti home and gazed back at the large power lines that stretched across their backyard and across a saltwater inlet to a large power plant. The object, by choice or by chance, had hovered directly above these power lines before angling upwards and out of sight. Little did I know then that I would witness this identical environmental situation many times during the course of future personal UFO investigations. I hadn't the slightest inkling then that this initial inquisitive visit to the Gilberti home would mark the beginning of a strange avocation—one that would involve me deeply in one of the most provocative research ventures of the twentieth century!

Upon completion of the report,[1] I decided to send unsolicited copies to the Air Force UFO Project Bluebook and to a civilian group called the National Investigations Committee on Aerial Phenomena (NICAP).[2] This, however, was not the end of the matter. I found that I could not get the incident off my mind. For sixteen years I had read and studied what others had written about UFOs. In a few cases, I had talked to people who claimed to have seen at some distance strange aerial objects that they could not identify. The Gilberti sighting, on the other hand, was startlingly different. This close-encounter case, if one disregarded the possibility of a hoax and took their verbal description at face value, left only one explanation. They had witnessed an alien, machine-like object seemingly under intelligent control. I had read about such incidents before, but I had always felt a certain nagging doubt about their authenticity. Only too often, the reports were written in popular form, without reference to such basic data as location, time and date. One wondered if such reports had been exaggerated through the passage of time or even deliberately by an over-zealous author. In most cases, one could never be sure about the matter. One was left completely dependent upon the veracity and credentials of any given author. However, when all was said and done, a small residue of reports always remained in which both author and witness credibility scored high. Such reports had elicited a continued interest in the UFO phenomena on my part.

My mind kept drifting back to Enrico Gilberti's initial attempts to describe the shape of the lighted object to me. I had asked him to compare it with some common, everyday item. He replied, "The lights were shaped like ice-cream cones but with their points cut off. Oh, I know. Have you ever seen a Turkish fez hat?" I acknowledged that I had. "They were shaped just like that," he said. "The wide base of each light was attached to the center of the top and bottom of the object."

"What about the object itself?" I asked. His answer was both classic and original.

"It was like two hamburger buns, one on top of the other, with a sandwiched piece of meat sticking out all around." Here was a genuinely honest attempt to describe an inexplicable but very real event within the context of the witness's common vocabulary and everyday experience.

This firsthand investigation of a reported close encounter with a UFO caused great consternation on my part. I asked myself how many other similar events were occurring and not being properly investigated? How could scientists and researchers ever be sure of their data if all they had recourse to was information contained in a brief newspaper account? In this case, it was no longer a question of my wondering whether the report was accurate or exaggerated. I had gone straight to the sighting location and interviewed the witnesses to my personal satisfaction. My contact with the incident made me realize that a definite need existed for the careful documentation of similar experiences. For myself, reliving their experience with them was the closest thing to actually observing a UFO myself. That hamburger whetted my appetite! I decided to continue careful documentation of UFO sightings occurring in my local area for possible use by military and civilian scientists. I would become a *flying saucer investigator!*

NOTES

1. Personal Files, UFO Report No. 63-1.
2. NICAP, 3535 University Blvd. West, Suite 23, Kensington, Maryland, 20795.

2

COLLECTING SPECIMENS

Raymond Fowler . . . whose meticulous and detailed investigations of New England cases far exceed in completeness the investigations of Bluebook.

J. ALLEN HYNEK[1]
May 23, 1972

This kind statement by Dr. J. Allen Hynek, formerly, for twenty-two years, scientific consultant to the United States Air Force UFO Project Bluebook, would hardly have applied to my activities a decade ago. I had much to learn. In the first place, I had no investigator's credentials. I had joined NICAP several years prior to initiating personal UFO investigations but had not served NICAP in any official capacity. NICAP membership is synonymous with becoming a paid subscriber to its UFO news bulletin. Secondly, I had no idea at that time as to what kind of information would be most valuable to UFO research. When investigating the Gilberti incident, I had hurriedly put together a UFO data questionnaire similar to that used by the Air Force. Coupled with these inadequacies was the fact that I was inexperienced as well as completely dependent upon newsclips and tips from friends for UFO sighting information.

Identified Flying Objects

I was not long in discovering that most UFO sightings were easily explainable upon serious investigation. A local advertising plane carrying a flashing illuminated sign at night created chaos. It generated UFO reports every time it was airborne. It was necessary to become thoroughly acquainted with its description and flight schedule. Also, it became equally apparent that a working knowledge of both astronomical and atmospheric phenomena was essential in UFO investigation. Many of the UFO sightings being reported to the newspapers and radio stations turned out to be the planets Venus and Jupiter or bright stars such as Sirius and Capella. Add to this list such things as fireballs (bright meteors), the northern lights (aurora borealis), and even the moon, and one can soon see what the UFO investigator has to cope with.

In one sense, it was discouraging for me to come to the realization that most people could be fooled by such commonplace phenomena. In another sense, however, it was most encouraging, for it clearly demonstrated that the majority of witnesses were accurately describing what they saw. The fault lay not in their description but in their inability to identify what they were observing. It is this very important factor that makes it possible for the UFO investigator to correctly evaluate most UFO sightings as either misidentification of man-made objects or misinterpretation of natural phenomena. Thus, one of the unappetizing aspects of UFO investigation is that for every apparently genuine UFO sighting, there are at least four others that can be attributed to misinterpretations on the part of the observers. Investigations of the latter, although providing a public education service, are largely a waste of personal time.

Another absolute necessity for the would-be UFO investigator is an intimate familiarity with the consistent characteristics exhibited by both IFOs (identified flying objects) and UFOs. Such knowledge serves to help in separating the wheat from the chaff at the very outset in the majority of investigations. This enables the investigator to concentrate solely on those sightings that appear to be genuinely unconventional in nature. If it were not for a continuing residue of such unexplainable events, I would have dropped the whole matter long ago. The remainder of this chapter records my involvement with a number of such incidents that took place during the year following the Gilberti "hamburger" episode.

A Strange Fishing Expedition

In a very real sense, I was about to embark upon a strange

fishing expedition for an elusive new species of fish—the UFO! In
its initial phase, specimens would be collected from the local
"pond" for a full year. This action was in direct response to well
over a decade of modern reports that a new species of "fish" had
been seen in many ponds throughout the world. This first en-
deavor would be my initial effort to discover if the *local* pond had
also been infiltrated by this unknown species. To do the job well,
I had to be very selective. Familiar fish would be immediately returned to the water. Only genuine *suspects* would be retained.

After the year was up, a return to port would be in order, to
conduct an initial examination of the "catch." What would be
found? Would the unknown fish be similar in physical appearance and behavior as those being reported outside of my local
area? Were there more than one type of fish involved? Had some
months and circumstances produced a better catch than others?
Was the government concerned about reports of these unfamiliar
creatures invading our waters? How would these initial findings
compare with what was being reported elsewhere? Answers to
these and similar questions will be sought within the UFO events
recorded in this chapter. Such answers had to be found in order
to determine whether or not the reported phenomenon was real
and to determine the need for and requirements of follow-up fishing expeditions. So, let's go fishing! The local pond in this chapter
pertains generally to that area within the boundaries of the state
of Massachusetts. The new species? UFO sightings. Our catch?
Well-documented reports.

During the spring of 1964, nationwide publicity was focused
on a series of reported UFO landings. Witnesses reported observations of a white egg-shaped craft on or near the ground. Investigators, in some cases, found unexplainable scorched areas and
markings seemingly made by quadruped landing struts. Such
reports originated from Socorro and La Madera, New Mexico,
Helena, Montana, and Newark, New York. Both the Socorro and
Newark reports featured small, four-foot-tall, white-coveralled
humanoid figures on the ground beside the objects seen by reliable
witnesses. Since detailed accounts of these events can be found
in the general UFO literature, these cases will not be touched upon

except for reference purposes. Suffice it to say that the April 24, 1964, Socorro, New Mexico, landing is one of the classical UFO-with-occupant cases reported in the United States. It was typical of similar events reported elsewhere throughout the world.

Although sightings were occurring in other parts of the United States, very few worthwhile reports had been brought to my attention during these early months of 1964. One would have thought that the publicity generated by the nation's wire services would have caused a flood of false reports locally, but this was not the case. Only one sighting was investigated and evaluated as being in the unknown category during this period. It involved only a strange light.[2] I had concluded that most "lights in the sky" reports were not worth investigating. However, a few involved very capable witnesses. Since there was always the possibility that such sightings might later supplement a close-encounter event, I did investigate those that appeared to be strictly unconventional in nature.

On May 18, an army reserve pilot and others sighted a silent, pulsating yellow light approaching Lawrence Airport at a speed estimated at 200-300 miles per hour. Captain Robert Smith told me that everyone had thought it must be an approaching aircraft's malfunctioning landing light until it abruptly performed a 360-degree turn with unchanging intensity and flashed away at a speed estimated at well over a thousand miles per hour. The object was silent and no sonic boom was heard. Other than this sighting and numerous false reports generated by the night-flying advertising plane, there were no "unknowns" investigated.

It was during these slow summer months that I was contacted by NICAP. I was told that the reports that I had been submitting to them were being received with great interest. Apparently, my reports had supplemented concurrent investigations being carried on by the Massachusetts subcommittee of NICAP. Arrangements were made for me to meet with Mr. Walter Webb, who was the chairman of this group. I was told that NICAP was interested in checking into my background and abilities for possible subcommittee membership. Needless to say, I was quite excited about this prospect.

I Am Investigated

Walter Webb arrived promptly on schedule at my home in Wenham, Massachusetts. Any apprehension about meeting him rapidly dissipated when I met this congenial, easygoing young man. Unknown to me then was the fact that Walter was one of the few persons intimately associated with the now-famous UFO-kidnapping case that had involved Mr. and Mrs. Barney Hill.[3] Walter explained to me that he was finding it increasingly difficult to serve NICAP as both subcommittee chairman and special adviser in astronomy. Since his primary interest lay in the area of special adviser, he had tried several times without success to recruit a chairman from within the ranks of the subcommittee. Astronomy was his chief interest and career. At that time, he was chief lecturer for the Charles Hayden Planetarium at the Boston Museum of Science. Since then, he has risen through the ranks to the position of assistant director. Before leaving, Walter told me that NICAP was impressed with my work thus far and asked if I would be interested in becoming an official investigator of NICAP. My answer, of course, was a resounding yes! He cautioned me that he could not promise anything but assured me that he would let NICAP know of my interest and that we would meet again.

I have introduced Walter Webb at this juncture in the book for two reasons. First, this initial meeting and the growing friendship that followed was instrumental in my becoming officially associated with the nation's largest private UFO research group —NICAP. Secondly, Walter Webb's first-hand investigations of UFO sightings reported within the New England area are among a number of reports in my files that deserve close scrutiny by scientist and layman alike. One such report shall be covered next, as we start to examine a series of incredible reports by credible people that suddenly commenced during the summer months.[4] At the time, I was unaware of this and didn't become involved until late summer and early fall, when the number of UFO sightings peaked for this area.

William Angelos, age twenty, and his mother were residing at an apartment complex in Lynn, Massachusetts. William had just completed his first year of study at the Franklin Technical Institute in Boston. He was looking forward to the change of pace that the summer months would bring. Their low, modern apartment building faced a paved parking lot set back off the street, which, in turn, was flanked on either side by two older apartment houses. The houses were close together and shaded by many trees, except at the parking lot, which was open to the skies.

"A Dome on an Inverted Dish"

On June 15, at 11:10 in the evening, William was watching television in the living room before going to bed. The room was dark except for some illumination from one lamp in a corner. His mother had gone to bed but was still awake. Suddenly, the living room was filled with a loud, intermittent roaring sound. The noise lasted for about five seconds and then abruptly died down. William rushed outside to investigate. Opening the door, he peered outside into the vacant parking lot. Astonished, he saw a red glowing light shaped like an inverted, truncated cone suspended above the parking lot about twenty feet away. As his eyes became adjusted to the darkness, he saw that it was attached to the bottom of a slowly rising domed oval object about fifteen feet in diameter.

"I Could Not Move"

William started down the steps toward the departing object. Simultaneously, he felt a tingling sensation begin from his feet and run upwards through his body. He stopped. He wanted to move but found himself completely immobilized. Stunned, he watched the object spew out a luminous white vapor trail and move away at great speed.

As the object moved off, William no longer felt the tingling sensation and found that he was able to move. He rushed in and told his mother what had happened and reported the incident to Logan Airport authorities in Boston on the following morning. The airport referred him to Hayden Planetarium, where Walter Webb was informed about the sighting.

During the course of his investigation, Walter managed to

find a supporting witness whose apartment faced the parking lot. She told Walter that at about eleven o'clock on that evening, she too was watching television. She stated that she was startled by an orange flash of light accompanied by a loud noise coming through the windows. Her first thought was that it was a plane flying into Logan Airport at an unusually low altitude. Although this was customary on foggy nights, she could not understand why it should be flying so low on a clear night. She was so annoyed that she almost reported the incident to airport authorities. She added that her television image fluttered during the brief period in which the noise was heard. Walter told me that the woman seemed honest and that she held a responsible position at the Lynn Hospital.

Interestingly enough, both NICAP and the Air Force were investigating a similar incident at Dale, Indiana, which had occurred on the night preceding the Angelos sighting.

"I Was Numb and Couldn't Move"

Charles Englebrecht, age eighteen, was alone in his home watching television. It was about nine o'clock in the evening. All of a sudden a bright light flashed through the window and the electrical power failed. Charles felt his way to the door and looked outside. About fifty feet away he saw a basket-ball-sized light hovering just above the ground. He started toward it but found he could not move, as a tingling sensation swept through his body. Dumbfounded, he watched the light rise and disappear over the barn, leaving an odor like sulfur or burned rubber in its wake.

Police Chief Leroy Musgrave reported that he could smell this odor at least a quarter of a mile away from the Englebrecht home. NICAP and Air Force investigators found a scorched area about the size of a salad plate surrounded by three shallow holes in the shape of an isosceles triangle. NICAP investigators evaluated this report in the "unknown" category and placed it on file at headquarters.[5]

One can already begin to sense that similarities do exist between the reported new species of "fish" both within and without the local pond. However, six more months of sampling remained before it would be time to analyze our catch of fish, so, let us get on with the job at hand.

Other than our friendly UFO, the night advertising plane, nothing of consequence was brought to my attention during the months of June and July. It seemed as if August would share the same fate, but the powers that guide the UFOs had other plans. On August 25, independently reported close-encounter sightings of apparently the same object caused alarm in two communities about thirty miles apart—Littleton and (would you believe it?) Lynn, Massachusetts, again!

Friday, August 28, found me busily performing my duties at my office in Waltham, Massachusetts. The telephone rang. It was Paul Winslow, a research engineer and fellow employee. He had heard of my interest in UFOs and had called to tell me of a series of unpublicized sightings that had taken place in his home town of Littleton. The twin sightings involved multiple witnesses between twelve and eighteen years old. Paul agreed to round them up at his home on the following day to be interviewed. He himself had personally cross-examined them to his satisfaction before phoning me. He knew one of the boys very well and thoroughly vouched for his integrity. I arrived at Paul's home early on the following afternoon. The boys' sighting account was both interesting and essentially consistent. I felt convinced that they were telling the truth about their strange encounter.

"A Cowboy Hat with a Bowl on It"

Norman Sheldrick, age twelve, was thumbing a ride home and was picked up by James Gaetz and John Thibeault. While driving along, they were amazed to see a low-flying oval object with lighted rim and gave chase. It descended to about two hundred feet over Porter Field just outside town. At first, no one dared to get out of the car. James honked his horn wildly in hopes of attracting somebody else's attention, but nobody was around. The object hovered over the field less than a thousand feet away and repeatedly went through a fluttering motion. Cautiously, the boys left the car and advanced towards it. As they approached it they could hear a low roaring sound.

Suddenly, it dimmed its lights and sped away over the treetops, melting out of sight into the darkness of the night. The boys ran back to the car and attempted to chase it once again but it had left the area. The time was about 9:30 P.M.

Meanwhile, John Marranzino had heard the car horn from his bedroom window, which overlooked Porter Field. Curious, he looked outside and was startled to see the strange, lighted object hovering over the field. When first seen, it had displayed many white lights around its perimeter. Only three lights were displayed as it fluttered like a falling leaf over the field. A steady red light shone to the left and right of the object and a bright white light was mounted on its dome. Size estimates varied from 75 to 125 feet in diameter, but it is possible that these were exaggerated guesses. Size is very hard to estimate unless an observed object is situated in front of some known structure. The boys described it as looking like a "cowboy hat" made of sheet metal with an inverted bowl resting on its brim. It had hovered momentarily over a church steeple before its descent toward the field.

I felt sure that others in town must have observed the low-flying craft and checked with the police to see if anyone had reported it. The police had received no such reports. I wondered then why more people do not report such apparently conspicuous and unconventional-appearing objects. Since then, experience has shown me that ninety percent of those people who are fortunate to see a UFO never report their experience for fear of ridicule and unwanted publicity. The remark "People would think I was crazy" is a common statement. Fortunately, in this case, it would appear that someone else had spotted the same object only an hour later at Lynn. I had no inkling of this, though, as I wended my way home from my trip to Littleton.

Arriving home, I found a telephone message waiting for me to call my brother John concerning another UFO sighting. I called back and found that he had heard a rumor at the factory where he worked that someone had recently seen a "flying saucer." Knowing of my interest, he had finally traced the story back to a friend of the witness, who refused to give out his name. I decided that the best thing to do was to personally confront him and try to at least obtain the first name and telephone number of the individual concerned. John arranged a meeting at the factory, and after much persuasion I obtained this basic information.

I phoned the witness. At first, he was very reluctant to talk about his experience and said that he wished he had never seen it. One could tell by his voice that he had been badly frightened. When he told me the date and time of his sighting, I gasped. He had seen an object similar to the Littleton UFO within an hour of that sighting! He, in turn, was very relieved to find out that someone else had seen something strange that night and was curious to find out more about it. This really broke the ice and we agreed to share information by meeting together at the home of his friend. He still would not give me his last name and address. I tried to obtain this data through the telephone company without success and even started a number-by-number search throughout the Lynn telephone directory. This proved unnecessary. Richard Pratt proved to be very cooperative when we met face to face and I assured him that there would be no publicity in the papers about his experience.

"An Egg with a Dome"

Richard Pratt drove into the driveway of his home, which nestled up against Lenox Hill in Lynn, Massachusetts. It was 10:30 and the weather was clear. He left the car and began walking to the house when suddenly a high-pitched, whining sound penetrated the still night air above him. Startled, he glanced upwards and stood petrified with fear as he watched a tilted, silvery, oval-shaped object slowly descending onto the top of the hill about two hundred feet away! A rim of soft white light ringed its perimeter and illuminated a domelike structure on top of the object. It halted momentarily above the hilltop and then dropped out of sight behind some trees.

The rest of Richard's story is a perfect example of the frightening effects that close-encounter UFO sightings can have upon some people. Richard told me that he ran into the empty house, locked the door, and sat with a loaded rifle on his lap until his parents came home! His mother and father were upset not only about what Richard had seen but also with his emotional reaction. They ordered him not to say anything to anyone about it. However, he felt that he had to tell someone so he had confided in his best friend. If this friend had not in turn told someone else, I probably would never have heard about the sighting. The witness, like many others in similar circumstances, did not want to be labeled a "nut." It was reassuring for him to learn about the Littleton event that had occurred just an hour before his frightening experience. Littleton was only about thirty miles west of Lynn. I made arrangements to meet with him again to examine the sighting area in the daylight. The rest of the evening was taken up in trying to locate other possible witnesses in the Lenox Hill area. I checked various establishments around the perimeter of the hill but could find no one who had seen the UFO. Richard had mentioned that there was a nursing home on top of the hill, so I decided to make this my final stop for the evening.

A long, winding driveway led up to the Lenox Hill Nursing Home. I must admit that I felt a bit uncomfortable entering a private mental institution to enquire about a possible *flying saucer* landing! As it turned out, the hospital administrator was very cooperative and allowed me to question a number of nurses. I finally found one that was on duty during the night of Richard's UFO sighting. Miss Jean Doucette told me that sometime after nine o'clock on that evening, she had distinctly heard a "high-pitched whistling sound"! She said that she had been too busy to think of investigating the unfamiliar sound and had dismissed it as some new type of fire whistle. I obtained a signed statement from her to that effect and wearily set out for home. On the way down the hill I caught sight of a fenced-in area to my left and stopped to investigate. My heart jumped! What I saw immediately brought the Gilberti incident to mind. The fence enclosed an electrical power substation that served underground power lines. Was this a coincidence, or was there some kind of mysterious connection between UFO sighting areas and electrical power lines?

Walter Webb was quite excited when he heard about another sighting in the Lynn area and joined me to examine the top of the hill during daylight hours. We reenacted the sighting with

Richard and took measurements. A search of the rocky hilltop
revealed no physical traces that might have been left behind by
the nighttime intruder. Richard told us that he and his friend
had unsuccessfully searched for evidence on the day immediately
following the sighting. In fact, one of the nurses I had questioned
at the Lenox Nursing Home had remarked that she had seen two
boys looking for something on top of the hill and had wondered
what they were up to. Before leaving, we spoke briefly to Richard's mother. She still was very concerned about Richard and
told us that he still seemed very nervous about it. We thanked
them for their cooperation and left for our respective homes.

The sighting time, direction and description ruled out the advertising plane. The manager of the Sky-Lite Company assured
me that his aircraft could not have been seen under the described
circumstances. What was it then? When asked how he would go
about constructing a model of what he had seen, Richard had
said, "I would take sheet metal and shape it into an egg and put
a dome cover on it. I would then wrap a thick metal bar around
its circumference." So, I added still another attempted description
of something inexplicable to my files. Both reports were sent to
NICAP for further evaluation.[6]

Walter felt that this recent sighting in Lynn was of particular
significance because it had taken place within only a quarter of
a mile from where William Angelos had sighted a similar object
just the month before. He pointed out some striking similarities
in a special report for **NICAP.**

1. Both occurred in the same area of Lynn.
2. Both occurred within the same time frame.
3. Both involved domed, oval objects.
4. Both witnesses felt the object was the size of a car.
5. Both objects descended from the WNW in apparent landing
   attempts.
6. Both were seen at close range near the ground.
7. Both emitted an audible sound.

Add to this list the similarities of the Littleton UFO and one could already see a pattern developing. The question was where would this strange type of domed oval object turn up next? It seemed that the wave of UFO sightings which had enveloped the western and midwestern United States earlier in the spring was now exhibiting itself on the eastern seaboard of Massachusetts. None of these local sightings had received publicity. They appeared to be spontaneous and genuine. A month was to pass before I would become involved with another close-encounter UFO sighting and some interesting run-ins with the United States Air Force. In the meantime, less spectacular, yet interesting UFO events continued. One of these involved a young amateur astronomer who worked at Hayden Planetarium as a volunteer helper.[7] Walter Webb knew him to be an accurate observer. This event took place at Melrose, Massachusetts, on August 26.

"It Wasn't a Star or a Planet"

Chris was observing the constellation Cassiopeia in the northeastern sky when he became aware of a "big red star" that wasn't supposed to be there. Picking up a pair of binoculars, he took a good look at the light source. It was a red ball surrounded by a yellow orange fringe. His curiosity aroused, he swung his telescope around and focused a 35-power eyepiece on it. The object began pulsating and started moving. He followed the silent, dark red object for three minutes before losing it in the distance.

At 35 power, an aircraft's identification lights would have been plainly discernible. In fact, it would have been next to impossible to observe an aircraft for three minutes with this magnification. I have attempted to follow aircraft and orbiting satellites in this same way and found it very difficult, as the object's forward speed is multiplied 35 times! Since the object behaved more like a satellite in orbit than a conventional aircraft, Walter checked with the Smithsonian Institution for possible satellite transits in the area. He found that the Echo I satellite had passed over eastern Massachusetts fifteen minutes after the sighting but that it was travelling easterly, not southerly. To obtain an exact plot of the object, Walter brought Chris into the planetarium and set the huge instrument to simulate the sky as viewed from Melrose on that night. Using an illuminated pointer, Chris traced the object's path across the planetarium sky while Walter obtained its elevation with the aid of auxiliary projectors. Walter's expert knowledge of astronomy, coupled with his ready access to Hayden Planetarium, proved to be a valuable asset to local UFO investigations time and time again.

Two nights later, another mystifying object was reported.[8] Paul Ellis, an aviation mechanic for United Airlines, sighted a "yellow ball" trailing a fiery exhaust cross the highway just ahead of him. The object did not "burn out like a meteor" but maintained a flat trajectory until it approached a hill, whereupon it rose slightly, clearing and disappearing behind the tree-studded hilltop. I have included this report primarily because of its interesting location. It was observed at the junction of Harwood Avenue and Route 495 in Littleton, Massachusetts!

Still another glowing-object-type sighting took place just a week later on September 6 at Medford, Massachusetts. Medford, interestingly enough, borders Melrose, where Chris McCarthy had viewed the yellow-ringed, red glowing object with his telescope!

"IT BOUNCED UP AND DOWN!"

It was almost midnight, and UFOs were the farthest thing from the minds of Tom Brooks and Anne Farell as they parked along the upper Mystic Lake in Medford. The sudden appearance of a bright, flying light jerked them both to their senses. Amazed, they watched a "bright, royal blue" object encircled by a rotating red light bounce up and down across the sky before disappearing behind a distant hill.

I asked Tom how he would construct a model of what they had seen. In the signed questionnaire, he wrote: "Place a blue Christmas bulb on a stick with a smaller red bulb about an inch behind it, and have the red light move slowly across and behind the blue one." I knew of no aircraft that carries a blue light and flies up and down across the sky like a bouncing Ping-Pong ball! The color, revolving red light, trajectory, and fifteen-second sighting duration seemed to rule out a fireball. I did know, however, that the up-and-down motion was a typical UFO characteristic. These factors and the surge of other UFO incidents being reported in eastern Massachusetts rated Tom and Anne's account a place in my file of "unknowns."[9]

The rest of September 1964 passed quietly, but October started with quite a surprise. My brother Richard sighted a UFO! His daytime sighting on October 1 was the prelude to a series of rather remarkable UFO incidents throughout the rest of that month. Richard's report[10] contains the following account.

"IT LOOKED LIKE A PHONOGRAPH RECORD!"

I had just driven into the rear parking lot of Sylvania on Endicott Street in Danvers. I was accompanied by two friends who were returning from lunch with me. We remained in the car talking for a few minutes when Mr. T. called our attention to a jet airliner flying over. One moment later, I looked up to see a dark, elliptical-shaped object passing through the sky in front of and below a large cumulus cloud. At first, I thought it was a sea gull, and since both Mr. T. and Mr. E. knew of my interest in UFOs, I jokingly said, "Look, there goes a flying disc." In a few seconds, I realized that it was not a gull and immediately tried to get Mr. T. to look at it. (Mr. E. was in the rear seat and had little opportunity to catch sight of it.) Mr. T. never got a close look at it. It looked metallic and elliptical in shape, like a phonograph record seen at an angle.

Richard, being an engineer, did not let the matter drop. He felt that enough data was readily available to obtain a rough estimate of the object's real size, speed, distance, and altitude. He was absolutely right. Very few people are able to accurately note the apparent size and elevation of an observed UFO in their excitement. Most do not remember whether or not an object passed in front of or behind something. Richard was a good observer with excellent vision. He was able to keep a level head and note these important pieces of raw data. He estimated that the flying disc had passed about five hundred feet under a cumulus cloud at an elevation of thirty degrees above the horizon. The disc's apparent diameter at arm's length was about 3/16 of an inch, or 30 seconds of an arc. A telephone call to the U.S.

Weather Service revealed that the scattered cumulus clouds were
at an altitude of 2500 feet. Using a simple trigonometric formula,
we estimated the diameter of the UFO to have been about twenty-
four feet. Further calculations indicated that it was about four
thousand feet away and flying at an altitude of roughly two
thousand feet. Estimated speed was about three hundred miles
per hour. (I mention these factors to emphasize the need for
UFO witnesses to keep their head and note such significant data
for subsequent analysis of their sighting report.)

Though Richard's experience could not be considered a close
encounter, it nonetheless added credence to my belief that some
strange things were occurring in the skies over Massachusetts.
They deserved serious attention. Stranger events were yet to come.
Another frightening encounter with a domed disc at close range
was a bare five days away. Sightings involving military aircraft
being paced by UFOs and my first encounter with an Air Force
UFO officer were to follow in rapid-fire succession.

First, the close encounter at Haverhill, Massachusetts:[11]

"LIKE A HALF BALL ON A FLAT PLATE"

It was 12:30 A.M. Robert Soucy drove his car eastward along
Broadway during the early morning of October 6. The area
was sparsely populated and bordered by cemeteries and tree-
studded fields. Robert's companion, William Chase, was gazing
aimlessly out the window when his eyes caught a glimpse of
something that sent a chill through him! Shocked out of his
lethargy, he yelled, "Stop the car!" Robert jammed on the
brakes and brought the car to a halt. "What's wrong?" "Look
back there, Bob, over those trees!" Robert looked back up the
road to where William was pointing and saw something glowing
in the air just off the road. Putting the car in reverse, he
backed up until it was broadside to the phenomenon and
flinched. There, hovering perfectly motionless at treetop level was
a domed, oval object several times larger than a car! The bottom
shone with a soft, silver glow. "It looked like a half ball on a
flat plate," Robert told me. "We both stared at it for about
twenty seconds and then got out of there real fast. No one else
was around and we were plenty scared. We drove right to the
police station and told them what was back there."

The police arrived on the scene at 1:00 A.M. but the object was no longer there. The officers who were sent to investigate told me that the witnesses were sincere and genuinely excited about what they had seen. The object had hovered over trees on the southern side of Broadway at a point about three hundred yards east from the junction of Broadway and Forest Street. A brook runs through this field, which in turn faces a cemetery on the north side of Broadway. I was unaware then that both cemeteries and bodies of water would figure in future UFO investigations.

During the next several days, two other UFO sightings took place in Massachusetts that still remain unique in my files. Both incidents involved civilians observing UFOs following military aircraft, and both generated great interest on the part of the United States Air Force.

October 7 was a beautiful, bright, sunny day. I would like to have been outside enjoying it but was very busy in my office at Waltham, Massachusetts. At 3:45 P.M. the phone rang. The excited voice on the other end belonged to Ken Lang, an engineer deeply involved in laser research. He told me that just fifteen minutes before, an employee had sighted a strange object trailing a low-flying aircraft. I thanked Ken for the tip and phoned the witness. Richard Forristall related the following story to me.[12]

"IT LOOKED LIKE A PENCIL"

I had just backed my truck up to the receiving area at the lab when I heard a very low-flying aircraft approaching. I glanced up through the windshield and saw it coming, but what surprised me was this "thing" without wings following it. I jumped out of the truck to get a good look. Whatever it was, it was grayish black and shaped like a stubby pencil with two short fins on its rear. It was approaching the plane from above and caught up with it. I watched them briefly until they both disappeared behind trees across the street. When I last saw it, the object was flying in formation with the plane, above and just behind its left wingtip.

I thanked Mr. Forristall and arranged a personal, on-site interview with him for the following day. I then quickly placed a

phone call to Hanscom Field, an Air Force base about two minutes' flying time from the sighting area. The base operations
officer seemed very excited when I informed him of the incident.
His first question to me was, "Did it drop anything?" I replied
that nothing had been seen dropping and asked if anyone in the
control tower had seen the approaching object. He told me that
no one at Hanscom Field had reported seeing it but asked me to
phone in a detailed account to the base UFO officer, Major
Brooks, after I had obtained more data from the witness. I agreed
to do this and asked him if any aircraft had landed there around
the 3:30 P.M. time frame. He stated that a C-119 and a C-47 had
landed at about that time.

On the following day, Mr. Forristall met with me at the sighting area and filled out a detailed questionnaire. His impression was
that the object had intercepted the aircraft and flew quite near to
it. After being shown both the C-119 and C-47 configurations, he
identified the aircraft as having been the C-119, a "flying boxcar."
A check with the FAA Control Tower at Logan International
Airport helped confirm this in that I was told that there had been
no commercial aircraft in the sighting area at that time.

Returning to my office, I phoned Hanscom Field and was
interrogated by the UFO officer, Major Brooks. He asked me the
same questions that I had asked the witness and again denied that
anyone on base or in the aircraft had seen the object. However,
even if they had, Air Force personnel were under strict military
intelligence orders not to admit such a thing to the public. Air
Force Regulation 200-2, which was in effect at that time, clearly
warned that:

> In response to local inquiries regarding any UFO reported in
> the vicinity of an Air Force Base, the commander of the base
> concerned may release information to the press or the general
> public only after positive identification of the sighting as a
> familiar or known object. Personnel, other than designated in-
> vestigators and those of the office of information, will not
> contact private individuals on UFO cases, nor will they discuss
> their operations and functions with unauthorized persons, unless
> so directed, and then only on a need-to-know basis.[13]

Thus, it is quite possible that the Air Force control tower operators guiding the C-119 on its landing approach observed both the aircraft and its strange companion. I was most curious about the initial reaction of the base operations officer when I reported the sighting to him. Based upon past experience, his questions should have first been directed to at least superficially establishing that such an event had indeed occurred. Instead, he immediately accepted my story at face value and excitedly asked, "Did it drop anything?"

Four days later, I sat at home in my study working on the Waltham report. A tape recorder hummed in the background, recording a radio talk show on UFOs. I was only half listening, in the event someone might phone the station about a UFO sighting. Only one caller did, but what he said literally sent the adrenalin pumping through my system. It was another sighting involving a UFO chasing military aircraft! I stopped typing and listened intently. The caller said that on the previous afternoon, he and two neighbors had watched dumbfounded as a white, disc-shaped object chased two supersonic jet fighters over the outskirts of Brockton, Massachusetts. I obtained his name from the station and set up an investigation for the following day.

"IT LOOKED LIKE AN UMBRELLA!"

Two thunderous booms pierced the stillness of a beautiful Sunday afternoon. David Hanson, Vincent Flaherty, and John (anonymous) were standing on David's front lawn. All three winced and jerked their heads skyward. Two swept-back-winged jet fighters spewing white contrails streaked across the clear blue sky. Directly behind and closing fast on the jets came a white, disc-shaped object. It caught up with the jets and abruptly stopped before dropping slowly straight down over the city. Astonished, they continued to watch as the jets continued on their course and the object leveled off at about five thousand feet and began a low, lazy, circular flight path. Suddenly, the object emitted a brilliant white flash and accelerated straight up with a blurring speed, disappearing from view in about two seconds.[14]

David told me that "the object looked like an umbrella and

was smooth all over." A spot in its midsection reflected light when it turned slightly. I wondered if this was from the often-reported central dome.

I had not been the only UFO investigator monitoring the radio show on UFOs. The Air Force had listened and had already interviewed Mr. Hanson before I talked to him on the following evening. He told me that he had been asked similar questions to the ones I was asking him. The Air Force major was particularly interested in whether or not the jets had turned around to search for the object. Unfortunately, David could not remember the major's name and he did not know where he was calling from. I had a pretty good idea who it was and decided to do a little detective work.

I phoned Major Brooks, the UFO officer at Hanscom Field. My question to him was simply, "Would it be possible for me to obtain additional information on a recent local UFO sighting that the Air Force was investigating?" He asked me for the date, time and place of the sighting and excused himself to look through his files. I heard him rustling through papers and then, after a pause, he said, "Mr. Fowler, I'm going to have to put you on 'hold' for a minute." Four minutes passed. I wondered what was going on. Air Force Regulation 200-2 specifically forbade his giving me any information at all. The real purpose for my call was to note his reaction and attempt to obtain any information that I could, regardless of regulations. Just as I began to wonder if I had been disconnected, Major Brooks' voice broke the silence. "I'm sorry, Mr. Fowler, but we have no record of the incident that you described." I reiterated that an Air Force major had questioned the witness, but he merely repeated his statement very firmly. I thanked him and hung up.

It was very strange that the good major had not asked me for any of the details relating to the Brockton sighting. This was puzzling because when I had informed him about the Waltham sighting just several days earlier, he had wanted all the information that I could give him. In fact, he had strongly encouraged me to phone in information on any future UFO reports. His not asking for further details was significant. According to AFR 200-

2, the UFO officer at the air base nearest any given UFO sighting was the *only* officer authorized to conduct an official investigation for Project Bluebook. Hanscom Field was the nearest air base. It is therefore most probable that the Air Force major that questioned Mr. Hanson was none other than Major Brooks himself!

These first contacts with Air Force UFO officers reflected a typical pattern that I was to witness many times on future such occasions. Project Bluebook was always a one-way proposition. Usually, they were happy to receive UFO information, but it was next to impossible to obtain such data from them unless the reported UFO had been positively identified. Later on, this frustrating situation would change drastically. The time would come when Air Force Intelligence would rouse me out of bed in the early morning hours to say, "A civilian just reported a UFO, Mr. Fowler." Cooperation such as this, however, was still many years away.

The year 1964 offered up just two more local UFO sightings evaluated as being in the "unknown" category. One of these took place on October 29.[15] Alfred Erickson was walking his dog along Rhinecliff Street in Arlington. Visibility was very poor and foggy clouds hung low over the neighborhood. Abruptly, Alfred stopped short in his tracks. He watched unbelievingly as a silent, stubby, cigar-shaped object descended slowly out of the cloud cover and hovered directly over his minister's house, a bare two hundred yards away! It glowed all over with a yellowish light and was tilted forward at a fifteen-degree angle. Two vertical black markings were located along its midsection, and at the end tilted downwards a darkened portion was noticed that looked like a cockpit. Alfred did not move a muscle and stared at it for a full thirty seconds before the mysterious craft shot upward and out of sight behind the thick clouds.

The last local sighting of the year in the "unknown" category took place on November 13 at dusk.[16] A bright red object having the apparent diameter of a harvest moon flew over Shutesbury, Massachusetts. Sighting duration seemed to rule out a fireball, and unconfirmed UFO landings in Brimfield and Sturbridge added to the mystery.

The highlight of November, however, was not a UFO sighting. It was official notification from NICAP that I had received the board of directors' approval to serve as the new chairman of the NICAP Massachusetts Investigating Subcommittee. Former chairman, Walter Webb, was to continue on as a special adviser for NICAP. My first assignments were to begin reorganizing the subcommittee at once and to represent the subcommittee with NICAP director Major Donald Keyhoe on a Boston radio station.

These two significant events mark the end of this chapter. Many months had passed since the Gilberti "hamburger" incident. My desire for involvement in similar enquiries had been fulfilled. A long chain of interesting and sometimes bizarre events lay ahead. A year's worth of UFO reports covering personal investigations lay in the past. The initial phase of the "fishing expedition" was over. It was now time to take a close look at what had been caught. I had just begun to break ground in this strange new avocation of "flying saucer investigator."

NOTES

1. J. Allen Hynek, *The UFO Experience, A Scientific Enquiry,* p. 136.

2. Personal Files, UFO Report No. 64-4.

3. The Hills experienced a terrifying close encounter with a UFO on the night of 19 September 1961. After the sighting, they could not account for two hours. Both developed psychological problems and submitted themselves to psychiatric treatment, which involved hypnotherapy. Under hypnosis, the psychiatrist extracted detailed and similar stories from both Barney and Betty. Essentially, they had been hypnotically kidnapped, taken aboard a UFO, submitted to two-hour physicals, and released with posthypnotic suggestions to forget the entire incident. The evidence is rather strong that this is what the Hills, even in their subconscious, believe happened to them. It is of particular importance that after the "posthypnotic block" was removed, both of the Hills ceased having their psychological problems. The book *Interrupted Journey,* by John Fuller, documents this incident.

4. Personal Files, UFO Report No. 66-6.

5. NICAP, 3535 University Blvd. West, Suite 23, Kensington, Maryland, 20795.
6. Personal Files, UFO Report(s) Nos. 64-10A and 10B.
7. Personal Files, UFO Report No. 64-11.
8. Personal Files, UFO Report No. 64-12.
9. Personal Files, UFO Report No. 64-13.
10. Personal Files, UFO Report No. 64-15.
11. Personal Files, UFO Report No. 64-16.
12. Personal Files, UFO Report No. 64-17.
13. Air Force Regulation No. 200-2A, 30 March 1964.
14. Personal Files, UFO Report No. 64-18.
15. Personal Files, UFO Report No. 64-19.
16. Personal Files, UFO Report No. 64-20.

3

EXAMINING THE CATCH

Unidentified Flying Objects: Relates to any airborne object which by performance, aerodynamic characteristics, or unusual feature does not conform to any presently known aircraft or missile type, or which cannot be positively identified as a familiar object.

USAF REGULATION 200-2

Establishing a Baseline for Comparison

In examining the "catch," I found that, including the Gilberti incident in 1963, fourteen objects conforming to the above official UFO definition had been personally investigated in 1964 within the confines of the state of Massachusetts. The next question to address was whether or not the objects reported in this localized sample were similar to the unidentified flying objects reported elsewhere. To accomplish this, it was necessary to establish a reliable baseline for comparison comprised of those UFO characteristics consistently noted by observers from all over the world. I turned first to the findings of the earliest known United States Air Force UFO Project on this aspect of UFOs.

PHYSICAL APPEARANCE

United States Air Force Technical Report Number F-TR-2274-IA had been released in February 1949. It was classified SECRET and entitled *Unidentified Aerial Objects—Project Sign.* This report surveyed 243 domestic and 43 foreign UFO sightings investigated by what was then known as the Air Material Command, which was headquartered at Wright-Patterson Air Force Base, Dayton, Ohio. It concluded that "The objects sighted have

31

been grouped into four classifications according to configuration:

1. Flying Disks
2. Torpedo- or Cigar-shaped
3. Spherical
4. Balls of light

Dr. G. E. Valley, who was a member of the United States Air Force Scientific Advisory Board and a consultant to Project Sign, wrote that:

> The most numerous reports indicate the daytime observation of metallic disk-like objects, roughly in diameter ten times their thickness. There is some suggestion that the cross-section is asymmetrical and rather like a turtle shell.[1]

Later Air Force statistics collected by a follow-up Air Force UFO project dubbed *Bluebook* indicated that of the 2,199 UFOs reported to the Air Force between 1947 and 1952: 47% were oval, 5% were cylindrical, and 24% were light sources or other shapes.[2] No shape was stated in 24% of the cases.

NICAP statistics are startlingly similar in that of 333 cases documented between 1942 and 1963: 58% were geometrical (i.e., discs, ellipses, etc.), 8% were cylindrical, and 34% fell into the category of light sources or other shapes.[3] Many of the discs were reported to have a central dome or superstructure on top.

BEHAVIOR

Statistical studies of hundreds of UFO reports have revealed typical *maneuver* patterns. The NICAP report entitled the *UFO Evidence*[4] includes the following consistent characteristics:

1. Hovering (or slow motion) followed by sudden rapid acceleration
2. Circling and pacing human vehicles
3. Satellite objects, associated with and maneuvering around larger central parent objects
4. A wobble on the axis, especially when coming to a sudden stop

5. A pendulum or falling-leaf motion
6. An up-and-down motion like a sine wave

EFFECTS

A chapter in an Air Force space science textbook in use at the Air Academy up until 1970 states that: "Some UFO Classification Systems do tend to have some common factors and a collection of these factors is as follows:[5] The text continues by listing some of the *effects* associated with UFO reports:
1. Electro-magnetic (compass, radio, ignition systems, etc.)
2. Radiation (burns, induced radioactivity, etc.)
3. Ground disturbance (dust stirred up, leaves moved, standing wave peaks on surface of water, etc.)
4. Sound (none, hissing, humming, roaring, thunderclaps, etc.)
5. Vibration (weak, strong, slow, fast)
6. Smell (ozone or other odor)
7. Flame
8. Smoke or cloud
9. Debris
10. Inhibition of voluntary motion by observers
11. Sighting of *creatures* or *beings*

CATEGORIES

One of the best attempts to classify UFO reports by *types* is by Dr. Jacques Vallée, a French mathematician and astronomer who has authored two fine books dealing with the scientific study of UFOs.[6] Vallée emphasizes that although UFOs are reported in different ways, they can nevertheless be reduced to a limited number of well-defined *types* whose characteristics recur again and again throughout the world. Vallée's investigation was based upon extensive material. He is one of the few scientists who have been given access to the unclassified portion of the Air Force UFO files. In addition, he has been privileged to draw upon both private and official data abroad. Vallée breaks reports of UFOs into five categories, or types, which I have summarized in the following table:

TYPE I.   The observation of an unusual object on the ground or
at close range to a person, construction, or vehicle

IA—Near ground
IB—Near water
IC—Intelligent signals
ID—Object scouting vehicle

TYPE II. The observation of a cylindrical or cigar-shaped object
often in a vertical mode and associated with a diffuse cloud
or vapor

IIA—Erratic flight
IIB—Stationary position—absorbing/ejecting smaller objects
IIC—Flight accompanied by formation of smaller objects

TYPE III. The observation of a stationary object in the sky

IIIA—Flight discontinuity (pendulum motion, bobbing, wob-
bling, falling-leaf motion.)
IIIB—Object halting in flight and hovering
IIIC—Object halting and changing shape or absorbing/eject-
ing smaller objects
IIID—Object halting and beginning dancing motion
IIIE—Object halting, circling, or changing course

TYPE IV. The observation of an object in continuous flight

IVA—Single object
IVB—Affected by aircraft
IVC—Formation of objects
IVD—Up-and-down motion

TYPE V.   The nighttime observation of peculiar light sources in
the sky

VA—Moving light source
VB—Starlike long hover
VC—Erratic or fast moving

A Comparison Against the Baseline

We shall now compare the fourteen specimens from our
localized sample with this overall baseline of UFO characteristics

in order to ascertain whether or not what our nets have caught is similar to the UFOs being reported on a global scale. A simple way to present an initial comparison is to construct a matrix listing the fourteen local UFO reports with a cross-reference to major baseline characteristics. Let us first consider the category of *physical appearance.*

LOCAL CONFIGURATIONS

Date	Place	Elliptical/Oval	Cylindrical	Light/Other
6/26/63	Weymouth	x (ringed)		
5/18/64	Lawrence			x
6/15/64	Lynn	x (domed)		
8/25/64	Littleton	x (domed)		
8/25/64	Lynn	x (domed)		
8/26/64	Melrose			x (ringed)
8/28/64	Littleton			x
9/06/64	Medford			x
10/01/64	Danvers	x		
10/06/64	Haverhill	x (domed)		
10/07/64	Waltham		x	
10/11/64	Brockton	x		
10/29/64	Arlington		x	
11/13/64	Shutesbury			x

COMPARISON WITH GLOBAL PERCENTAGES

	Local Sample (1963-1964)	NICAP (1942-1963)	Air Force (1947-1952)
Elliptical/Oval	50%	60%	47% (61%)*
Cylindrical	14%	9%	5% (7%)*
Balls/Light, Other	36%	31%	24% (32%)*

Proportional assignment of 24% (no shape reported)

The results of my initial comparison against the baseline were, to say the least, very interesting. UFO shapes and their statistical percentages based on the fourteen local specimens were startlingly similar to global samples taken by NICAP and the Air Force. Looking back, the local sample could also be seen to contain most of the consistently reported behavior and effect characteristics of UFOs reported on a worldwide basis. Indeed, each of the fourteen local sightings readily falls into one of the categories in Vallée's UFO classification by type. Six of the reports are divided evenly between the Type IV and V categories, but the remaining eight are all of the Type I vintage! Type I reports are truly puzzling, for they involve the observation of an unusual object on the ground or at close range to a person, construction, or vehicle. Such reports of objects so close at hand leave little room for either misinterpretation of natural phenomena or misidentification of man-made objects. One is forced either to reject such reports out of hand as hoaxes or hallucinations or else to accept them at face value. To adopt the latter position would be tantamount to admitting that unknown, unconventional, vehicle-like objects were actually observed!

In comparing this local sample with the global baseline of *physical appearance, behavior, effects,* and *categories,* it was hard to escape the obvious compatibility that existed between them. The internal consistency that existed just within the eight Type I cases was also striking! In five cases, people from different areas with different backgrounds all reported seeing metallic machine-like objects hovering near the ground. Four of the reported objects had prominent central domes, and in four cases witnesses reported hearing similar but unconventional sounds emanating from the objects. Also of significance is the fact that two silvery, domed oval objects with glowing rims and making strange sounds were seen at two widely separated locations by two completely independent sources on the same date and within one hour of each other! Two other independent reports involving objects chasing military aircraft were made within four days of each other! It is important to note that the majority of these cases received no newspaper publicity at all. Only a few cases made the local newspaper that was distributed only within the particular sighting area.

Back to the Drawing Board!

Although the results of "examining the catch" were personally gratifying, I was only too aware of the shortcomings that such novice UFO investigations posed. There was a lack of time and experience. The Air Force and NICAP questionnaires that I had been using seemed inadequate. Both overlooked UFO *effects* and were not conducive to obtaining accurate data relating to the angular size of the reported object. Conversely, I had no established UFO reporting network. I wondered how many reports I had missed. I had to rely almost completely on chance newsclips, rumors, and a few personal contacts. Results of the "fishing" expedition showed definite signs that the "local pond" was indeed being infiltrated by the same unknown "species" being reported elsewhere in the world. However, to better ascertain that this was truly the case, a larger sample needed to be collected, compared, and tabulated. I could neither do this alone nor rely on the haphazard methods employed during the past year. A definite need existed for *more fishermen and better nets!*

NOTES

1. U.S. Air Force, Air Material Command Technical Report No. F-TR-2274-IA, *Unidentified Aerial Objects, Project Sign*, Appendix "C," p. 19 (Release date: February 1949).
2. U.S. Air Force, Air Technical Intelligence Center, Project Bluebook Special Report No. 14, *Analysis of Reports of Unidentified Aerial Objects*, p. 28 (Release date: 5 May 1955).
3. NICAP, *The UFO Evidence*, Section XII (Patterns), p. 143.
4. *Ibid.*, pp. 152-156.
5. Department of Physics, USAF Academy, *Introductory Space Science, Volume II*, p. 456.
6. J. Vallée, *Anatomy of a Phenomenon and Challenge to Science*.

4

MORE FISHERMEN AND BETTER NETS

Time is but the stream I go a-fishing in. I drink at it, but
while I drink, I see the sandy bottom and detect how shal-
low it is. Its thin current glides away . . . I would drink
deeper, fish in the sky whose bottom is pebbly with stars.
                                                    THOREAU

I Will Make You Fishers of—?

How did one go about the unorthodox business of selecting
flying saucer investigators? This was the puzzling question that
faced me in October of 1964 as I looked back over the chain of
events that had culminated in my appointment as a NICAP subcommittee chairman. The former subcommittee had broken up,
and past attempts to reactivate its members proved to have been
fruitless. NICAP promised to notify me of prospective candidates
who came to their notice, but I had no idea how long this would
take. I finally decided that the best course of action was to concentrate upon obtaining initial investigators from among personal
acquaintances who had technical backgrounds. Donald Meyers,
the research engineer who had tipped me off about the Littleton
sightings, was the first to acept the challenge. My brother Richard,
a chemical engineer, followed suit. His curiosity was already
whetted by his daytime sighting of a flying disc over Danvers.
Next to join us was Lee Comly, an aeronautical engineer. Shortly
thereafter, Larry Spencer, Sylvania graphics art director, and project engineer Martin Shapiro were added to our ranks. Larry
helped greatly in the preparation of visual aids material for UFO
reports and presentations. Martin's experience included radio and

38

radar research at Harvard Observatory. Detailed resumés of these gentlemen's backgrounds were sent to NICAP headquarters for approval.

Have Subcommittee—Will Travel

By mid-November, the subcommittee was approved and issued instructions and ID cards. The number of "fishermen" had increased sixfold, but there still remained a need for "better nets." Somehow we had to let the local public know who, what, and where we were if we were to catch "fish." It was at this point that Walter Webb suggested I contact Bruce Kincaid. Bruce had been instrumental in helping organize the initial Massachusetts subcommittee in the fall of 1960. His background was in business administration. Although he was soon to embark upon a career as a naval officer, he nonetheless agreed to provide assistance until that time. His past investigating experience and keen interest in promoting the subcommittee proved to be most fruitful. In just a short time, Bruce set up a dinner meeting with Jim Westover, one of the most popular radio talk show masters in Boston. I was able to brief Jim about NICAP in general and to outline specifically what we were trying to accomplish in Massachusetts. Jim showed great interest and graciously invited both Bruce and me to appear on the popular "Night-Line" talk show in Boston. Bruce, however, did not stop there. He then phoned Major Donald Keyhoe (USMC, Ret.), then director of NICAP, and arranged his participation with us on the program via special telephone hookup. The show was scheduled for November 30.

Subcommittee organization and training were well underway when Bruce and I nervously entered the broadcasting studios of radio station WEEI to appear on "Night-Line." We had extra cause to be apprehensive. Earlier that day I had phoned Dr. Donald H. Menzel, director of Harvard Observatory, and invited him to telephone in his views on UFOs during the show. Menzel was and still is the most outspoken scientist in debunking UFOs. The very suggestion that the reported UFOs could represent real unknown physical objects caused this rational scientist to go into

a highly emotional state. Since I could not at that time understand why most scientists seemed to ignore the rapidly accumulating evidence for UFO reality, I felt that an encounter with
him would be most enlightening. It would also provide me an
opportunity at the very outset to discuss this matter personally
and publicly with one of our nation's leading astronomers.

Dr. Menzel was flabbergasted that I should invite him to participate. Looking back on the situation, I suppose that to him it
was rather like a Christian layman asking the devil himself to
join in a public debate over the trustworthiness of the resurrection
accounts recorded in the Bible! Needless to say, Menzel eagerly
accepted such an opportunity. Keyhoe was equally shocked when
I informed him of these circumstances during a preshow debriefing by phone. He felt strongly that such a confrontation with
Menzel would take up precious time that could be otherwise used
to present a good, solid case for the UFO. In a sense, this turned
out to be true. Bruce and I turned out to be just passive spectators of an intense duel between the leading representatives of
two opposite and extreme positions.

Major Keyhoe vigorously presented evidence that our government was concealing the fact that "flying saucers" were from
outer space. His documentation, if taken at face value, was impressive. Menzel, on the other hand, proceeded to brand *all* UFO
reports by reliable persons as being just honest misinterpretations
of natural or man-made phenomena. It was clear from the very
beginning that neither person was really listening and evaluating
what the other had said. Each spokesman had strong preconceived beliefs from the very start. The correct approach seemed
to lie somewhere in the middle of these two extremes. It was pre-
mature to emphatically pronounce, without scientific proof, that
UFOs were alien space vehicles. Likewise, it appeared equally
presumptuous to declare that all UFO reports were the products
of hoaxes, hallucinations, and misinterpretations just because the
majority of investigated cases proved this to have been the case.
Menzel would automatically rule out the possibility of the Type
I or close-encounter cases as actually having occurred as reported.

To defend his position, he had to label such cases as being either hoaxes or hallucinations. In other types of puzzling reports, he seemed to really stretch the reported data in order to make it fit his hypothesis. Conversely, Keyhoe refused to admit the possibility that a nighttime sighting of a *fireball* might appear to be a strange vehicle, even to experienced airline pilots. All of this just further strengthened my contention that it was imperative to build up a record consisting of carefully investigated and painstakingly documented UFO reports.

Many of the UFO sightings being reported at that time in the pages of NICAP literature were outwardly impressive but not properly documented by actual field investigation. Some were merely rewritten newspaper accounts. On the other side of the coin, even many of the official Air Force UFO investigations appeared superficial, although this might have been a cover-up for a more serious parallel investigation. In either case, a civilian scientist was caught in the middle. UFO reports were being generated on every side, and he was continually being asked by the press to explain them. On the one hand, our Air Force publicly damned their existence and restricted military personnel from UFO discussions with the public. On the other hand, civilian organizations and sensational magazines were spouting forth a voluminous amount of data about UFO sightings but were not taking the trouble to thoroughly document them for serious consideration by civilian scientists. Publicity given personalities such as the late George Adamski, who claimed to have flown in flying saucers, dealt the final death blow to any open scientific discussion on UFOs.

My few words with Menzel before he terminated his very lengthy telephone call amounted to merely stating that an examination of the better cases *as a whole* indicated an overall consistency within the reported data. I further emphasized that it was not enough to just examine each UFO report in isolation apart from the overall record but that a total analysis was necessary to establish whether or not UFOs existed in physical reality. Neither Menzel nor I had an inkling that almost a decade later we would meet face to face before TV cameras to do battle on these very same points. Again, much to his surprise, it would be by my invitation.

Bruce and I spent the latter half of the program answering the questions of interested callers and discussing the function of the NICAP investigating subcommittee. This first radio show helped give us the "better nets." It put us on the map for thousands of radio listeners in eastern New England. My home address and telephone number were given out over the air as focal points for receiving UFO reports. By the end of 1964, the initial subcommittee applicants had received training, and we were *ready to travel!*

5

THE GOAL:
SCIENTIFIC RECOGNITION
OF A NEW SPECIES

Our acceptance of any concept always seems to pass through three phases: At first, it is declared impossible. Then, as supporting facts accumulate, their interpretation is said to be erroneous. But finally, everybody says blandly, "We knew it all the time."

IVAN SANDERSON[1]

The Dilemma—No Hardware

Suppose some stranger invited you to go fishing for a strange *new species* of fish in a certain large lake. For the sake of argument, we'll say that you are a seasoned marine biologist and an ardent fisherman. Your first response would probably be: "New species? How can this be? I have fished this lake with my colleagues for many years and have never heard of any new species being caught in that lake! When was such a fish caught and who caught it?"

You would then probably sit back and listen in utter incredulity as the stranger proceeded to tell you that such fish had indeed never been caught but that many reliable persons had reported them. At that point, if you hadn't politely excused yourself from such nonsense, you may have enquired further about these fish stories.

"What do these fish look like?" you ask.

"Well," says the stranger, "they really don't look like ordinary fish at all. People who report seeing them say that they don't have tails or fins."

43

"Whoa! Stop right there!" you interrupt. "How could they swim? What makes you think they are fish?"

"What else could they be?" the stranger retorts. "They are seen swimming in lakes. In fact, they are said to swim faster than any known fish. Some say they are able to make sharp right-angle turns without even slowing down! And, do you know what? Witnesses say that for all their speed, they don't even cause the tiniest ripple in the water!"

You start to walk away, but the stranger grasps you by the shoulder and whispers in your ear, "Some even claim to have seen them swim out of the lakes and lie at the water's edge for short periods of time!"

Thinking that you have stumbled upon the dregs of a liars' club convention, you hurry away from this irrational soul, but not before he shouts: "If you don't believe me, ask Tom Savage! He saw one last year and belongs to an organization that is trying to prove their existence."

"Tom Savage?" you muse to yourself. "Why, I know Tom. He's won the local fishing derby several times. Surely Tom wouldn't get mixed up in such rubbish as this!" You promptly try to forget about this stupid incident until you come across Tom one day and proceed to ask him about an eccentric man who told you the wildest tale you have ever heard. "Why, he even said you were mixed up in this, Tom!" Tom then remarks that he had thought these bizarre reports were just so much hogwash until he himself had seen something very strange. He then proceeds to tell you about it in an embarrassed half whisper.

"I was fishing in a quiet cove one morning just after sunrise. The water was crystal clear and the white sandy bottom could be clearly seen. I was all alone except for an old-timer who was in another boat anchored not too far away. Then, without any warning, a large, elongated fish appeared moving along the sandy bottom. It was the weirdest fish I had ever seen. My first thought was that it must be a huge northern pike, but as it came closer it appeared to be silver and had neither fins nor tail. It appeared to propel itself by squirting out some kind of white liquid. Suddenly, it stopped and slowly turned upright in a vertical position, as if it were going to lunge upward to grab something on the surface. Then something most incredible happened. I thought I was losing my senses. It began ejecting from its rear a number of small, perfectly round, finless silvery fish, which sped off in all directions. I turned to watch them for just a moment and then turned back to take a better look at what seemed to have been the mother fish. It was gone! No ripples, no wake, and no sign that it had been there, except for a rapidly dissipating cloudy substance, which I assumed came from it when it propelled itself away. I yelled over to the old man: 'Did you see that?' He yelled back: 'I'll say I did to you, but I'd never admit it to anyone else. I'm sure glad you saw it too, young man, because I thought I was seeing things!' "

Now, if we continued this fish story further, we might find that the marine biologist would be tempted to ask Tom about similar reports being studied by the organization that he belonged to. Tom then would introduce him to a variety of bulletins, news-clips and paperback books that told of many boaters, bathers, hikers, and fishermen who had indeed reported seeing these strange fish in lakes all over the world. However, when he looked for the evidence to support these fantastic claims about USFs (unidentified swimming fish), all that was offered were a host of fuzzy photographs and poorly documented accounts. Looking further, he would find that some governments, seemingly in response to public pressure, had actually sponsored study programs in an attempt to account for the deluge of USF reports. Results of such studies were just as he suspected. The majority of reports could be attributed to misidentifications of common fish, reflections, shadows, and just plain hoaxes. He would be most amused to find that many USF buffs were claiming that these government studies in actuality had found proof that USFs were real and that they were coming from another dimension! The USF buffs accused the government of being afraid to release their findings to the public and demanded congressional hearings to force the Department of Fisheries to declassify its secret studies. Some of them even maintained that this department had actually caught some USFs and were secretly studying their remains!

This would be quite enough for the marine biologist. He would quickly conclude that USF reports resulted from a widespread craze fostered by cults who promoted the semireligious belief that earth was being visited by strange lifeforms from a parallel universe. If, by some chance, people like Tom Savage really had been seeing such strange fish, one would someday be caught for scientific examination. In the meantime, he had no more time to read about, let alone study, such poorly documented reports. He had a career and had established credentials in the study of *real* marine life that one could photograph, catch, and physically examine in the laboratory. He wasn't about to tarnish his reputation by getting involved with USFs. He had no time for *paper fish!*

Perhaps this analogy has helped illustrate the dilemma that the physical scientist faces when initially confronted by the *strangeness* of the UFO phenomenon. Entrenched in a busy career and dedicated to the scientific method, as well as to maintaining a good reputation with his peers, he has more than ample reason to avoid the subject of UFOs like the plague. The few UFO reports that he has been exposed to are poorly recorded. Most photographs are indistinct or obvious fakes, and the government officially maintains that UFOs do not exist. Topping this all off is the fact that two decades of UFO sightings have passed and still no one offers the scientific community any physical proof. This is the crux of the dilemma—*no hardware!*

The Alternative—Credible Software

SAUCER "CRASHES"

What about the reports that UFOs *have crashed* and that they *are* being studied in secret by government authorities? Other than some ultrapure magnesium fragments said to have fallen from an exploding UFO, there is no proof in civilian hands that the remains of flying saucers are being studied. The magnesium fragments were retrieved by fishermen at Ubatuba Beach, Brazil, in 1957.[2] Studies have indicated that magnesium of this purity could have been produced by terrestrial manufacturers such as DuPont. However, it remains an enigma as to how Brazilian fishermen could obtain samples of such. Recent studies have indicated that the fragments were of magnesium manufactured by a new technique known as "directional casting."[3] This technique was definitely not employed as early as 1957! Thus, the fragments remain a mystery and certainly provide supporting evidence to the fishermen's UFO report. However, "crashed saucers" being studied secretly by the military thus far belong strictly to the rumor mill. I have been twice confronted with such incredible reports.

A DESERT IN MEXICO

The first such confrontation involved an alleged flying saucer crash just outside of Mexico City. Back in the late 1940s, newspapers, magazine articles, and a sensational book called *Behind the Flying Saucers* told of such a crash. Although the book's author was known for his shady dealings in other ventures, the book itself did much to help spread this rumor. The remains of the crashed saucer and its dead three-foot silver-suited occupants were said to have been taken away in trucks to the United States for study. Strangely enough, I became personally involved with a similar story from an apparently highly reliable source. After I had presented my UFO lecture at a well-known church in Boston, the then assistant minister took me aside and told me the following fantastic story. I have deliberately changed names and places to assure the anonymity of my source and the witness concerned.

I became good friends with Jack Williams while we were both stationed at the Pentagon. Both of us were in Naval Intelligence. Jack told me that while on assignment in Mexico, he had received an urgent message to report to a designated area at once to assist in the investigation of an air crash. By the time Jack arrived, the crash area had been roped off and personnel were loading remains of an oval object and its occupants into trucks. He was waved off as he drove up to the area, but he continued

on and stopped to ask questions. He was quickly ordered out
of the area by a superior, who told him not to mention what he
had seen to anyone.

The minister seemed to be serious enough, so I proceeded to ask
where the witness might be located. He told me that he and Jack
had not corresponded for years but that he might still be living
in retirement at Belfast, Maine. I thanked him and later actually
located Mr. Williams and talked to him by phone. He was very
cordial when I mentioned that I had recently met and talked with
his old friend. However, his cordiality instantly changed to cold-
ness when I mentioned the crashed UFO incident. He told me that
he did not know what I was talking about and that his friend must
have made some kind of a mistake. I then called back the minister,
who assured me that there had been no mistake and that Jack
was probably just reluctant to talk about it since he was receiving
a Navy pension.

INCIDENT AT MATTYDALE

The second confrontation with such a rumor took place in
1967. One of my investigators, Nathan Gold, brought it to my
attention. Nat, a senior scientist with Polaroid, had heard it prior
to his becoming a member of the NICAP subcommitte. He told
me that he had brought along his telescope to a father-son Cub
Scout banquet and had become engaged in a conversation about
astronomy with a Mr. Bill Marsden. Somehow the topic of UFOs
came up, and Bill told Nat that back in the 1950s, both he and
his wife had seen what appeared to be a crashed flying saucer on
the ground. Nat told me of this incident shortly after he joined
the subcommittee, and I asked him to interview the Marsdens
about the incident. Nat found that both Mr. and Mrs. Marsden
were well educated and held responsible jobs. Mrs. Marsden held
a degree in law from the University of Breslav in Germany and
had held a position in the German army for several years. Mr.
Marsden held a bachelor's degree in physics and was the manager
of information services at a major electronics firm. A check of
personal records indicated that the alleged incident must have oc-

curred at Mattydale, a suburb of Syracuse, New York, sometime between October, 1953, and May, 1954. The following excerpts from a written and taped interview with the Marsdens provide a good summary of their strange encounter.

> About 3:00 A.M., on a Sunday morning, my wife and I were returning from visiting friends. We had not been drinking. As I crossed the throughway towards the airport [Hancock Field] going uphill, I noticed flashing red lights at the intersection at which I had to turn to go to Mattydale. I thought there was an accident. There seemed to be at least four or five police cars. As I approached the turning point, I slowed more than normal to avoid trouble with the accident. But there was no accident that I could see. After turning left, I looked over my right shoulder and saw an object which appeared to be twenty feet in diameter and possibly fifteen feet high at the center and having phosphorescent lights of several colors spaced over the surface. The light from these light sources was strong enough to make clearly visible quite a few men walking around the object and examining it. Some were uniformed and some were not. One man had what appeared to be a large press camera with a strap and was taking pictures. My wife remarked that it must be the Canadian AVRO disc that she had read about. On Monday morning, I did not find any news on it, so I called the city editor and asked if he knew anything about it. He said he didn't but would send a man to the sheriff's office to find out about it. I decided then to call the sheriff myself. I described the scene to the officer who answered. He said, "Yes, we know about that, but it is a military secret and we cannot discuss it." I hung up and called the editor back. He had done nothing since my first call, but when I told him what the police officer said, he was very interested and said that he would look into it immediately.
>
> On the way home from work, I puposely went by the area to examine the field. The weeds were freshly trampled down around a slight ravine. The walls of this ravine were packed down in two spots where the object had apparently rested. Tire tracks indicated that a vehicle had entered the area from one street and left toward the other. [Later, his wife said she had stopped by and examined the area and confirmed what he had seen.][4]

The city editor was in turn told by the police and the Air Force that no such incident had occurred. The sheriff denied that anyone in his department had told Mr. Marsden that the incident was a military secret. Mr. Marsden told us that after that he felt he had best drop the whole matter. He did not want the editor to think that he was some kind of a nut.

So, chalk up another sample of the "crashed saucer" rumor. NICAP attempted to locate the sheriff for questioning through its local subcommittee in Syracuse, but investigators found that the sheriff had since died. However, just prior to writing this chapter, I made an all-out personal effort to locate men on the Syracuse police force who were veterans from those days. I located several, including the former deputy sheriff, who is no longer involved with law enforcement. He denied any knowledge of the incident but did ask why I was enquiring into something that had happened so long ago. Only two men presently serving on the police force remembered something similar that had happened. The former dispatcher told me that he remembered that sometime back in those days, a weather balloon had come down, a wing tank had fallen off a plane, and a plane had crashed in the woods. A captain told me that he had not joined the force until 1957 but had heard talk about a *bomb report* that seemed to concern the same account. He stated that someone had reported that a *bomb* was lying in a field in the sighting area. Police officers were dispatched but radioed back that the object did not look like a bomb. They contacted the Air Force, who in turn took it off, stating that it was a dummy bomb filled with sand that had accidentally dropped from an aircraft near Hancock Field.

I contacted Mr. Marsden again after this recent probe and chatted about the case. Since I had just studied the original report in detail, I was very impressed with the matter-of-fact and accurate description the witness gave of the incident as he reminisced with me. Then I sprung the balloon, wing tank, and bomb explanations on him. I proposed that he might have seen one or the other objects reflecting the police cruisers' flashing lights. He merely replied that this was a good theory but that the object they had observed stood much higher than the men who encircled it. In addition to this, he further stated that the craft carried multicolored lights and was definitely shaped like a *bowl inverted on a bowl,* with a clearly defined edge where the bowls touched.

The incident at Mattydale became a deadend, like many of the other "flying saucer crash" rumors that have come to researchers through hearsay. Apart from the Ubatuba, Brazil, fragments possessed by the Aerial Phenomena Research Organization (APRO),[5] we must conclude that no UFO hardware is positively known to exist. If such evidence has been found, its presence and subsequent analysis results have been kept secret. Evidence for the physical reality of unidentified flying objects must be found elsewhere.

ALTERNATIVE EVIDENCE

"Elsewhere" brings us right back to the "paper fish" that our imaginary marine biologist refused to have anything to do with. The typical scientist would have concluded quite correctly that UFOs, for all intents and purposes, exist only in the form of verbal and written *reports.* But isn't it possible that he was being a bit hasty? His conclusion was based upon the fallacy that *all* reports and photographs were poorly documented. We should not blame him for such an evaluation, because it was usually the sensational, unsupported type of UFO accounts that had received the greatest publicity. He perhaps would have rejected newspaper accounts of the Gilberti "hamburger" incident as just a fantastic claim by wild-eyed people. However, what if he had been sent a detailed report by a competent, trusted investigator who had obtained his data firsthand from an on-site field investigation of the incident? He may still have rejected the report as impossible nonsense, but it also might have caused him to think a little more seriously about the subject.

If hundreds of similar well-documented reports were brought to his attention, it would hardly be scientific to ignore them. Upon serious examination of such reports, he would discover multiple witnesses and independent groups of respected citizens from all walks of life, all giving overall consistent testimony about structured, unconventional objects seen in the air and on or near the ground. He would also find that the reports were worldwide in scope. In some cases there would be a variety of additional evidence to support the witnesses' claim: similar burned and depressed physical traces at reported UFO landing sites; reliable supporting radar data; effects on electrical systems; animal and bird reactions; and even truly unexplainable photographs. As he enquired further, he would find that a number of competent colleagues in the field of science had also witnessed strange aerial phenomena but were afraid to publicize their experience for fear of professional and public ridicule. Hopefully, the growing UFO record would at least instigate private scientific UFO studies that would eventually lead to open international study by the civilian scientific community. It is obvious that a *crashed saucer* would constitute *proof* of UFO reality and motivation for a top priority investigation. Most likely this could be going on in very highly classified military projects, but why should the civilian scientist hesitate to investigate the growing data that is presently available? In my own mind, there was strong UFO evidence to be obtained, providing that one made the effort. I hoped to become a major contributor of such evidence, for it was clear to me that the only valid alternative to the dilemma of no hardware was *credible software!*

The Result—Data for Analysis

DATA COLLECTION

Since the inception of the present subcommittee nearly a decade ago, the methodology for investigating and documenting reported UFO sightings has vastly improved with time and experience. Most of the original members have left this area and have since been replaced by equally competent and dedicated investigators. An extensive UFO reporting net work has been built up throughout the state of Massachusetts. Personal lectures, follow-up radio and television appearances, and personal involvement with an Air Force scientific study of UFOs have helped elicit aid from local and state police as well as from government agencies and military installations. Over the years, a more detailed and efficient questionnaire was worked out to assure that truly pertinent UFO sighting data is correctly recorded for analysis.

DATA ANALYSIS

All UFO sightings reported to the subcommittee must survive an initial evaluation before being assigned to a field investigator. The UFO's description is checked against astronomical phenomena, aircraft, weather balloons, flares, and a variety of other possible stimuli in order to account for what is reported. After field investigation, if a reported object still remains unidentified, a detailed report is typed up and sent to NICAP and interested scientists. Unsolicited copies of these reports are also sent to the Air Force Foreign Technology Division at Wright-Patterson Air Force Base, Dayton, Ohio. Such reports contain signed witness questionnaires; maps, photographs and measurements of the sighting area; and background data on the witnesses. UFO configuration, category, time, weather, effects, witness background, and sighting locale information are all meticulously recorded for analysis by interested researchers. Chapter twelve contains such an analysis based upon a decade of personal UFO investigation.

As 1964 drew to an end, the Massachusetts subcommittee might well have been compared to a bunch of naval recruits just out of boot camp and going to sea for the first time! We were totally unaware that a UFO hurricane was blowing up and that we would soon be riding some of the largest UFO waves in recorded history. If ever there was to be an optimum time to collect evidence toward the obtaining of *scientific recognition of a strange new species*—this would be the time!

NOTES

1. Ivan T. Sanderson, *Uninvited Visitors*, p. 4.
2. Coral E. Lorenzen, *The Great Flying Saucer Hoax*, pp. 89-135.
3. David R. Saunders and R. Roger Harkins, *UFOs: Yes*, pp. 170-74.
4. Personal Files, UFO Report No. 53-1.
5. Aerial Phenomena Research Organization, 3910 E. Kleindale Road, Tucson, Arizona, 85712.

PART II

RIDING
THE UFO WAVES

It is important to recognize that UFO waves are sudden peaks of the number of sightings that come as an addition to a constant phenomenon of low intensity, but whose abnormal character can hardly be denied.

JACQUES VALLÉE
Anatomy of a Phenomenon (1965)

6

WE SET SAIL

I understand that you are extremely active in this field, one which requires persistence and patience in separating fact from interpretation of facts and winnowing out, whenever possible, the often considerable honest errors in the making of observations. May I wish you luck in your continued efforts.

> J. ALLEN HYNEK
> Personal correspondence
> April 15, 1965

An Encouraging Bon Voyage

The above letter from astronomer Dr. J. Allen Hynek was a great source of personal encouragement and served as a fitting bon voyage to our motley crew that had just set sail into the year 1965. This initial contact with the then chief scientific consultant to the Air Force was prompted by my investigation of a UFO sighting reported from Bethel, Vermont. We had hardly cleared the harbor, as it were, when word of this incident came to Walter Webb at Hayden Planetarium from Edward Knapp, Vermont Commissioner of Aeronautics. The sighting was initially received with great interest, because it involved reliable and independent groups of witnesses. A description of the sighting follows.

Dr. Richard S. Woodruff, Vermont State Pathologist and staff member of the University of Vermont College of Medicine, was driving back to Burlington with a Vermont State Trooper. He had just testified before a grand jury at Brattleboro. As they were driving along Route 12, a sharply defined object glowing orange red came rapidly into sight and crossed the highway in front of them. It appeared to be oval. The trooper shouted, "My God, did you see that?" No sooner had he spoken than a second object came into view, followed shortly by a third one! All were similar and followed the same flight path, climbing slightly and moving from west to east before fading into the distance.

Additional witnesses to this strange phenomena were located later. Four men traveling in another automobile in front of the doctor and the trooper stated:

> We were driving along the flat between Bethel and Randolph when all of a sudden an object crossed in front of us. It was reddish pink . . . and crossed from west to east . . . about 75-100 feet off the ground. Before we made the corner to the bridge, a second one shot across . . . and just at the top of the hill, we saw another one.[1]

Another witness turned out to be the Randolph chairman of the Board of Selectmen, who related to me:

> I was reluctant to tell anyone other than my wife until I read the report in the paper. To me, they appeared brilliant red and perfectly round.[2]

In reference to one witness's suggestion that the objects might have been tracer bullets, the selectman said:

> I ruled out any type of tracer bullet since they give out a long white trail to the point of impact.[3]

Large meteors, called *fireballs,* were immediate suspects, because the sighting date fell into the general time frame of the annual Quadrantid meteor shower. However, because of the overall description of the objects, coupled with the caliber of the witnesses involved, I filed a report with NICAP and the Air Force Project Bluebook. The Pentagon promptly responded in a letter from Major Maston Jacks, who wrote: "The Air Force evaluates this sighting as a probable observation of meteors associated with the Quadrantid Meteor Shower."[4] Dr. Woodruff, when informed of the Air Force explanation, retorted:

I am amazed that the major could not come up with a better
answer than this. I have seen numerous meteors in the past
. . . I feel most definitely that they were not meteors.[5]

I promptly prepared an analysis of the Quadrantid meteor
possibility in the light of both astronomical and witness data and
sent it off to the Pentagon. Apparently, it caused the good major
to scurry to astronomer-consultant Hynek for help, who in turn
wrote me a letter asking for more data on the case. He agreed
with me ". . . on the basis of what limited information I have that
the sighting was not of ordinary meteors, particularly the Quadran-
tids."[6] He went on to explain that "the *bolide* [fireball] hypothesis
is not entirely ruled out."[7] Actually, both of us knew that the
probable answer to this question lay in the accuracy of some of
the witnesses' statements to the effect that the object had passed
in front of distant hills. If this were indeed true, it would indicate
that the objects were close at hand rather than fireballs located
a great distance away. Many reported fireballs that appear to the
observer to be landing just a few blocks away are, in reality, hundreds of miles away. I wrote right back to Hynek, stating that:

This is one of the many UFO reports that are borderline cases.
As you know, an outline of facts tending to negate the Quadrantid meteor theory was compiled and included in our
report to NICAP and Bluebook. We pointed out that these facts
in themselves did not prove that the objects were not meteors
but that the Air Force evaluation was at least questionable. It is
interesting to note that our New England newsclip service did
not pick up any reports of this phenomena and the Smithsonian
Institution received no reports of a bolide on that date.[8]

It was the last two factors that finally influenced me to evaluate
this sighting as being in the "unknown" category.

Operation Hynek

The true significance of the Bethel, Vermont, sighting, however, was the beginning of a personal dialogue with a scientist
who was officially involved in UFO research. Dr. Hynek's public

statements about UFOs, for the most part, seemed to have been
that of an honest skeptic tempered by Air Force public information policy. Here, in a real sense, was the prototype of our imaginary marine biologist from the analogy used in the last chapter. The
very fact that he had accepted a position as scientific consultant
on UFOs to the Air Force indicated to me that Dr. Hynek must
have had some interest in the subject. Walt Webb disagreed with
me. By a strange quirk of coincidence, Walt had actually worked
for Dr. Hynek shortly before the surprise launch of the Russian
Sputnik. Walt felt that Hynek's position with the Air Force was
largely one of convenience. Project Bluebook's location at Dayton was close by to Ohio State University and afforded Hynek
an easy opportunity to be a paid consultant. Walt insisted that
Hynek then had treated the subject very lightly. Nonetheless, it
seemed inconceivable to me that Hynek, like our analogous marine biologist, could not help being influenced by the better UFO
reports investigated by Bluebook. I dismissed Hynek's skeptical
attitude as being part and parcel of an overall governmental policy
to play down the UFO problem publicly while carrying on a secret
study in a serious manner. In any event, I was encouraged that Dr.
Hynek had at least been reading the reports I had faithfully been
sending to Bluebook over the past two years. Later, I made it a
standard operating procedure to send him personal copies of all
significant reports. *Operation Hynek* proved to have been a wise
decision, for it eventually resulted in some very interesting devel-
opments that related directly to the fulfillment of my goal, i.e.,
scientific recognition of a new species.

A Storm on the Horizon

Meanwhile, January and February 1965 proved to have been
the beginning of a series of UFO *waves* that persisted well into 1967.
The initial activity in this country centered in the southeastern
states of Maryland, Washington and Virginia. The proximity of
NICAP headquarters enabled staff members to coordinate local
subcommittee investigations of UFO fly-overs and landings. One
of these landings involved *occupants.*

William Blackburn, a resident of Waynesboro, Virginia, was working at the Augusta County Archery Club off Route 250, near Brands Flats, when at approximately 5:40 P.M. on January 19, 1965, he saw two objects in the sky.

One of these UFOs, the smaller of the two, descended to the ground and landed approximately eighteen yards from the witness. From it emerged three beings of extraordinary appearance, each about three feet high. They were dressed in clothes of the same shiny, peculiar color as the object. One had an extremely long finger on one hand. The beings' eyes were particularly penetrating; according to the witness, "they seemed to look through you." As the creatures approached the witness, to within twelve yards, he froze in fright, a double-edged axe in his hand. After uttering some unintelligible sounds, the beings turned and reentered the object through a door that appeared to "mold itself into the ship." The object then ascended and disappeared.[9]

The witness told assistant NICAP director Richard Hall and other staff members that he had been interrogated by members of a government agency whom he would not identify, although he said he was told not to say anything further about his sighting. NICAP found strong evidence to support the witness's report of being silenced.

In the meantime, Air Force public information officers from the Pentagon were very busy offering irrational explanations for increasing numbers of observations being made by some very rational observers. In some locales, UFO sighting incidents were so high that frightened citizens took the matter into their own hands and began forming armed vigilante bands. The following newspaper item from the *Richmond Times-Dispatch* will give the reader some insight into what forms public reaction has taken when confronted with the unknown at close hand:

UFO REPORTS CALLED DANGER IN AUGUSTA

Staunton, Jan. 28—Reports of UFOs throughout the state but particularly in this section of the Shenandoah valley—"have gotten completely out of hand" and are now "dangerous to county residents," Sheriff John E. Kent of Augusta county said Thursday.

Kent's remarks were prompted by a complaint on Thursday

that several persons in the Brands Flat area of the county armed themselves Wednesday night and were looking for creatures which were supposedly landed last week by UFOs.

The sheriff further stated that even if the vigilante bands did sight *little green men from space* that they "had no right to mow them down." The tension became so great that the Fredericksburg justice of the peace asked Attorney General Robert Y. Button to give his opinion on the matter. Button stated: "There apparently is no state law making it unlawful to shoot little green men who might land in the state from outer space"!

While the UFO storm raged on the horizon, all remained quiet on the New England front. Other than the Vermont incident, January passed without any further fanfare. Our subscription to a New England newsclip service indicated that very little publicity was being given to the rash of sightings in the southeastern United States. News coverage appeared to be confined to just those newspapers operating within the confines of the immediate sighting areas. The silence was broken on February 18 when we received a newsclip from the *Haverhill Gazette* captioned "6 Youths see Flying Object"—which involved an alleged UFO sighting by six boy scouts conducting a patrol meeting.[10] I phoned the prime witness, Gary Smythe, and with his father's consent set up an interview for February 20. Upon arriving at the Smythe residence, I found members of the press waiting to interview me. They were interested in both the sighting and the local activities of NICAP. An article soon appeared in the *Gazette* that described my investigation in some detail.

A Saucer with a Dome!

The boys were in the midst of the game-time period during a weekly scout meeting in Gary Smythe's backyard at Groveland on February 16. At about 8:10 P.M., Gary saw a strange, lighted object approaching at low level and shouted to the others to look. The object passed low over a nearby barn and disappeared behind a row of tall trees behind the Smythe home. The boys rushed through the trees to an adjoining field just in time to see it disappearing behind distant trees. The sighting duration was less than a minute. I monitored independent attempts on the boys' part to draw the object. All drawings showed an object looking like a *dish inverted upon a dish*. Five noted that it carried a large rear white light and a bright blue light on its leading edge. All except one drawing showed a *central dome* on top of the object. Two noticed the outline of *glowing ports* around the object's perimeter, and one told me that he had heard a sound emanating from the object like a *soft hum*. Most felt it was from 150 to 500 feet high as it passed over them. The weather was excellent for such an observation. The U.S. Weather Service told me that visibility was good, with high, thin scattered clouds at 13,000 feet. The moon was only one day past full moon, and its gibbous phase brightened the night sky. Gary's father, who is acquainted with all the boys, told me that he was convinced that they were telling the truth. Their excitement impressed him so much that his first reaction was to phone the police, who in turn informed the newspaper.

I was personally convinced after my investigation that the witnesses had essentially described exactly what they had observed. Their drawings and descriptions looked startlingly similar to those contained within other reports on file, i.e., a domed disc with a glowing rim which made a humming sound. I hoped that the follow-up newspaper story would encourage other possible witnesses to file a report, but no one did. This silence on the part of UFO observers is typical. Most people are very reluctant to report seeing a "flying saucer"!

The following months, prior to my vacation in July, produced nothing substantial for the most part. A total of one fireball, two meteors, Jupiter, and the night-flying advertising plane appeared on the *solved* side of the scoreboard. The sightings in the southeastern part of the United States had abruptly ceased. My records show that only two other sightings remained unsolved for this period. One of these took place at Bradford on May 14.[11] Bradford, like Groveland, is a suburb of Haverhill.

Cup-and-Saucer-Shaped

Richard Miller and Philip Economous were playing golf at the Bradford Country Club. The weather was absolutely clear with no clouds and a blue sky. Philip happened to glance up and was shocked to see a dull silver-colored, noiseless object that looked like a "cup inverted on a saucer." It was perfectly motionless and just seemed to "hang there in the air." As they gaped at it in near unbelief, it suddenly sped away and out of sight behind trees "faster than a jet!" Hardly had it disappeared when it shot right back along the same flight path, hovered momentarily, and then shot off and out of sight again. This time it did not return. Actual hovering time was estimated to have been between six and nine seconds each time. Neither witness would guess at the object's real size and distance, but both agreed it was close enough to clearly see its strange shape.

The other sighting was reported by a minister's wife and took place on May 22 in Beverly, Massachusetts, at 5:00 P.M.[12] The day was humid and a thick mist hid the sun from view.

"I THOUGHT IT WAS A DIRIGIBLE!"

We were riding toward Beverly on Bridge Street in Salem in a line of thick traffic. It was about 5:00 P.M. on a Saturday night. We had come to a stop because of a "walk" light. I just happened to look up over the corner of a house on Bridge and Arabella Streets, and out of sort of a mist, in the direction of the Salem Power Plant, I saw what I thought was a blimp or dirigible. There were no wings. It seemed to be only a little higher than the smoke stacks of the power plant and was a dull luminous color. I called my husband's attention to it, but he could not see it from his side. It didn't seem to move but stayed right there for as long as we were stopped at the light. As we started up, I said to my husband, "Turn down this street [Arabella Street] so we can get a better view of it." But, as we turned, it just seemed to vanish.

The minister and his wife then drove along the coast to see if it could be seen again, but to no avail. Finally, they drove up to the Coast Guard station located just behind the power plant and enquired about the object.

A guard met us at the gate and we told him what I had seen. He asked a few questions and said they had no other report of it as yet. Then he said that their two helicopters were out somewhere looking for "something" but declined to say anything about it. I asked him if they used dirigibles anymore, but he said, "No, not for years." I did not hear any sound from this craft because of the noise of the traffic. Even though the day was misty, I had a very good view of it and cannot understand how it could have disappeared in just about a few seconds.

I must admit that I was a bit disappointed as our family prepared to go to the White Mountains in New Hampshire for a vacation. I had hoped that the large number of well-witnessed low-level UFO sightings that had occurred earlier in the year within the southeastern section of the U.S. was indicative of the kind of reports we might receive in Massachusetts. However, this had not been the case. The few sightings investigated thus far in 1965 were a far cry from this. The Bethel, Vermont, sighting was well witnessed but offered little detail about the objects seen. Those sightings that had offered more detail were not witnessed by adults. Although personally convinced that the youthful witnesses were sincere and generally accurate in their descriptions, I felt that most UFO researchers would not take such reports too seriously. This is unfortunate, because in many cases sincere youngsters are more apt to describe exactly what they see rather than introduce preconceived data elements into the matter. In any event, I packed my family into our over-burdened station wagon and headed north, leaving Bruce Kincaid behind to coordinate subcommittee activities. Unfortunately, other members were also vacationing during this period, which left Bruce in a very vulnerable position.

"Darling, Have You Seen the Paper?"

The trip to the mountains was pleasant and uneventful. We booked some nice cabins just outside of Jefferson, New Hampshire, which provided a beautiful panoramic view of the surrounding countryside. It actually felt good to get away and forget about UFOs for awhile. On the following day, we arose early to find a place to eat breakfast before attending church in Whitefield. After eating and while I was waiting to pay the cashier, my wife went over to the newspaper stand to glance at the front page of a Boston Sunday newspaper. Probably against her better judgment (bless her), she came back to tell me that there were UFO reports all over the front page of both Boston papers! I quickly went over and purchased the papers. My heart sank. Here I was, miles away on vacation, and UFOs were being reported all around the Boston area! Not only that, but coverage was given to sightings in the Antarctic, where scientists had seen and photographed a *lens-shaped* glowing UFO that interfered with communications equipment and sensitive magnetometers at the base. Another report involved sightings in Portugal and one in the Azores, where electric clocks had stopped while the object was overhead. The 1965 wave had started. Before it ended, people from all over the world would be sighting and photographing UFOs. Observations and photographs would be made by our astronauts and be considered "a challenge to the analyst"[13] by professional scientists examining the negatives. I was in a quandary. Vacation time was a precious commodity and I was not about to return to Massachusetts. In just a few days we were planning to visit my parents in Bar Harbor, Maine. The UFO storm that had been brewing on the distant horizon had suddenly hit my own locale, and I wasn't there to help Bruce cope with it.

Swamped by IFOs

I contacted Bruce by phone just as soon as we arrived in Maine. He excitedly told me that the situation was hectic. All the publicity on UFOs had created a secondary effect. People who normally would not have been out looking for UFOs *were* out looking and reporting almost anything that moved as a "flying saucer"! Bruce complained that he was accumulating a long list of witnesses' names but could not possibly conduct interviews with all of them. I told him to do the best that he could and suggested he keep trying to contact other subcommittee members as they returned from their vacations.

Separating Wheat from Tares

When I arrived home from vacation, the subcommittee had received dozens of reports. Out of these, only ten were actually investigated. Close examination of the accumulated data indicated that the storm had washed up all kinds of junk along with the UFOs. It was now just a matter of sorting it all out. Most of the early evening reports of a bright light in the western sky were obviously of Venus. Others turned out to be aircraft, the Echo I satellite, and (you would never guess it) the moon! The latter was described as a glowing object hovering behind the clouds and glowing "brighter than the moon"! However, some forty percent of the July sightings remained "unknown." Curiously enough, most of these incidents took place in the early hours of the morning. The first of these reports was of the *nocturnal light* variety.[14] Normally, most "lights-in-the-sky" reports are ignored, but the witness in this case was a private pilot, so I dispatched Larry Spencer to investigate. The sighting involved a strange yellowish light that moved on a straight course but with a bouncing up-and-down motion. It was seen by Harriette Rober from Sherborn at 10:30 P.M. on July 15 and later at 2:00 A.M. on July 16. She observed both or the same object(s) through binoculars and was convinced that they were not conventional aircraft by their appearance and erratic flight paths.

The second report evaluated in the "unknown" category occurred on July 19 in Watertown.[15] The witness, Miss Sally Ann McPherson, was a Northeast Airlines stewardess. The sighting account had appeared in the *Boston Globe,* dated July 21, and was forwarded to the subcommittee by the newsclip agency. I set up an appointment with the witness through her mother, who told me that because she "liked the sound of my voice" she would let me talk to her daughter. Mrs. McPherson said that she was worried about all the phone calls that the newspaper article had instigated. She had even discouraged an Air Force captain from Hanscom Field and a professor from M.I.T. from talking to Sally. At that point I was glad that she "liked my voice"!

I arrived early at Sally's house on a hot, humid August afternoon and talked with her mother on a screened porch until her daughter arrived home from work. Soon a car pulled into the yard and a very attractive brunette walked up the walk to the porch. She was very cautious at first and asked me many questions about NICAP, the possibility of adverse publicity, etc. However, I soon won her confidence and she related her UFO experience to me.

"LIKE AN ALUMINUM BALL"

I was lying in bed, sort of half-asleep. It was just about 4:00 A.M. when I saw this bright light suddenly shine through my bedroom window. I moved to the foot of the bed and looked out the window. There, moving along the western horizon, was an object like a white, silvery aluminum ball except that sometimes it would glow all colors of the rainbow.

The multicolored globe had moved about thirty degrees above the horizon and disappeared behind a tree that grew close to the house. Sally told me that she had first viewed it through a screened window but had quickly opened the window to get a better look. No sound was heard. The object glowed brightly at times and would change color by going through the whole spectrum before returning to a white metallic color. A personal check of her detailed report against astronomical phenomena and the possibility of a weather balloon reflecting the sun's rays before actual sunrise proved negative. Sally told me that she had never seen anything like it before but had talked with an airline pilot who had observed UFOs. Her estimate that the object's apparent size was as "large as a silver dollar" held at arm's length was probably a bit exaggerated, although it did indicate that its angular size was quite large. The interview ran much later than I had initially expected, and I arrived home late for supper to a very patient and understanding wife. (That is, until I told her that interviewing pretty airline hostesses was one of the fringe benefits of UFO investigation!)

Another "unknown" sighting in July involved a bright green glowing object hovering over the home of a security officer and his wife in Framingham on July 29.[16] It hovered and then moved away and then returned along the same path at a speed "ten times faster than an aircraft!" The witnesses told me that it changed color from green to orange to red as it approached and shot away over the horizon. It was also reported by another observer from nearby Route 20.

The last unexplained sighting in July took place over North Weymouth on July 31. It occurred not far from the locale of the Gilberti "hamburger" incident. The account appeared in the Quincy *Patriot Ledger,* and I asked Bruce Kincaid to investigate and document the following account.[17]

The witness, Edwin Finley, was a twenty-year Navy veteran who had been formerly a senior inspector of ships. His wife's heart condition often caused him to get up during the night to care for her. During the early morning hours of July 31, at about 3:12 A.M., Mr. Finley was up caring for his wife. Glancing out the window, he was surprised to see a large glowing object in the southern sky.

"AN OLD-FASHIONED WASHTUB"

I went and got a pair of 8x60 German navy field glasses and observed the object for about four minutes. Through the glasses it looked like a glowing fruitbasket or old-fashioned washtub. It varied in color from silver on top to orange and red on the bottom. The object itself glowed. There were no separate lights like an airplane carries. It seemed at times to be bright as the sun or an acetylene torch. Its elevation was 60-70 degrees and it moved slowly, first one way then another. It hovered momentarily at several points along its path before disappearing from view. I continued to watch, and at 4:20 A.M. I spotted the same or similar object. As I watched through the glasses, I saw two smaller silvery objects fly directly over the larger one in a criss-cross pattern. Suddenly, the large object moved off very fast and disappeared from view.

Bruce examined the field glasses and sighting stance. The glasses were of a fine quality, and a good view was afforded from the window through which the witness had observed. The sky had been clear. He agreed with Mr. Finley who said, "I know an airplane when I see it. I'm sure this was no plane. It makes you wonder."

It's the Real Thing!

The July sightings had much in common, and, as Mr. Finley so aptly said, "it makes you wonder." But still lacking were the multiple-witness, close-encounter types of sightings that we had hoped to document. The IFO nuisance continued, but there were a few more "unknowns" in August. During the early morning hours of the thirteenth, Donald O'Leary was gazing out a large, open window at the Nissen Baking Corporation. Shortly before 1:00 A.M., he was startled to see a large, low-flying, noiseless, reddish tinged, white glowing object suddenly appear from above the building he was in and move downward away on a 45-degree trajectory. He yelled for Lester Mitchell to come and look. Together they watched it level out and change direction on a low horizontal flight toward two large *power cable towers* about a mile away. It disappeared from sight behind trees about a half mile away.[18]

A week later, on August 20, a former navy *aircraft spotter* reported seeing a strange object hovering over Haverhill while he was driving home from work between 5 and 6 P.M.[19]

"Two Saucers Facing Each Other"

There were four of us in the car but I was the only one to see it. We came out of Andover going into Bradford [a suburb of Haverhill, Massachusetts] on Route 110. We had almost reached the crest of the hill when I saw it. The object at first looked like a conventional airliner, but on second sight it looked different. The thing that was missing was the rudder. I have been to *spotter's school* in the navy and still remember the instructor saying: "look closely and don't guess." The object was like *two saucers facing each other,* but not touching. It had the color of brushed aluminum or grayish silver. The total time of my sighting was approximately fifteen to twenty seconds. The sky over the city held one large dark cloud. This object was over that cloud in clear daylight. I had my eyes off it for just one moment to apply my brakes as I was coming up on another car. When I looked up again, the object had vanished as if into thin air. I said nothing to my passengers about this for fear of ridicule.

The month of August continued with the usual IFO sightings. The advertising plane and the bright star Arcturus were added to the subcommittee scoreboard. Then, it happened. A close-encounter UFO sighting in broad daylight at Derry, New Hampshire. It was the real thing! Although witnessed by youths, it was a dramatic preview of two adult witness close encounters that would follow in rapid succession. One of these would become known as a UFO *classic.* But first, the Derry sighting.

It was several days after Labor Day when I returned home from the office to find a letter from NICAP waiting for me. Enclosed was a newsclip captioned "Girl Scouts spot UFO in Derry." The story went on to relate how Dorothy Doone, age thirteen, and Patricia Walton, age twelve, of Malden, Massachusetts, saw nine strange, low-flying *humming* objects while on vacation at East Derry, New Hampshire. The objects were described as looking like *big black domes.* I located the Doone family through the Malden Girl Scout headquarters. Girl Scout officials knew the family well, as Dorothy's mother had been a Scout leader for seventeen years.

I phoned Mrs. Doone and found out that an additional daughter, Shirley, had also witnessed the weird flying objects. An interview was arranged at the Doone home for September 9. No sooner had I arranged this meeting when more newsclips arrived from NICAP concerning what appeared to be a dramatic close-encounter UFO sighting that had taken place at Exeter, New Hampshire. I quickly put in a telephone call to Walt Webb, who agreed to investigate this incident over the forthcoming weekend. I was relieved about this as I had been promising to take my family to the zoo at Benson's Animal Farm for months but had kept putting it off because of UFO investigations, report writing, and lectures. I felt that I would have my work cut out for me just to document, type, and mail out the Derry report by the weekend. In any event, I arrived at the Doone residence, where I met with Mrs. Doone, her daughters Dorothy and Shirley, and their girlfriend Patricia Walton. They told me of the frightening experience they had undergone while vacationing at Derry.

East Derry is mostly country and woods. The three girls were staying at a cabin with Mrs. Doone. It was hot and muggy. Lightning flashed and distant rumbles of thunder could be heard as an intense electrical storm slowly approached the area. Dorothy, Shirley and Patricia were hurrying to fetch water from the public well before the storm broke. The time was about 6:40 P.M. and the clouds grew darker as they crossed the fields. Suddenly, Dorothy stopped and pointed toward the south. Coming almost directly at them were what appeared to be very low-flying aircraft. Fascinated, they wondered why the planes were flying so low. Their fascination rapidly changed to hysteria, though, when they realized that the approaching objects were not airplanes!

"LIKE OVERGROWN BUBBLES"

> As they got closer, we got scared. There were nine of them and they were not planes. They looked like big, black, overgrown bubbles with silver tails. Before we could run, they passed right over the field next to us, making a sound like a swarm of bees. Then, a big spark jumped between the last three objects. We started running for the cabin!

The nine objects had no wings, propellers, rotors, rudders, insignia, or landing gear. They flew at an altitude of about three hundred feet from the ground and passed within only four hundred feet of the awe-stricken girls. No sound was heard until just as they passed by, and then only a strange *buzzing sound*. The girls ran almost a mile before reaching the cabin to tell Mrs. Doone what they had seen. Each object consisted of a very straight, slim, silvery fuselage with an upright pointed fin at the rear. Oversized dark domes like "bubbles painted with black paint" were located at the front of each object. Each fin was shaped like an inverted vee and had a red pulsating light on top and a green pulsating light on the bottom. The slim, sticklike fuselages continued right under the glasslike domes, giving them a flat, silvery bottom. The thunderstorm broke about thirty minutes after the sighting.

My first thought was that the girls must have observed nine helicopters, but as I listened to their story, examined their individual drawings, and cross-checked details, I became more and more convinced that they had witnessed some very unconventional flying objects. All were familiar with airplanes and helicopters. Mrs. Doone told me that when they ran into the camp, they could hardly tell her what had happened. She told me that as soon as she had calmed them down, she asked her oldest daugh-

ter, Dorothy, to sketch the objects. She had no trouble doing
so. Dorothy's original sketch agrees essentially with the individual
sketches drawn for me during the interview. The only difference
was that the girls were a bit unsure as to what part of the objects'
fins produced the one-to-two-second continuous spark. Mrs.
Doone was a great help to me in that she did not attempt to coach
her children and was able to give me a very good description of
the sighting area, with which she was intimately familiar.

One could conclude that the objects were helicopters and that
the account was grossly exaggerated. The "lightning-like spark"
could have actually been lightning flashing directly behind the last
three helicopters. However, this does not seem to have been the
case. In the first place, the objects were reportedly very close at
hand. Each appeared to be as large as two cars placed end-to-end
at a distance of four hundred feet. One would have easily seen
and heard the clatter of helicopter rotors at that distance. I
checked with Lee Comly, the subcommittee aeronautical engineer, and an Army pilot about the possibility of the objects'
having been helicopters. Both pointed out that the pulsating red
and green lights on the fins did not correspond with the posi-
tioning, number, and color of conventional taillights.

Next, I enquired into the possibility that the objects were
airplanes. Airplanes seemed to be the least likely answer, because
the objects had no rudder, no wings, and no visible means of
propulsion. Aircraft engines would have produced a tremendous
conventional sound at that range. The objects, however, were
completely silent until they were broadside to the witnesses. One
newspaper account suggested that they were probably some kind
of aircraft out of Grenier AFB near Manchester, New Hampshire, but added that "others had been reporting flying objects"
and that "the girls' sightings should not be totally dismissed."
Grenier AFB was about ten miles northwest of the sighting area
and Pease AFB about thirty miles northeast of the area. A check
with the Air Force indicated that Grenier Air Force Base had
been deactivated and was civilian except for a small reserve wing
of C-119 Flying Boxcars. There were no military helicopters stationed there.

It was hard for me to believe that the witnesses had sighted nine helicopters flying so low in such close formation shortly before a severe thunderstorm. Other than a few Coast Guard helicopters and a civilian taxi helicopter in the Boston area, there just were none supposed to be flying in that area. One very rarely sees more than one helicopter flying at a time. Nine helicopters would be most unusual. I felt sure that the incident was not a hoax. After taking all data into consideration, I evaluated the Derry incident as falling into the "unknown" category of UFO sightings.

The next few days found me checking out, typing, and reproducing the Derry report.[20] Papers were scattered pell-mell all over the living room floor that Friday night when my wife gently reminded me that we were "bringing the children to the zoo in the morning"! I told her that I would stay up late in order to get copies of the report prepared for mailing in the morning, just so we could all go to the zoo. Then disaster struck! The telephone rang. It was Walter Webb. He told me apologetically that circumstances had forced him to cancel his trip to Exeter on the following morning and asked whether I could go. This immediately put me into an all too familiar, frustrating situation. UFOs, which officially did not even exist, nevertheless managed somehow to continually disrupt my already busy family and church life! Walter urged me to go or send someone else, as it would be at least two weeks before he could go himself. In the meantime, the newspaper reports about the already one-week-old Exeter incident seemed to demand prompt on-site field investigation while the event was still fresh in the witnesses' minds. It was too late to assign anyone else and Walter had not even made any appointments with the witnesses. I thanked him for calling and hung up. What was I to do? Should I go to Exeter tomorrow or the zoo?

NOTES

1. Personal Files, UFO Report No. 65-1.
2. *Ibid.*
3. *Ibid.*

4. Personal Correspondence, dated 27 January 1965.
5. Personal Correspondence, dated 9 February 1965.
6. Personal Correspondence, dated 15 April 1965.
7. *Ibid.*
8. Personal Correspondence, dated 1 May 1965.
9. NICAP, *UFOs: A New Look,* p. 30.
10. Personal Files, UFO Report No. 65-3.
11. Personal Files, UFO Report No. 65-10.
12. Personal Files, UFO Report No. 65-11A.
13. Edward U. Condon, *Scientific Study of Unidentified Flying Objects,* p. 208.
14. Personal Files, UFO Report No. 65-14.
15. Personal Files, UFO Report No. 65-15.
16. Personal Files, UFO Report No. 65-21.
17. Personal Files, UFO Report No. 65-22.
18. Personal Files, UFO Report No. 65-24.
19. Personal Files, UFO Report No. 65-26.
20. Personal Files, UFO Report No. 65-29.

7

TO EXETER OR THE ZOO?

Congressman Bates: *I have here a [report] from a constituent of mine. . . . I would like to get unanimous consent to insert [it] in the record.*
Chairman Mendel Rivers: *Without objection.*

UFO Congressional Hearings,
HOUSE ARMED SERVICES DOCUMENT 55,
5 April 1966

Behind "the Incident at Exeter"

"BUT, DARLING, YOU PROMISED!"

"Who was that, dear?" my wife Margaret asked as I returned to collating the Derry report on the living room floor.

"That was Walter," I replied. "He says he can't investigate that sighting in Exeter tomorrow." Then the question that I dreaded to answer came sailing across the room.

"Well, it can be investigated some other time, can't it? You don't have to go, do you? Remember, we're going to the zoo tomorrow!"

I explained that I wasn't sure what to do and that the sighting appeared to be highly significant, if the newspaper accounts were accurate. She then reminded me of the many times that newspaper reports of UFO sightings turned out to be a garbled version of the actual facts. Indeed, Walter himself had not seemed that impressed and had pointed out similar arguments to me. However, I had also been urged to look into the sighting by a friend whose niece was a policewoman at Exeter. Her niece had told her that the Air Force had already investigated. My mind was in turmoil, so I changed the subject and continued working on the Derry report. Margaret went to bed. By the time I retired,

I had made up my mind that the Exeter sighting could not be put off until later. It had to be investigated now before the trail got cold.

My wife was still awake as I set the alarm for 5:00 A.M. "What have you decided, dear?" she yawned.

"I'm sorry, dear, but I feel that I must get to Exeter just as soon as possible. I'm leaving early in the morning to allow plenty of time to locate the witnesses."

"But, darling, you promised we'd be going to the zoo with the kids tomorrow!"

"I know," I said, "and if this were just a run-of-the-mill type of UFO report, we'd still be going, but I feel strongly about this one." I told her that we could go out for a family ride elsewhere if I got back from Exeter in time. She accepted the situation, but I know that she was bitterly disappointed. It was at times like this that I wondered what on earth I was doing in this business of investigating *flying saucers!* For some deep-seated reason, I seemed addicted to UFO investigation. To me, the very existence of UFOs, if proved, could very well be the most important scientific discovery that mankind had ever made. If they proved to be extraterrestrial vehicles, the implications were beyond comprehension!

"GOOD MORNING, OFFICER!"

The alarm clock jolted me out of a sound sleep. It seemed as if I had just set it! It was mighty tempting to just turn over and go back to sleep. I was dead tired, but my conscience was wide awake and putting in overtime, telling me what a *fink* I was for not taking the kids to the zoo. But I slipped out of bed, showered, shaved, ate and was soon on Route 95 heading towards Exeter. To tell the truth, I was really wondering whether I shouldn't have waited until definite appointments had been set up with the witnesses. No one knew I was coming, and I had no assurance whatsoever that I would be able to talk to any one of them. My approach to this case was highly unorthodox. I had made it a personal rule never to send an investigator to the field without first performing a telephone investigation and setting up definite witness interviews in advance. In this case, I had done neither. Here I was, well on the way, and there was no turning back. I headed directly for the police station. "Who knows?" I thought, "perhaps Officers Bertrand and Hunt will be on duty and be willing to talk right now."

The little town of Exeter at 6:40 A.M. on Saturday morning, September 11, was dead. It was still fairly dark, and neither traffic nor pedestrians were to be seen. I parked in front of the police station, took a deep breath, and strode into the front lobby, trying to look as official as possible. I dropped my NICAP ID card in front of the semiconscious policeman hunched over the front desk. He looked up, startled. Before he had a chance to say anything, I said in the most authoritative tone I could muster, "Good morning, officer, my name is Raymond Fowler. I represent the National Investigations Committee on Aerial Phenomena in Washington and have a few questions to ask about a UFO sighting in this area!"

"The National what?" he said.

I then proceeded to tell him about NICAP and our interest in documenting the Exeter case.

"Oh," said another officer who had been standing unnoticed on the other side of the room. "You're with that Major Keyhoe's group."

I replied in the affirmative and asked if it would be possible to talk with Officers Bertrand and Hunt.

The officer at the desk chuckled. "That's Hunt right there!"

I turned to look at Hunt, who had just turned a shade of red.

"Well," I said, "can we sit down and talk about it?"

"What's there to talk about? It's all in the papers," he cautiously replied.

I showed him the standard, eight-page Air Force questionnaire and explained that I wanted him to fill it in and sign it. It took a bit of convincing at first, but he finally agreed to do it.

Officer Hunt explained that he had been called to the UFO sighting area to assist Officer Bertrand, who had radioed the station for help. Bertrand had gone to a field earlier with a teenager, Norman Muscarello, to investigate the boy's story that a

UFO had chased him. While walking in the field with Norman, the UFO had suddenly appeared again and made passes at them. "By the time I got there," Hunt said, "the object was moving off to the tree line, performing fantastic maneuvers. It made right-angle turns and sort of floated down like a falling leaf. Then it took off toward Hampton and chased another guy in a car." Hunt then gave me directions to Norman Muscarello's house. He said that if I returned to the station at eight o'clock, he would phone Officer Bertrand and ask him to cooperate with me. I thanked him and headed off to Muscarello's house.

The house was unlighted when I arrived and knocked on the door. Mrs. Muscarello warily opened the door just a crack and we talked. She would not let me in and seemed very upset about all the phone calls and publicity. She told me that Norman had left the state and would not return until September 14. She related to me that both Air Force and Navy officers had visited to question him. I obtained Norman's account through her and made arrangements to talk to him personally at a later date. I then returned to the police station, where Hunt called Bertrand and persuaded him to talk with me. Hunt went off duty and I left for Bertrand's home, whose address, believe it or not, was *Pickpocket Road!*

Officer Bertrand invited me in and proceeded to interrogate *me!* He explained later that he wanted to assure himself that I wasn't "some kind of a nut." He told me that several days after the sighting, a man had driven into his yard in a car that had a sign on it reading "UFO Investigator."

"Somehow, the guy persuaded me to let him into the house, and he made some real crazy remarks. He really scared my wife. He told her that perhaps 'they,' the *UFO operators,* were after me!"

"Oh, I think I know who that was," I said. "Was he a real friendly looking fellow with a bald head?"

"Yeh, that's what he looked like. When he said that to my wife, that was enough for me. I got rid of him real fast! You seem to be serious about this, and I'm willing to tell you exactly what happened but no more. I don't want to speculate about it. If

you'll drive me down to the field where I saw this thing, I'll fill
out your forms and talk to you about it."

As we drove to the field, Bertrand told me how he had come
upon a woman parked in an automobile on Route 101 about an
hour before his own experience.

"I thought she had car trouble, but she was real upset and
told me that a red glowing object had chased her! I looked
around but didn't see anything except a bright star, so I sent
her home. Then, about an hour later, I got a call from the station
telling me to report in at once. A kid had just come into the
station all shook up about some object that had chased him."

"What on earth was a kid doing out that time of night?" I
asked.

"He was hitchhiking between Amesbury and Exeter along
Route 150. He'd been visiting a girlfriend." Bertrand continued
and related to me how he had gone back to the station, picked
up Norman, and brought him back to the field where he had
seen the UFO. "I know this kid," he said. "He's real tough. It
would take a lot to scare him, but something must have really
scared him. He could hardly hold his cigarette and was as pale
as a sheet! Whoops, slow down. This is the place, right here."

I turned around and parked at the head of a field that lay
between the Clyde Russell and Carl Dining farms. Bertrand continued his story as we sat in my car.

"Norman and I came out here and I parked right about
where we are parked right now. We sat looking for several minutes but didn't see anything unusual. I radioed the station and
told them that there was nothing out here. They asked me to take
a walk into the field for a quick look before coming back in. I felt
kind of foolish walking out here on private property after midnight, looking for a *flying saucer!*"

Bertrand then suggested that we go out to the field so that
he could show me where he and Norman had been. We got
out of the car and strolled into the field toward a corral.

"We walked out about this far," he said. "I waved my flashlight back and forth, and then Norman shouted—'Look out, here

it comes!' I swung around and could hardly believe what I was seeing. There was this huge, dark object as big as that barn over there with red flashing lights on it. It barely cleared that tree right there, and it was moving back and forth."

"What did you guys do when you saw that thing?" I asked.

"Well, it seemed to tilt and come right at us. Norman told me later that I was yelling, 'I'll shoot it! I'll shoot it!' I did automatically drop on one knee and drew my service revolver, but I didn't shoot. I do remember suddenly thinking that it would be unwise to fire at it, so I yelled to Norman to run for the cruiser, but he just froze in his tracks. I practically had to drag him back!"

"How close was the object to you then?" I asked.

"It seemed to be about one hundred feet up and about one hundred feet away. All I could see at that point was bright red with sort of a halo effect. I thought we'd be burned alive, but it gave off no heat and I didn't hear any noise. I called Dave Hunt on the radio. He was already on his way out here and arrived in just a few minutes. Whatever it was, it must have really scared the horses in that barn."

"Why do you say that? Did you hear them from here?" I asked.

"Yeh, you could hear them neighing and kicking in their stalls. Even the dogs around here started howling. When Dave arrived, the three of us just stood there and watched it. It floated, wobbled, and did things that no plane could do. Then it just darted away over those trees toward Hampton."

"What did you do then?" I asked.

"Well, we all returned to the station to write up our report. We'd only been back a short while when a call came in from the Hampton telephone operator. She told us that she'd just talked to a man who was calling from a phone booth and was very upset. He said that he was being chased by a flying saucer and that it was still out there! Before she could connect him with us, the connection was broken. We went out looking for him and even went to the hospital to see if he'd been brought in there, but we never found out who he was."

As Bertrand and I walked back toward my car, I was thinking to myself, "This really happened! He's reliving a real event!" My heart was literally pounding in empathy as we sat down in the front seat to fill in forms and continue the interview. I sat there entranced, wistfully looking at the field while he pencilled in answers on the questionnaire. As he passed me the forms, I remarked to him, *"This one will go down in UFO history!"*

I spent the rest of the morning interviewing people in the general locale. Some had already been questioned by the Air Force just a week ago. Bertrand had also mentioned these investigators, who had questioned him and Officer Hunt just a day after the sighting. The Air Force team had told them to keep quiet about the incident so that it would not get printed up in the newspapers.

"We told them that it was a bit too late for that," Bertrand had recounted to me. "A local reporter was in the station that night and had tipped off the Manchester *Union Leader*. It was really funny. We were all standing there talking about what had happened when someone pointed at the front window. We all jumped! There was this reporter peering through the glass at us with a helmet and tight jacket on! He had motorcycled all the way up from Manchester."

I laughed, "Thought the spacemen had landed, huh?"

I finally arrived back home just before three o'clock in the afternoon, weary and with an empty stomach. Margaret was worried when I hadn't shown up for dinner, and I had been too busy to think to call. After gobbling down some warmed-up leftovers, I informed her rather hesitatingly that we'd have to take a raincheck on the afternoon drive because I had to get back to Exeter to take some photographs. I'm afraid at that point, she definitely did not share my enthusiasm! I explained to her that I had discovered a set of power lines that crossed the road about a half mile from the field where the object had been seen. It looked to me as if they might have passed just behind the trees from where the object had first appeared. In any event, I wanted to walk back there and check this aspect of the sighting out, as well as take some photographs of the sighting area. I phoned my brother

Richard to assist me, and off I went to Exeter again. I wasn't usually so callous in putting flying saucers before family, but this was an exceptional case! We took some photographs and then drove down the road to where the power lines crossed Route 150. Leaving the car, we began hiking along the lines until stopped short by a swamp. Our feet were soaked as we headed back to the car, but it was a worthwhile jaunt. The power lines *did* pass directly behind the field. When I arrived home bedraggled and wet, Margaret just gave me that "you must be nuts" look and shook her head.

The Saturday Review *Calls*

I worked on the initial report for the next few days and managed to mail it out early Tuesday morning.[1] By Thursday, I had recevied a most encouraging response from Richard Hall, acting director of NICAP. It contained news about an excellent opportunity.

September 15, 1965

Dear Ray:

Your excellent report on the September 3, New Hampshire sightings has been received. You certainly are to be commended for a prompt and thorough investigation. The information is most interesting and will be of great value. We are fortunate to have people of your ability donating their services to us.

Mr. John Fuller of *Saturday Review* may be in touch with you about these sightings. He is doing a straightforward column on the recent wave of sightings. . . . We are cooperating fully. Thanks again for your hard work on our behalf.

Sincerely,
Dick Hall

"The *Saturday Review*?" I thought. "What an opportunity to aquaint its readers with cases like Exeter!" I showed the letter to my not-too-sympathetic-about-Exeter wife, who said in effect, "I'll believe it when I see it!" Well, she believed it several days

later as she was scurrying around busily preparing for the writer
from *Saturday Review*. John Fuller had indeed phoned. He
told me that he did not want to write about the Exeter incident
until he personally had thoroughly reinvestigated the case to his
own satisfaction. I agreed to provide him with a Xerox copy of my
initial report along with any follow-up data that might come in.

John arrived at our home for dinner on the following weekend
armed with a tape recorder and notebook. He explained to me
that he had been reading about the increase in UFO sightings
with great interest. An overwhelming curiosity had prompted him
to track down and document at least one specific case. "To be
quite frank," he said, "I'm very skeptical about this subject." We
all liked John. He took the time to chat with the children and my
wife. It was readily apparent that he was interested in getting to
know us as people as well as using me as a source for information
about the Exeter UFO sighting.

John left for Exeter armed with my report and copious notes.
He talked with the witnesses, local newspaper editors, and Air
Force officers at Pease AFB. He phoned back afterwards to tell
me that he was absolutely convinced that "these people really
saw something!" One thing led to another. John's story soon appeared in the October 2, 1965, issue of the *Saturday Review*'s
"Trade Winds" column. Then *Look* magazine asked John to return to Exeter to obtain additional material for an in-depth story
on the incident. Soon after, *Reader's Digest* printed a summary
of the *Look* article, and the G. P. Putnam publishing company
commissioned him to write a book based upon the Exeter sighting.[2]

John soon made a return visit to us and secured information
from my files relating to other sightings for use in his book. He
insisted that I would be given full credit. "You are going to be
the hero of this book," he said. To me, all of this seemed too
good to be true. The results of my personal efforts coupled with
the support of the subcommittee had hitherto been known and
used by a small segment of the public via the auspices of NICAP.
Now, in just the space of several months, my reports had suddenly become the basis of national magazine articles and the later

best-selling book, *Incident at Exeter,* by John Fuller. However, the crowning event was yet to take place, as we shall soon see.

On April 5, 1966, the House Armed Services Committee unanimously voted my entire report on the Exeter sighting into the *Congressional Record* during the first *open* Congressional hearings on UFOs! By that time, the report had grown considerably and contained a blow-by-blow description of a fight with the Pentagon, whose initial evaluation of the incident was "stars and planets twinkling!"[3] I found out several years later that the local commander at Pease Air Force Base had not even sent the base's report out to Project Bluebook when the Pentagon issued this misleading statement. The same source told me that after this press release was made, an urgent wire from Bluebook came into Pease Air Force Base that reprimanded the commander for not being more punctual in submitting the report through channels. Then, since the "twinkling star" answer was obviously contrary to the well-publicized facts, the Pentagon tried to explain away the sightings as military aircraft.

Each of these attempts to explain away the Exeter sightings was proved erroneous, and a fully documented account of my running battle with the Air Force became part of the *Congressional Record.* This battle was won, but not without much effort on the part of myself, the witnesses, and John Fuller.

My Report Goes to Congress

The House Armed Services Committee opened the public segment of the UFO hearings at 10:35 A.M. on April 5, 1966. Those persons mentioned in connection with my report on the Exeter UFO sighting were: Congressman William H. Bates, Massachusetts; Honorable Harold Brown, Secretary of the Air Force; Dr. J. Allen Hynek, Scientific Consultant to the Air Force; and General McConnell, USAF. During Dr. Hynek's testimony, my former congressman, the late William H. Bates, interjected my report into the hearings. Let us join the discussion at this point.

> *Mr. Bates:* But the interesting thing, of course, is we have so many prominent people in the scientific world here who have

taken a position, a rather strong position—I have here a letter
from a constituent of mine. He is a project administrator or
engineer in the MINUTEMAN program. That is a responsible
position, would we say?
General McConnell: Yes.
Mr. Bates: On the basis of scientific ability he has been
given a rather important position toward the security of this
country; is that correct?
Secretary Brown: I would like to know who he is and what
his responsibilities are before I comment on this, Mr. Bates.
Certainly, from the information contained in the letter you
quote, he appears to occupy a position of some responsibility.
Mr. Bates: It does seem to be. And as I read the letter
which he has written to me, it is certainly written by a well-
educated person. And, of course, we hear all kinds of comments
on the other side of the same issue now. With this Lunar II
excursion around the moon, people say, "I suppose the people
up there are making the same kind of reports as the doctor
has just made to us." They are making these kinds of statements.
Doctor, to be more specific, the paper which I have—Mr.
Chairman, I would like to get unanimous consent to insert in
the record the information which has been provided to me.
The Chairman: Without objection.[4]

Since a substantial portion of this letter appears in the introduction to this book. I have omitted it here. Thirty-four pages were
inserted into the *Congressional Record* at this point that thoroughly documented the Exeter sighting. Included within the report
were letters to and from the Air Force from myself and from
Officers Bertrand and Hunt. They centered around the ridiculous
"explanations" that the Pentagon had offered for the sighting.
One of the first attempts to cover up what really happened at
Exeter appeared in local newspapers on October 6.

The unidentified flying object spotted in this area by many
residents has finally been identified. It's a flying billboard which
contains 500 high-intensity lights that spell out an advertising
message.[5]

I was horrified when I saw this and immediately wrote to newspapers in the area to put the matter straight:

At the time of the September 3, 1965, UFO sighting I checked with the manager of "Sky-Lite Aerial Advertising Co." and its aircraft was not flying on this night. On October 9 I went over the advertising plane's flight paths between August 1 and October 8. The plane was not even airborne between August 21 and September 10.

In all fairness, this explanation did not seem to have originated from the Air Force. It seems to have been the attempt by an over zealous newspaper reporter to come up with an explanation for the sighting. It is curious to me that he did not discover that the plane was not airborne during the time frame of the Exeter sightings. It could have been just poor documentation on his part. However, about two weeks after my letter dismissing the advertising plane was printed in the local news, the Pentagon issued a number of explanations for the incident, They included· "a high altitude Strategic Air Command exercise" and a temperature inversion which causes "stars and planets to dance and twinkle." These explanations came directly from Washington and were prominently displayed in the papers around the Exeter area.

PENTAGON DOESN'T BELIEVE
UFO EXETER SIGHTINGS

Washington, D.C.—The Pentagon believes that after intensive investigation, it has come up with a natural explanation of the UFO sightings in Exeter, N.H., on September 3. . . . The spokesman said, "We believe what the people saw that night was stars and planets in unusual formations."[6]

Some intensive investigation! Does this sound like high-altitude aircraft or stars and planets twinkling?

It was coming up over a row of trees. There was no noise at all. It was about one hundred feet in the air and about two hundred feet away from us. I could see five bright red lights in a straight row. They dimmed from right to left and then from left to right. . . . It lit up everything . . . it was silent. The horses started kicking and making an awful fuss, and the dogs in the farm started barking. The kid froze in his tracks, and I grabbed him and pulled him toward the police car. I reached for my revolver and then thought better of it. Then Officer David Hunt arrived in another patrol car. We sat there and looked at it for at least ten minutes. My brain kept telling me that this doesn't happen—but it was right in front of my eyes. There was no tail, no wings, and again no sound. It hovered there, still about one hundred feet away, sort of floated and wobbled. I don't know what it was. All I can say is that it was there, and three of us saw it together.[7]

This official release from Washington was all too familiar and completely frustrating. The witnesses felt that such statements jeopardized their hard-earned reputations as responsible police officers. In response to a request for further information about the Strategic Air Command aircraft exercise, Project Bluebook forwarded the following information:

Big Blast *Coco,* a SAC/NORAD training mission, was flown on 2-3 September, 1965. By 03/0430Z, the operational portion of the mission was complete . . . . The town of Exeter is within the traffic pattern utilized by Air Traffic Control in the recovery of these aircraft at Pease AFB, N.H. During their approach the recovering aircraft would have been displaying standard position lights, anti-collision lights and possibly over-wing and landing lights.[8]

Undaunted, Bertrand and Hunt drafted another letter to Project Bluebook and outlined the facts of the matter. Excerpts from this letter are as follows:

. . . we have been the subject of considerable ridicule since the Pentagon released its "final evaluation" of our sighting . . . both Ptl. Hunt and myself saw this object at close range, checked it out with each other, confirmed and reconfirmed the fact that this was not any kind of conventional aircraft. . . . Since our job depends on accuracy and an ability to tell the difference between fact and fiction, we were naturally disturbed by the Pentagon report. . . . What is a little difficult to understand is the fact that your letter (undated) arrived considerably after the Pentagon release. Since your letter says that you are still in the process of making a final evaluation, it seems that there is an inconsistency here. . . . Since one of us (Ptl. Bertrand) was in the Air Force for four years engaged in refueling operations

with all kinds of military aircraft, it was impossible to mistake
what we saw for any kind of military operation, regardless of
altitude. . . . Immediately after the object disappeared, we did
see what probably was a B-47 at high altitude, but it bore no
relation at all to the object we saw. . . . Another fact is that
the time of our observation was nearly an hour after 2:00 A.M.,
which would eliminate the Air Force operation Big Blast. . . .[9]

Outflanked by Bertrand's discovery that the alleged Air Force
aircraft were not even airborne during the time that he, Muscarello, and Hunt concurrently observed the object, Bluebook
gave some ground, but not much! In regard to the earlier sightings
by the woman motorist and Muscarello (when alone), the Air
Force still maintained those two had seen the aircraft!

The early sightings . . . are attributed to aircraft from operation
Big Blast "Coco." The subsequent observation by Officers
Bertrand and Hunt occurring after 2 A.M. are regarded as un-
identified.[10]

This was incredible to me but typical of the Air Force pattern of
playing down and debunking reliable UFO sightings. I felt that
I could not take this matter sitting down and drafted a long letter
to the Office of the Secretary, Department of the Air Force.
Among other things, I pointed out the following facts:

The UFO sighted by Norman Muscarello was identical to the
UFO sighted later by Muscarello, Bertrand and Hunt. Norman
observed the UFO at close range during his initial sighting.
There is no question in my mind that the same or similar object
was involved in both of these particular sightings. The number
of pulsating lights, the yawing motion, the same location, etc.,
make this so very apparent. Since I did not interview the *un-
named woman*, I am not certain of the details . . . . but according to Officer Bertrand, the object . . . was very similar
to the UFO they sighted later. I might add that another witness,
a male motorist, also sighted a similar object. He tried to phone
the police from a pay station at nearby Hampton, N.H., but was
cut off. Later he reported the incident to U.S. Air Force
authorities at Pease AFB. The chances are astronomical that six
people, entirely independent of each other, should report the

identical description of a UFO within the span of several hours in the same general area.[11]

The Air Force never answered this letter. They probably wondered how I knew that the male motorist had reported the object to Pease Air Force Base, because he had been strictly instructed to tell no one about the incident. I found out about this when lecturing to a management club from a major firm located in the area. One of the managers, a good friend of the witness, informed me. The man's name cannot be revealed.

The Exeter incident is typical of hundreds of other cases in which our government is forced, because of national security policy, to deny the existence of UFOs at the expense of witnesses' reputations. After a dogmatic explanation is issued from the Pentagon, it takes nothing short of an act of Congress to change it. Fortunately, through public, witness, and Congressional pressure, the Air Force was forced to back down in this case. Needless to say, this is an exception rather than the rule. Let us continue to examine the House Armed Services hearings on UFOs. The following statements were made after my detailed report on Exeter had been presented and voted into the *Congressional Record:*

> *Mr. Bates*: In reference to the so-called sighting in New Hampshire, Doctor, you are familiar with that case?
> *Dr. Hynek*: Yes, sir; I am familiar with the case.
> *Mr. Bates*: You have examined it?
> *Dr. Hynek*: No, I have not been there to examine it. Much of my information is based upon the rather excellent account that Mr. John Fuller has given of it in *Look* magazine. I cannot vouch for the authenticity of his statements, but I have talked with Mr. Fuller, and he apparently has tried to do a very thorough job in talking with people in New Hampshire.
> *Mr. Bates*: Are you familiar with Mr. Raymond E. Fowler?
> *Dr. Hynek*: I have had some correspondence with him, but I have never met him.
> *Mr. Bates*: Is this . . . case one of the five percent that have not been identified, or within the ninety-five percent on which you have reached a decision?
> *Dr. Hynek*: It is, I believe, to the best of my knowledge, listed as unidentified.

Mr. Bates: This one is still unidentified?
Dr. Hynek: Yes, sir.
The Chairman: In other words, you make no bones about it, you cannot explain it?
Dr. Hynek: That is correct.[12]

The interested reader should secure a full copy of these controversial hearings for his information. They contain statements made by persons intimately associated with the Air Force investigations of UFOs that are in utter contradiction to documented facts in formerly classified and unclassified source material.

What If?

To Exeter or the zoo? I cannot help but wonder how things would have turned out if I had brought my family to the zoo on that eventful day. One thing was certain. The sighting at Exeter and my subsequent investigation had opened the way for public governmental and scientific discussion of my reports on a national scale. It was indeed a giant step forward in my personal efforts to obtain *scientific recognition of a new species—the UFO!*

NOTES

1. Personal Files, UFO Report No. 65-31.
2. John G. Fuller, *Incident at Exeter*, New York: G. P. Putnam's Sons, 1966.
3. *The Haverhill Gazette*, October 27, 1965
4. *House Report No. 55: Unidentified Flying Objects*, Hearing by Committee on Armed Services of the House of Representatives, Eighty-Ninth Congress, Second Session, April 5, 1966, pp. 6009, 6010.
5. *The Amesbury News*, October 6, 1965.
6. *The Haverhill Gazette*, October 27, 1965.
7. House Report No. 55, p. 6015.
8. *Ibid.* p. 6040.
9. *Ibid.* pp. 6039, 6040.
10. *Ibid.* p. 6039.
11. *Ibid.* p. 6042.
12. *Ibid.* pp. 6042, 6043.

8

THE NORTHEAST BLACKOUT

The Federal Power Commission . . . had many dozens of sighting reports for that famous evening . . . five witnesses near Syracuse, New York, saw a glowing object within about a minute of the blackout.

DR. JAMES E. MCDONALD
House Symposium on UFOs
July 29, 1968

The Build-up Continues

Local UFO sighting reports continued after the Exeter incident. During the month of September, a number of "unknown" cases were logged by the subcommittee. Two encounters with UFOs involved motorists and associated *electrical effects*. One of these took place on the same night as the Exeter case just twenty miles away to the southeast at Ipswich, Massachusetts! I dispatched Bob Jackson, a detective who had joined our ranks, to investigate this case. A summary of his report follows.

"IT MADE MY HAIR RISE!"

Shortly after 1 A.M., schoolteacher Dennis Winters drove along Route 133 towards his home in Ipswich. Shortly before coming over the crest of a hill, near the Candlewood Golf Course, he began to experience an unusual physical reaction. A weird feeling of uneasiness swept over him. He felt the hairs on the back of his neck stand up on end. Coming over the hill, he noticed a glow over the golf course. As he rapidly closed on the light, he was alarmed to see a phosphorescent object suspended just above the ground. He was so taken back by this sight that he veered almost off the road. Barely straightening out, he sped away in utter terror, not even looking back. He described the object as looking like an "inverted saucer with a flat dome." The dome had at least five "oval-shaped windows" around its periphery which emitted a whitish glow. The whole object was surrounded by a grayish glow with a reddish tint around it. The object appeared to be about forty feet in diameter.[1]

Another sighting involving electrical effects took place in mid-September and was investigated by Walter Webb.

THE SUDBURY CAR CHASE

It was raining hard as taxi driver Ronald Schofield drove home from work southwards along Dutton Road in Sudbury. As he reached an intersection near the famous Longfellow's Wayside Inn, the car engine began to skip. Puzzled, he turned west onto lonely Wayside Inn Road, hoping that his car would make the remaining five miles home. It got worse, so he stopped to see if he could locate the trouble. Ronald shifted to "park," turned off the headlights except for the parking lights, and left the car engine running. Stepping out of the car he noticed a light shining down from above his head and heard a "soft, high-pitched whining sound." Startled, he glanced up into the rain and gaped in utter astonishment. There, hovering about two hundred feet overhead, was a large, glowing, disc-shaped object! It was two car lengths in diameter, and a dull glow seemed to emanate from its edge. Yellowish "sparks" flashed around in a circle on its bottom, which extended about three-quarters of the way out from the center. He stated that "nine or so" of these sparks moved around the object in perfect sequence. Terrified, he jumped back into the car, turned the headlights on, and "floored the gas pedal!" He did not look back. As he sped off, the headlights and dashboard lights were abnormally dim but they brightened as he moved away from the UFO. The engine ran perfectly thereafter.[2]

Reports continued to flow in during this month. Misidentifications of the Echo satellite, the bright star Vega, a Coast Guard helicopter, and some searchlights added to the confusion and frustration involved in weeding out the IFOs. For example, on September 25 at 6:45 P.M., I received a phone call from Edward Preston, who lived in the neighboring town of Danvers. He told me excitedly that his family and neighbors were watching a bright, stationary object in the sky. I ran outside and looked toward Danvers. Sure enough, there it was, almost directly overhead in the still lighted early evening sky. It seemed to be perfectly stationary, so I dashed inside and brought out a six-inch astronomical telescope. In less than ten minutes, I was gazing through a 40-power eyepiece at a *weather balloon* reflecting the rays of the setting sun. It seemed to be on a tether and carried an instrument package that was swinging wildly in the wind. Suddenly, it exploded into thousands of pieces, creating a beautiful shower of rainbow-colored fragments. However, not all the sightings that continued to be reported could be so easily explained.

The Power Plant Sightings

The New England Power Station at Salem, Massachusetts, had received international fame among UFO researchers on July 16, 1952. During one of the largest UFO sighting waves on record, Coastguardsman Shell Alpert photographed four white glowing egg-shaped obejcts hovering over the adjoining power station. The objects were sighted visually at 9:35 A.M. by a power company work team and a number of Coastguardsmen. Years later, I was told by Coast Guard officials that the Air Force was furious with the commanding officer of the station for releasing the photograph to the *Salem News*. When Air Force investigators arrived at the station, the front gates were closed and no one was allowed to leave or enter the Coast Guard base. Subsequently, the Pentagon issued contradictory statements, first that the "photos were double exposures"[3] and later that they were "light reflections on the window through which they were taken."[4] This was absurd. While lecturing on UFOs at this Coast Guard station, I was told that men were observing it from the dock where amphibian aircraft were moored. These explanations also ignored the workers in the yard of the power plant who also had observed them outside. The supervisor of this work team told me that the objects were so bright that their reflection off some tanks they were working on caused him to look up and see them! *(See picture section.)*

On the evening of October 2, 1965, the Salem Police and the

Coast Guard station received telephone calls reporting a strange object hovering over this same power station! This sounded most interesting, as back in May I had investigated a report of a dirigible-shaped object over this power station. The police were only able to give me one witness's name. Other callers had refused to give their names for fear of ridicule. I contacted the young witness's father, a professor of meteorology at Salem State Teachers College. He graciously allowed me to interview his sixteen-year-old son, James Centorino, who related the following experience to me.

"IT WAS SHAPED LIKE A CIGAR"

It was about twenty minutes after eight. I was riding my bike up Columbus Avenue on the way home when I saw two bright lights over the three smokestacks of the power plant. Each stack has two red lights, but I couldn't figure out what the white lights were. There seemed to be a dark shape between them, so I cycled down to the plant and up to the fence around it for a closer look. I was only several hundred feet from the stacks and could see a dark, cigar-shaped object which had a slight hump toward its rear. A white light was attached to each end. It was hovering at a 45 degree angle about fifteen feet above the stacks. When I got off my bike to go up closer to the fence, it made a sound like air being let out of a balloon. It rose up in the air for about a hundred feet and shut off its lights. I could just barely see it moving away into the darkness.[5]

The object was estimated to be twenty to thirty feet long by comparing them to the stacks. The weather was good with some broken clouds. James informed me that they had been "cirrocumulus" clouds—like father, like son! He impressed me as being an exceptionally bright and sincere young man. I received the immediate impression that he was carefully relating a true account of what he had experienced. He told me that after the object moved off, he bicycled home and phoned the police. In checking with the police, I obtained confirmation that James and an anonymous woman had phoned in to report the object. The police told me that they in turn had notified the Coast Guard, who had told them that they had received many calls about the strange object. I phoned the Coast Guard in an attempt to obtain the names and addresses of these callers. Although they admitted receiving the calls about the UFO, they informed me that regulations did not permit them to give out information of that nature. I was told that the crew on night watch had relayed the data to the Air Force at Hanscom Field in Bedford. I then phoned the Air Force UFO officer at Hanscom Field, but he stated that he could not comment upon the matter. A personal check with the power station revealed that nothing unusual was seen or noted by the night shift on the sighting date.

RETURN VISIT?

Another report of *strange lights* over the New England Power Plant was brought to my attention in November.[6] Francis Burnham was driving in the rain along Dearborn Street in Salem with his wife and two children at about 7 P.M. Two bright lights hovering over the power plant caught their attention. Curious, Francis stopped the car and got out to get a better look. The plant was about one-mile away and the lights appeared to be hovering just a few hundred feet above it. One was white and the other red. They seemed to be about one hundred feet apart from one another. All of a sudden, the lights took off from a dead standstill to a speed *three times faster than a jet* and disappeared in the distance towards Boston.

The local sighting build-up, associated electrical effects, and reports of UFOs over power plants and power lines was typical of others occurring elsewhere in the Northeast. At this time, however, I was not aware of the overall situation. One of these other sightings took place directly over power lines near a power sub-station at Clay, New York, on November 9. What happened less than a minute later has now become an historical event.

What Happened to the Lights?

THE CLAY "FIREBALLS"

Clay, New York, lies just outside of Syracuse and is the location of a power substation that serves as a junction plant for two

345,000-volt power lines running from Niagara Falls to the Mohawk Power Corporation at Clay. Just prior to the Northeast Blackout, at 5:15 P.M., pilot Weldon Ross and a passenger were flying toward Syracuse to land at Hancock Field. As their aircraft passed over power lines near the Clay substation, they were shocked by the sudden appearance of a huge, *bright red fireball* about one hundred feet in diameter ascending from just above the power line! A moment later, the Northeast Blackout occurred! Thirty-six million people lost electrical power over an area of eighty thousand square miles. Meanwhile, at Hancock Field, Deputy Aviation Commissioner Robert C. Walsh was busily occupied in putting on emergency lights at the darkened airfield. At about 5:25 P.M., he was amazed to see a similar *fireball* just a few miles south of Hancock Field. It also was in the vicinity of power lines coming into the area from the Niagara Fall power station. Ton minutes later, he saw still another one! The Aerial Phenomena Research Organization (APRO), based at Tuscon, Arizona, stated after investigation that:

> Putting all this information together in a pattern, it appears that three separate "balls of fire" were seen in the vicinity of the power line that evening. The first failure, felt in Canada, was about 5:16. The second big failure, after several other areas experienced the blackout, was New York City at about 5:27. In other words, *two fireballs coincided with two facts*: the blackout in Canada and the New York blackout.[7]

I was driving home with a car pool from work when the lights went out in Massachusetts. We thought it was just a local breakdown until we noticed that each community we passed through was darkened. When I arrived home, I found my family huddled around some candles waiting for me. At the time, I half-jokingly said to my wife that UFOs might be responsible! Although she took it as a joke, I kept going out and gazing at the sky. I could not help but think about the developing pattern that seemed to link many UFO sightings with power lines and power stations. Little did I know then that UFO events were occurring simultaneously with the blackout! Interestingly enough, John Fuller was in southern New Hampshire researching UFO sightings for his book, *Incident at Exeter.* During his stay there, he came across many such reports of UFOs hovering and moving over power lines.

RECONSTRUCTING THE CRIME

The first sign of trouble was noted at 5:15 P.M. at Consolidated Edison in New York. According to reports, the plant manager was very pleased with "very orderly peak period" as darkness fell and the city lights were being turned on. They had "an excellent reserve in the system." Abruptly, the city lights dimmed and brightened again! Officials quickly checked the city's generating facilities for trouble, but everything was operating normally. However, monitoring instruments showed an immense flow of current to the north. The plant manager called the Syracuse station, who informed him that points north were indeed experiencing trouble. Before New York could take remedial measures, the city was plunged into darkness at 5:27 P.M.!

Consolidated Edison told the press that there was no equipment failure noted and placed the blame on northern transmission lines in Canada being somehow grounded out. This in turn caused the tremendous power drainage. The Canadians, however, pointed out indignantly that the blackout struck there at 5:15 P.M., a full twelve minutes before New York experienced total power failure. In Toronto, a government electric power commission told the press that they blamed a "high voltage line *south* of Niagara Falls." They stated that a "surge of electricity" had hit the electrical system in Ontario which "flowed in the opposite direction to the normal flow at that hour." Alarmed, Canadian technicians had opened switches in order to save equipment from being damaged. This caused much of Ontario and Toronto to be blacked out at 5:15 P.M. The reader will take note that "south of Niagara Falls" was *in the Clay area* near Syracuse where the *fireballs* were observed! Annoyed, officials at Syracuse countered with a statement by Edward Hoffman, assistant to the chief system electrical engineer. Hoffman acknowledged that some local generators had indeed gone out of step with the interconnecting system but maintained that this trouble was *secondary* to *"some kind of distur-bance* somewhere that caused the generators to get out of step. The source of this disturbance is not known."

The day following the blackout found everybody trying to explain what could have happened to representatives of a federal probe initiated by President Johnson. Canada complained that American officials "have clammed up tight" in releasing data to them concerning what had happened. Then, paradoxically enough, the Canadians attributed the power loss to a relay at Queenston, Ontario. This was quickly followed by a joint American-Canadian statement that they "still don't know the origin of the source of power that ripped out the relay." Still later, the Texas White House stated that "the trouble had been traced to a Niagara Mohawk substation *at Clay,* ten miles north of Syracuse!" No sooner had this statement reached the press than another announcement was released, stating that the announcement about Clay was "again in error."

In April of 1966, contradictory statements were still being given to Congress regarding the cause of the Northeast Blackout. On the one hand, F. Stuart Brown, chief of the Federal Power Commission's Bureau of Power, still blamed Canada. He maintained that the blackout was "due to the unfortunate action of some relays which served to unload the lines unexpectedly" from the Adam Beck Generating Station at Queenston, Ontario. On the other hand, Oscar Bakke, eastern regional director, gave testimony to the same House Appropriations Subcommittee that was in direct contradiction to the Federal Power Commission chief's statement. He told Congress that the operators of the power system even at that late date still insisted that the power blackout simply should not have, indeed *could* not have, occurred. Even as I write, there is still no unanimity regarding its cause. Were the *Clay fireballs* and other UFO events during that fateful evening of November 9, 1965, coincidental or causal?

Major Blackouts Continue

Most people are totally unaware that major blackouts occurred elsewhere throughout the world on November 9 and the days that followed throughout the rest of 1965 and into 1966. A partial listing of some of these follows.

Date	Place	Duration	Circumstances
Nov 9	Stockholm, Sweden	+ hour	Tunnel collapse
Nov 9	San Salvador, Sal.	1 hour	Not disclosed
Nov 11	Toledo, Ohio	− hour	Reason unknown
Nov 15	London, England	+ hour	High consumption
Nov 19	Lima, Peru	− hour	System failure
Nov 26	St. Paul, Minn.	− hour	UFOs overhead
Dec 2	Texas, New Mex.	− hour	Regulator failed
Dec 4	East Texas	− hour	Relay tripped
Dec 26	Buenos Aires, Arg.	+ hour	Line failure

In several of these blackouts, agreement could not be reached regarding the *initial causes* for relays to trip, which in turn caused overloaded regulators and transformers to malfunction. The blackouts had their amusing moments as well. When the East Texas power failure occurred, Joseph C. Swidler, Federal Power Commission chairman, was explaining the massive New England power failure of November 9 to President Johnson on his ranch in Texas! The most interesting of these blackouts occurred at St. Paul, Minnesota. NICAP investigation revealed the following:

> Power failures, simultaneous with UFO sightings, were reported by the Northern States Power Company, police and numerous residents. The sudden failures knocked out house lights and appliances. The area hardest hit was Totem Town, on Highway 61. Residents reported all lights out as *objects* giving off blue and orange flashes appeared overhead. The power company said it was unable to determine the blackout cause.[8]

The first failure took place shortly after 8 P.M., when Nick DeVara and Mark Wilcox reported seeing a huge, blue light, "like someone welding in the sky." Just as the glowing object passed overhead, the lights at an adjoining service station went out! Several minutes later, a bit to the north, another blackout occurred. Mrs. Don Housh of 1875 Hoyt Avenue reported that at 8:15 P.M. all house lights and appliances went dead. Again, concurrently with the power blackout, witnesses also observed a bright blue, glowing UFO. Other observers included a motorist whose car lights and radio failed as the object passed overhead! Prior to the November 9 blackout, the most recent UFO-linked power failure had taken place at Cuernavaca, Mexico, on September 23, 1965. Among the many witnesses were the governor, Emilie Riva Palacie, the mayor, Valentin Lopez Gonzalez, and a military zone chief, General Rafael Enrique Vega. In a report to NICAP, it was stated that the lights of Cuernavaca went out while a glowing, disc-shaped object hovered at low altitude. A number of UFO-related blackout cases occurring before 1965 are on file at NICAP.

In 1957, lights went out at Mogi Mirim, Brazil, as three UFOs passed overhead; also in 1957, power failure was reported at Tamaroa, Illinois, after a hovering UFO was seen. On August 3, 1958, city lights failed in an area at Rome, Italy, when a luminous UFO went overhead. A similar failure was reported at Salta, Argentina, on July 22, 1959. According to an August 17, 1959, news report from Umberlandia, Minais Gerais, Brazil, *automatic keys at a power station turned off* as a round-shaped UFO passed above, following a trunk powerline. After the UFO disappeared, the keys went on automatically, restoring normal service.[9]

Blackouts continued into 1966. All of southern Italy lost power for up to two hours on January 8. The cause of this blackout was not announced by officials. Over a million people were affected in Naples alone as firemen answered dozens of calls to get people out of elevators stalled between floors. On January 13, the Telstar communications satellite tracking station and a 75-square-mile area in Franklin County, Maine, lost power for seven hours. No explanation could be found, and the power was restored for no apparent reason! A frustrated spokesman for the Central Maine Company blamed the failure on "an apparent equipment failure which somehow corrected itself." Even Vietnam was not exempt from the mysterious UFOs and associated power failures. One such incident occurred in mid-June 1966. I was fortunate enough to have interviewed one of the witnesses, Sergeant Wayne

Dalrymple. NICAP first learned about the sighting from a NICAP member who mailed a copy of Wayne's letter to his parents describing the bizarre incident. Since it was written just after the UFO sighting took place, it is well worth reading before discussing the case further. The letter is postmarked June 20, 1966, and was mailed from Nha Trang, Vietnam. Pertinent excerpts are as follows:

> Well, now for the big news. Last night about 9:45 P.M., this camp, which has about 40,000 men went into a panic and, believe me, I was scared . . . too. We got a big generator in last week along with a movie projector and some movies and we were outside watching one of them when a real bright light came from out of nowhere. At first we thought it was a flare which are going off all the time and then we found out that it wasn't. It came from the North and was moving from real slow to real fast speeds. . . . Some of the jet fighter pilots which were here . . . said it looked to be about 25,000 feet and then the panic broke loose. It dropped right towards us and stopped dead still about 300 to 500 feet up. It made this little valley and the mountains around look like it was the middle of the day. It lit up everything. Then it went up and I mean up. It went straight up completely out of sight in about 2-3 seconds. Everybody is still talking about it and everybody is going to be outside looking tonight. What really shook everyone is that it stopped, or maybe it didn't, but anyway *our generator stopped* and everything was black and at the Air Force Base about ½ mile from here *all generators stopped* and two planes that were on the runway ready to take off, their engines stopped. . . . There wasn't a car, truck, plane or anything, that ran for about 4 minutes. There are 8 big bulldozers that are cutting roads over the mountain and they *stopped* and their *lights went out too.* A whole plane load of *big shots from Washington* got here this afternoon to investigate. It's on the radio over here. Is it at home? I swear, if somebody says they saw a little green man, I won't argue with them.[10]

Wayne estimated that the glowing object was about fifty feet in diameter, but no detail could be seen behind the round-shaped light. The aircraft that were affected were Skyraiders. The bulldozers were similar to civilian D-9s and were clearing an area to install Hawk missiles on Oak Hill. A total of six 100-kilowatt, independently operated, diesel powered electrical generators failed. All power and equipment functioned perfectly about four minutes after the UFO left the area. Wayne, in the course of his military duties, checked each generator out for defects. They were found to be in good order and experienced no further malfunctions. Fortunately, no aircraft were airborne in the area at the time of the incident! However, a Shell oil tanker anchored offshore experienced a complete power failure simultaneously with the blackout on shore!

Two successive two-hour power failures crippled the states of Nebraska and Missouri in July of 1966, and two million people in Rome, Italy, lost power for an hour on October 16. Although conventional explanations were forthcoming in some cases, it is of extraordinary interest to note that the streak of major power failures throughout the world in 1965 and 1966 just happened to coincide with the heaviest concentration of UFO sightings in modern history!

I MAKE THE HEADLINES!

It was during this concentration of sightings that I found myself constantly bombarded with requests for interviews with newscasters, talk shows, and newspapers. One of these interviews was conducted by the Boston *Daily Record* on Saturday, April 16, 1966. The editors were particularly interested in the growing amount of observational evidence that appeared to link UFO reports with coincidental electrical interference and power failures. Two reporters were dispatched to my home to examine reports of local and international incidents. It proved to be a long interview. Photographs were taken of me peering through my telescope, and I supplied them photos of an alleged UFO trailing an RB-57 aircraft. I stressed that there was no absolute proof that UFOs caused such side effects but was able to demonstrate to them that an abnormally high rate of strange coincidences nevertheless existed. *(See Figure 1, first page of picture section.)*

A very busy weekend passed and I arrived at work on Monday morning to find people giving me strange looks and smiles as I passed through the corridors to my office. I half wondered what was wrong with me and casually checked my clothing, hair, beard, etc. I seemed to be all in one piece! I entered my office and stopped dead in my tracks. There on my desk was a copy of the *Daily Record* with my picture staring back at me from the front page. I picked up the paper and read the glaring headlines—NOW IT IS REVEALED—UFO SPOTTED AT GREAT BLACK-OUT SITE. I quickly turned to the story inside the paper. It was a well-written article. It provided a brief historical overview of the UFO mystery, my local investigations, and the complete story about the *fireballs* over Clay, New York. Only one thing was wrong. Somehow, the writer had interchanged the Niagara Power Station with the Clay Substation. I reached for the phone and called the paper to question them on this accuracy but could not reach the night editor until evening. He apologized for the mix-up and told me something very interesting. He said that the front office had been called by the Air Force and severely criticized for printing the story. In the meantime, the national wire services had picked up the story and it was being carried in newspapers coast to coast! I telephoned NICAP headquarters and apologized for any inconvenience that the speculative article might be causing them. I wondered if I had overreacted to the mounting circumstantial evidence relating to UFOs and blackouts. My goal was scientific recognition of a *new species*—the UFO. I feared that publication of my speculative thoughts on a nationwide scale might alienate my past and any future reports from further scientific discussion. I was soon to find, however, that I had nothing to fear. Some respected scientists were coming to the same conclusion. A few actually spoke out openly both to the scientific community and to the Congress of the United States!

World-Famous Scientist's Warning

GREEK UFO INVESTIGATION

On February 24, 1967, members of the Greek astronautical society were highly interested as they listened to conference speaker Professor Paul Santorini. Santorini, the most respected scientist in Greece, explained to them that back in 1947, the Greek army had supplied him with a team of engineers to investigate the *flying objects* that were believed to be Russian missiles flying over Greece. The professor made this startling revelation during the course of his address:

"NOT MISSILES"

We soon established that they were not missiles. But, before we could do any more, the Army, after conferring with foreign officials, ordered the investigation stopped. Foreign scientists flew to Greece for secret talks with me.[11]

A newspaper account indicates that the Pentagon and U.S. scientists were among the foreign personnel who conferred with the professor. This indicates that selected members of the civilian scientific community were working on the UFO problem for the Department of Defense prior to the inauguration of the U.S. Air Force Project Sign, which began in 1948.[12]

"WORLD BLANKET OF SECRECY"

The professor further informed his startled colleagues that "there is a world blanket of secrecy" concerning UFO activity because authorities were unwilling to admit the existence of a force against which earth had "no possibility of defense." The learned scientist added that his studies indicated that, for the time being, *aliens* were probably "visiting earth to collect plant and animal specimens" but that their future purposes, if any, were entirely unknown to us.

"UFOS CAUSED POWER BLACKOUTS"

He warned that

Power blackouts in New York in November 1965 and in the eastern U.S. and Mexico about the same time, were possibly caused by UFOs flying along power lines.

I must admit that I was suspicious at first when I read a newspaper account based upon Dr. Santorini's address, so I decided to check upon its accuracy firsthand. I obtained the professor's address from the Greek Embassy in Washington and sent him a copy of my manuscript to proofread for accuracy. He graciously made corrections as required and wrote:

> In the meantime, since my conference to which you refer, many things have happened. The UFOs are certainly a reality. Many of the observations are certainly conclusive but a lot of nonsense has been published. I have the impression that your book, together with Professor Hynek's book, will do much good.[13]

Dr. Paul Santorini's credentials proved to be impeccable. Among his personal scientific achievements were the development of the first proximity fuse to explode the Hiroshima A-bomb at a predetermined height and a centimetric radar system (between 1936 and 1940) that was superior to the British system at the outbreak of World War II. He is a fellow of many academies and learned societies, has a six-inch entry in the *International Who's Who* (London) and in similar references, has represented Greece at a great number of international congresses, and is the author of more than three hundred scientific papers. Albert Einstein was his former physics teacher in Zurich and a personal friend.

Professor Santorini was over seventy years old when he gave this address. He perhaps dared to speak out so openly because of his unchallenged position in the scientific world. His reputation had been well earned. He had nothing to lose. Younger scientists interested in the UFO problem conducted their studies privately. Those scientists working on restricted military UFO projects were not allowed to make any positive comments on the UFO situation. In actuality, UFOs are treated as a threat to national security. This aspect of the situation will be covered thoroughly in chapter thirteen of this book. Adding to the secrecy surrounding UFOs were the fanatics and showmen claiming *contact* with the spacemen. Their well-publicized incredible statements have produced an aura of ridicule around the subject that makes it that much harder for serious researchers to become publicly associated with UFOs. However, in spite of such obstacles, some scientists still have the courage of their convictions to speak out. The late Dr.

James E. McDonald was such a man. McDonald was a senior scientist at the Institute for Atmospheric Physics at the University of Arizona. His interest in UFOs caused him to devote several years of full-time study to the subject. He too had noticed the UFO/power line pattern.

Congress Asks Why?

My first contact with Jim McDonald was a phone call shortly after John Fuller published his book, *Incident at Exeter,* in the spring of 1966. He was interested in my opinion of the many sightings John had documented in this book. He also asked me for copies of any UFO reports that I had investigated which involved power lines and power stations. No mention was made of the Northeast Blackout at that time, but it was very encouraging for me to see that a respected scientist shared my curiosity about the connection between UFOs and power sources. From that time on, Jim's name joined Dr. Hynek's name on my UFO report distribution list. Thereafter, we kept up a voluminous correspondence and compared notes by phone concerning many of my reports. One of the highlights of 1967 for me was a personal visit from Dr. McDonald. I found him to be an intense and meticulous individual who was absolutely convinced that UFOs were the greatest scientific problem of our time. His full-time study of UFOs had taken him all over the country and even abroad to Australia. He was clearly frustrated over the military approach to the problem and the reluctance of other scientists to speak out openly on the subject. Jim told me that he found it hard to understand why Air Force consultant Dr. Hynek had not spoken out more and sooner on the UFO problem.

I mention Jim at this point because he was the first well-known scientist in the United States to publicly suggest that UFOs might have been responsible for the great Northeast Blackout. The date was July 29, 1968. The occasion was a UFO symposium requested by the Committee on Science and Astronautics, of the U.S. House of Representatives. Jim was one of twelve scientists asked to contribute to these hearings. The House Committee met

at 10:05 A.M. in room 2318 of the Rayburn House Office Build-
ing. The Honorable J. Edward Roush presided over the hearings.
At this pertinent point in the hearings, committee member William
F. Ryan (N. Y.) was questioning Dr. McDonald.

> *Mr. Ryan:* Let me ask a further question. In the course of
> your investigation and your study of UFO sightings, have you
> found any cases where contemporaneously with the sightings of
> UFOs, allegedly, there were any other events which took place
> which might not be related to the UFOs?
> *Dr. McDonald:* Yes. Certainly there are many physical ef-
> fects. For instance in Mr. Pettis' district, several people found
> the fillings in their mouth hurting while this object was nearby,
> but there are many cases on record of car ignition failure. One
> famous case was at Levelland, Texas, in 1957. Ten vehicles
> were stopped within a short area, all independently, in a two-
> hour period. There was no lightning or thunderstorm, and only
> a trace of rain. There is another which I don't know whether
> to bring to the committee's attention or not. The evidence is
> not as conclusive as the car-stopping phenomenon, but there
> are too many instances for me to ignore.[14]

Then McDonald dropped his bombshell. His statement to
Congress on the Northeast Blackout would follow mine across
the nation by two years via the national press services!

> UFOs have often been seen hovering near power facilities. There
> are a small number, but still a little too many to seem pure,
> fortuitous chance, of *system outages,* coincident with the UFO
> sighting. One of the cases was Tamaroa, Illinois. Another was
> a case in Shelbyville, Kentucky, early last year. Even the famous
> one, the New York Blackout, involved UFO sightings. Dr. Hynek
> probably would be the most appropriate man to describe the
> Manhattan sighting, since he interview several witnesses involved.
> I interviewed a woman in Seacliff, N.Y. She saw a disk hovering
> and going up and down and then shooting away from New
> York just after the power failure. I went to the Federal Power
> Commission for data. They didn't take them seriously although
> *they had many dozens of sighting reports* for that famous eve-
> ning. There were reports all over New England in the midst
> of that blackout, and five witnesses near Syracuse, N.Y. saw a
> glowing object ascending within about a minute of the blackout.

. . . It is rather puzzling that the pulse of current that tripped the relay at the Ontario Hydro Commission plant has never been identified, but initially the tentative suspicion was centered on the *Clay Substation* of the Niagara Mohawk network right there in the Syracuse area, where unidentified aerial phenomena was seen by some of the witnesses. This extends down to the limit of single houses losing their power when a UFO is near. The hypothesis in the case of car-stopping is that there might be high magnetic fields, DC fields, which saturate the core and thus prevent the pulses going through the system to the other side. Just how a UFO could trigger an outage on a large power network is, however, not yet clear. But, this is a disturbing series of coincidences that I think warrant much more attention than they have so far received.

Mr. Ryan: As far as you know, has any agency investigated the New York blackout in relation to UFOs?

Dr. McDonald: None at all. When I spoke to the Federal Power Commission people, I was dissatisfied with the amount of information I could gain. I am saying there is a puzzling and slightly disturbing coincidence here. I'm not going on record as saying, yes, these are clear-cut cause and effect relations. I'm saying it ought to be looked at. There is no one looking at this relation between UFOs and outages.

Mr. Ryan: One final question. Do you think it is imperative that the Federal Power Commission, or Federal Communications Commission, investigate the relation between the sightings and the blackout?

Dr. McDonald: My position would call for a somewhat weaker adjective. I'd say extremely desirable.

Mr. Roush: Thank you, Dr. McDonald.[15]

I personally would go a step further than Dr. McDonald. It is *imperative* that this relationship be thoroughly studied. My intuition, based upon years of careful study, tells me that highly classified governmental studies already have and are being conducted in this area. In any event, NICAP and other civilian agencies continue to collect UFO reports indicative of the UFO/ power line/blackout pattern.

A question immediately arises *if* UFOs are physical craft controlled by superintelligent beings. Are the power outages and other forms of electrical interference caused *intentionally,* or are they just an associated *side effect* of the UFO? Observational evidence seems to indicate that both aspects might be involved. This is dead serious. Modern countries have become almost totally dependent upon electricity. Chaos results without it. *If* UFOs are extraterrestrial vehicles, one can only hope and pray that the intelligences that control them are neither unintentionally nor intentionally hostile to man and his environment.

NOTES

1. Personal Files, UFO Report No. 65-30.

2. Personal Files, UFO Report No. 65-32.

3. Letter to NICAP member (Maj. Carl R. Hart, USAF, Public Information Division, Office of Information, to George D. Fawcett, February 12, 1963).

4. Letter to NICAP member (Maj. Maston M. Jacks, USAF, Public Information Division, Office of Information, to John P. Speights, August 5, 1963)

5. Personal Files, UFO Report No. 65-39.

6. Personal Files, UFO Report No. 65-41A.

7. *The APRO Bulletin,* November-December, 1965.

8. *UFO Investigator,* NICAP, November-December, 1965.

9. *Ibid.*

10. Personal Files, UFO Report F66-1.

11. *Sydney Sun,* Australia, February 25, 1967 (as edited by Professor Santorini, August 6, 1973).

12. *Sydney Sun,* Australia, February 25, 1967.

13. Personal correspondence, dated 6 August 1973.

14. *House Report No. 7, Symposium on Unidentified Flying Objects,* Hearings before the Committee on Science and Astronautics, U.S. House of Representatives, Ninetieth Congress, Second Session, July 29, 1968, p. 31.

15. *Ibid.,* pp. 31, 32.

Record *Boston* American

10 Cents Everywhere　　★　　Monday, April 18, 1966　　56 Pages

NOW IT IS REVEALED

UFO Spotted At Great Blackout Site

iery Ball Above iagara Station

STORY ON PAGE TWO

ELUSIVE UFO'S — Raymond E. Fowler, left, Wenham, chairman of committee that probes reports of unidentified flying objects, faces puzzling incidents such as photo of plane above, with arrow pointing to object at its right. Unidentified object behind plane is shown below in blown up photo. Story, Other Photo, Page 2.

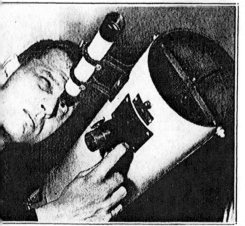

Fowler Peers Through Telescope For UFO Objects
Record American Photo Leo Tierney

Top of the News

'LOST' boy bound for Florida with dad —**Page 2**

JACKIE, Princess Grace steal show at glittering Spanish ball —**Page 3**

FIRES kill man, rout mother and 5 children. —**Page 5**

HANOI SUBURB airbombed by U. S, Reds charge —**Page 2**

RED SOX lose 5th straight —**Back Page**

CELTICS lose in overtime —**Back Page**

One of four overexposed but successful photographs taken near
Trindade Island on January 16, 1958, by a Brazilian IGY expedition.

The enlarged photograph shows an object identical to the "hamburger"
shaped UFO described in Chapter One.

An official U.S. Coast Guard photograph taken of Four UFOs near the New England Station, Salem, Massachusetts, July 16, 1952.

A police skindiver searching for a cylindrical-shaped UFO which entered ice-covered Sunset Lake, Cape Cod, Massachusetts on January 7, 1971. (photo by John Kerr)

9

THE INCREDIBLE MONTHS

While . . . current cases investigated . . . did not yield impressive residual evidence . . . to support an hypothesis that an alien vehicle was physically present . . . the 1966 incident at Beverly, Massachusetts . . . would fit no other explanation if taken at . . . face value.
SCIENTIFIC STUDY OF UFOs
University of Colorado

March Comes In Like a Lion!

March and April 1966 were without a doubt two of the most incredible months I have ever encountered as a *flying saucer investigator!* The quotation prefacing this chapter relates to just one of a series of low-level and well-reported sightings that I investigated during these extraordinary months. I brought the Beverly sighting to the attention of the Air Force-sponsored University of Colorado UFO Project, which, in turn, conducted a reinvestigation of the event. Project scientists were very impressed. January and February had proved to be uneventful. My family activities were actually normal for a change. Then March came along. March came in like a lion!

In March, a concentration of sightings in Michigan became front page newspaper stories throughout the United States. A crowd, including investigating police, had witnessed three UFOs hovering over a swamp near a *radio telescope installation.* One hovered almost at ground level while two others hung in midair just above it. Frank Mannor, who knew the swamp well, advanced toward the UFOs with his son. As they approached the oval domed objects, the UFOs flew off with a whining sound like a *ricochet-*

111

ing bullet! Although the Michigan sightings made the national news, local papers elsewhere were reporting the same type of objects being observed in their own localities. One was shot at near Bangor, Maine, as it hovered over a field near a road. A lone motorist stopped his car to watch it. Curious, but frightened, he took a 22-caliber pistol from his glove compartment and stepped outside for a closer look. Simultaneously, the object began moving toward him. It was so low that it was heard scraping the bushes! The terrified witness began firing at it and could hear bullets ricocheting off metal as it passed overhead. The UFO climbed up and out of sight at a terrific speed. It was described as appearing metallic, oval in shape, and exhibiting a central dome on top. There were so many UFO sightings in this area of Maine that the mayor of Brewer erected a giant billboard that welcomed the UFOs and invited them to settle down in Brewer. *Plenty of land here,* it read! Meanwhile, most of the month of March passed without fanfare in Massachusetts. It was uncanny because during the wave in 1965, UFO publicity had instigated a flood of *IFO* reports. Even this type of report was conspicuously absent. Just when I had about given up hope of anything occurring close enough to investigate, I received word of a significant sighting.

It was Monday, March 21. I had just got home from work and about to sit down for supper when the phone rang. It was for me. "Try not to be too long, dear, as supper is about ready," my wife said as she handed me the phone. An excited voice greeted me on the other end.

"Hello! Mr. Fowler? This is Gene Bertrand calling from Exeter. They're back again!"

"What's going on up there?" I asked. "I haven't talked to you for a long time."

Officer Bertrand then told me that members of the Exeter Police Department and a newspaper reporter had observed a strange glowing object maneuvering over *power lines* late Sunday night and early that very morning!

"No one wants any publicity about this, even the reporter," he cautioned.

I assured him that the witnesses would be kept anonymous

and made arrangements to interview them on the following evening.

Investigator Jack O'Neill and I headed directly for Exeter after working hours on Tuesday evening and grabbed a snack along the way. We arrived at Sergeant——'s home early in the evening and he told us what had occurred in detail.

"A Lighted Egg with a Dome"

I was checking doors in town on Sunday night. It was sometime after ten o'clock when I saw this flash of light out of the corner of my eye. I looked up and saw a fast-moving white light falling vertically in the west. It looked like a shooting star but didn't burn out. It seemed awfully close so I decided to go up to Beech Hill and have a look for it. When I got there, I saw it moving back and forth near a big bright star. It looked like a lighted egg and had rotating lights around the middle.

"What color were the lights?" I asked.

They would change from red to white to blue to green and then back to red again. Then, it just dropped straight down real fast and stopped just above some power lines. I drove down the hill and looked up along the power lines toward Brentwood. It was hovering.

"Officer Bertrand told me that others had seen it," I said. "How did this come about?"

"Well," he replied, "I radioed the station and asked them to send someone out there with some binoculars."

While he waited for assistance to arrive, the sergeant told us, the object slowly ascended. It leveled out and moved into the eastern quadrant of the sky and then moved in a semicircle into the western quadrant again. About this time, one very skeptical police lieutenant and a patrolman arrived on the scene with a pair of binoculars. Through the 7-power glasses, the object was seen to be clearly *egg-shaped* with a brighter white *dome on top*. The rotating lights, especially red, were very prominent but no other details could be seen because of the object's brightness. The skeptical lieutenant was no longer skeptical! After the object receded into the distance, the policemen returned to the station, where the lieutenant told them that there was to be no publicity concerning the incident. The resultant notoriety and problems they had undergone after the classical sighting at Exeter just a year before still tasted bad in their mouths. The lieutenant did not want to go through all that again!

Jack and I then drove over to Gene Bertrand's home. He informed us about the part he had played in this more recent sighting.

> I came on duty and everybody was talking about it. I thought they must have seen the red lights on the antenna tower at Raymond but they said they were familiar with that. What got to me was the fact that the lieutenant was impressed. He'd always been skeptical.

"You said that you saw the object, too, when I talked to you on the phone last night. When did that happen?" I asked.

> I went out to Beech Hill with the sergeant and a newspaper reporter. We watched for a while and saw this light appear over the distant treeline. It would stop, bob, and then swing back and forth like a pendulum. I managed to get the binoculars on it. It seemed to be football shaped.

Betrand then told us that the object ascended into the eastern portion of the sky and hovered momentarily at about an 80-degree elevation before moving out over the ocean and fading into the distance.

Jack and I returned to our respective homes at a very late hour. On the next day, I checked the object's position against bright stars and planets. During his initial sighting, the sergeant had seen the object near a *bright star*. This, in actuality, was the *planet* Jupiter, which later had set in the west about 12:54 A.M. Venus, an extremely bright planet, did not rise in the east until approximately 3:13 A.M. The weather was perfectly clear with northwesterly winds between five to ten knots. The movement, size, motions and directions that the object was seen in ruled out an astronomical explanation. Aircraft and balloons also did not fit the witnesses' observation data. Both Jack and I felt convinced that this sighting fell into the "unknown" category.

No sooner had I put the *new* Exeter report[1] into the mail, than I received a phone call tip from Jim Westover, talkmaster of the Boston "Nightline" radio talkshow. He had heard that UFOs had been sighted at Haverhill, Massachusetts, on the evening of March 29. This growing number of UFO reports in the Haverhill area was puzzling. I immediately put in a call to the Haverhill police. They confirmed that a reported UFO sighting had indeeed been logged at 10:30 P.M. as a result of a phone call from a Russell Conway. After talking to Mr. Conway by phone, I dispatched Jack O'Neill to Haverhill to investigate. The description of the reported object was very similar to what the Exeter police had observed a week earlier.

"A GLOWING OBJECT CIRCLING"

According to Russell, age seventeen, he was getting out of a friend's car about five hundred feet from his house. It was just after nine o'clock. Glancing up, he saw a bright glowing object circling overhead at about eighty degrees above the horizon. It was almost overhead. Fascinated, he watched the object change colors in perfect sequence. He told Jack that

> The light was first a dim white which brightened and dimmed to nothing and was replaced by first a green, then a blue and back to a white light again.

It kept going through this pattern. The circles circumscribed by the object became large as he ran to his house to inform his parents. Mrs. Conway came out in time to watch the strange glowing object abruptly stop and hover for several minutes before suddenly accelerating from a standstill to a blurring speed. It moved out of sight and over the horizon in about three seconds flat! A short glowing blue vapor trail left behind in the object's wake quickly dissipated.

Weather conditions again were perfect for viewing. It had been fair and cool. Interestingly enough, just after the UFO had vanished in the distance, a car had suddenly arrived at the Conway residence. It was Mrs. Conway's nephew who had left the Conway home just prior to the UFO sighting. He excitedly told them that he had just seen a similar object.

During the course of our investigation, it was learned that the nearby Merrimack police had sighted a similar object earlier that same evening at eight o'clock. Mr. Wilfred Lavalley and Officers Frank Matthews and Wallace Spencer all described viewing "a flying white light with blue and red lights rotating around its circumference."[2] Not too many miles farther south, the newly organized NICAP subcommittee for New Hampshire had its hands full. Their files show that on this same date and within the same general time frame, multiple witness sightings were occurring at Eliot, Maine, and North Hampton, New Hampshire!

"A FOOTBALL WITH A DOME"

At 7:50 P.M., Mrs. Madeline Huntress was proceeding along Goodwin Road, Route 101, at East Eliot, Maine. Noticing some lights over some *power lines* up ahead, she continued to observe until she passed close enough to see "an object shaped like a *football* sitting on high power line poles or very close to the wires."[3] She slowed the car for a better look and stated further that "It appeared 20 to 30 feet in diameter and had a *dome* and five or six ports through which a bright white light was shining."[4] She described the object's surface as being a dull silver color like *crumpled aluminum foil*. Frightened, she hurriedly drove home and told her husband. Significantly, and unknown to Mrs. Huntress, others in Eliot were also observing the same or a similar object!

A group of six witnesses watched two bright red glowing objects performing strange maneuvers and making a *pinging sound* like sonar. The time was sometime between 7:30 and 8:00 P.M.![5] Again, around eight o'clock, another witness in Eliot reported seeing a "bright white light with a red light on top moving like a shooting star."[6] Suddenly, it stopped for a moment and took off at great speed into the distance. Just across the border, at nearby Hampton, New Hampshire, Mr. Rodney Grimsley reported seeing two noiseless oval objects. Each carried "a red light revolving counterclockwise."[7] Mr. Grimsley watched in amazement when one of the objects descended and began pacing his car at treetop level for about a thousand feet before accelerating up and out of sight!

March 29, 1966, was indeed a banner day for local UFO reports! But the strangest of all has not been told. Earlier on this fateful day, during the late afternoon hours, one of the most bizarre sightings that I have ever investigated took place in this same general area. The exact location and the names of the witnesses must be kept confidential to protect them and their property from possible curiosity seekers. The principal witness approached within twenty-four feet of an extremely unconventional appearing object on the ground. It took off at lightning speed with a *whining sound* and left its calling cards behind—a shallow, smoothly blown-out depression and imprints from what appeared to have been tripod landing gear!

THE UFO IN THE WOODS[8]

I consider this sighting to be one of the most significant cases in my files because it involves a very unorthodox appearing object (even for a UFO!) seen on the ground at extremely close range for several minutes before it took off. Other witnesses *heard* its strange whining sound and saw the physical traces it left behind just moments later. A most thorough investigation has indicated that a hoax or misinterpretation would have been next to impossible under the overall circumstances. The unusual incident was brought to my attention by investigator Nat Gold, a senior scientist employed by a very well-known camera company. An acquaintance of Nat's, who does consultant engineering, had told him a most intriguing story. He said that he had become good friends with a manager within a large industrial firm while doing consultant work. The manager had confided with him about a *landed* UFO that his son had come across while walking in the woods with his dog. Although the witness's father had told very few people about this experience, Nat, through his friend, sought his cooperation with me in conducting an investigation. Since a number of years had passed since the incident, he agreed to let me interview his son and others indirectly involved provided full anonymity was guaranteed. A detailed investigation was launched by myself and a scientist named John Oswald, who has conducted research into a number of UFO sightings that have taken place in the area around Exeter, New Hampshire. Included within this study was the monitoring of a network of electromagnetic UFO detectors. A paper describing John's work is being prepared for possible publication. NICAP has published summary data on his experiments. However, this is another story; let us discuss—*The UFO in the Woods*. (See figure 2.)

The circumstances. On March 29, 1966, at approximately 4:15 P.M., the witness (age ten) was walking with his Dalmation dog in a woodlot behind his home toward a small pond. He walked this route a few times a week.

The initial encounter. When turning off a rough woods road onto a path leading up a long wooded ridge, he noticed something *silver* on top of the ridge, which he first thought was radar chaff caught in the branches of a tree. He moved off onto the path and could then see that it seemed to be a roughly spherical mass of shredded silver material affixed to the top of a vertical silver rod that stuck up out of what appeared to be the top of a box about one hundred twenty feet away. As he walked closer, the silver rod could be plainly seen. It was about the same thickness as a pencil and about one-and-a-half feet in length.

The boy's next thought was that this "thing" must be some experiment placed there by a neighbor, a consultant physicist, who lives on an adjacent farm. The physicist was known to conduct experiments in his electronics laboratory located in a barn on his property. The witness took his eyes off the "box" for a moment and when he looked at it again, the silver shaft had disappeared. He was only seventy-five feet from the object at this point, according to on-site measurements taken by John and myself.

As he continued to walk up the path toward the object, he saw that it was a box shaped like an *el* lying on its side with

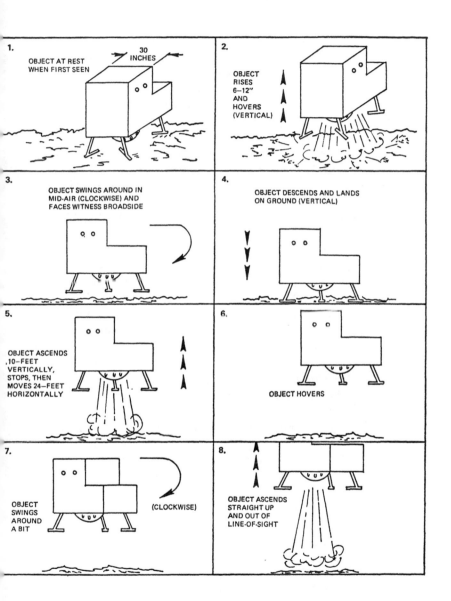

FIGURE 2

tripod legs. Curious, he increased his pace while his dog ran ahead and began sniffing it. Apparently not interested, it continued on its way into the woods. When he got within twenty-four feet of it, he stepped off the path and stepped slightly behind two trees. It was at this point that he realized he was not sure what it was he was looking at.

The object's first movements. Suddenly, without warning, there was a terrific blast of air from the direction of the object, and pine needles and cones flew helter-skelter. Simultaneously, there was a short *high-* then *low-*pitched sound—WHO-O-OP—WHE-E-E!—as the object lifted off the ground about a foot, stopped in midair, swung around in a clockwise motion and settled down on the ground again! This maneuver was about four seconds in duration. The object had risen with a perfectly vertical motion in an unwavering, mechanical-like manner. It was all too obvious that this object had nothing to do with his neighbor's experiments. The thought that it must be some kind of Air Force hovercraft raced through his mind as curiosity suddenly changed to terror! He did not know whether to run or what to do! Then, strange *electric-like* sounds came from within the "box" and he froze to the spot!

Detailed object description. The witness found himself facing the intermittently humming object about broadside, i.e., with its longest side about parallel with him. He got a good look at this side of it. On the upper left side, which was higher, there were two round black *holes,* which seemed to be just under an inch in diameter. These appeared to be definite openings, not just markings, and were recessed into the object about an inch. They were spaced about six inches apart and centered in the upper left portion appearing like *eyes* watching him. He saw nothing inside these holes.

Centered and attached to the middle of the object's underside was a round appearing section protruding downwards that looked like a *dishpan* or flattened dome. It was about two feet in diameter and had three two-inch openings spaced around that part of the circumference facing the witness. The holes were more egg-shaped than round and were like an egg standing on end. He never noticed if there were similar holes continuing around the circumference of this domelike protrusion.

The color of the *boxlike* part of the object was a brownish hue that blended well with the trees. Its surface was somewhat like that of unevenly rusted steel but looked more like the pitted surface that *cork* displays. It looked more nonmetallic than metallic. The object had definite sharp edges, i.e., its extremities were not rounded. The domelike section appeared to be of similar material but darker and more like metal. The tripod legs were square shafts about one inch in diameter. They apeared to be about one foot long and were attached to the bottom of the object around and slightly away from where the *dome* was attached. Each leg angled out slightly and had a pad attached on the end. The pads were about one foot long and about two inches square. The legs were attached about three inches inwards, and about nine inches of the pad toed inward, forming vee shapes relative to one another. They appeared to be constructed of a very dull, nonshiny metal.

Intermittent sounds come from object. While wondering what to do next and thinking about turning around and running, the boy hesitated as he heard a series of intermittent *electric-like* sounds coming from within the object. A "humming" was as close as he could describe these sounds, although he felt this was not a satisfactory description. The sound stopped and started three to four times in a random rather than in an evenly timed fashion for about one minute. The longest of these humming periods was estimated to be about fifteen seconds in duration when John and I timed the witness's reenactment of the event.

Last observed movements (vertical-horizontal-vertical). Suddenly a huge blast of air rushed out from the domed underside of the object sending pine needles flying about in all directions! The witness compared the blast of air to facing a stiff wind or standing about fifty feet from moving helicopter rotors. Concurrent with this blast of air was the same sound he had heard when it had ascended before but much louder. The loudness and pitch increased as the box-shaped craft ascended. He saw no lights, flame, or exhaust and smelled nothing unusual. The object rose in a perfectly straight vertical fashion until it reached an altitude of about ten feet. It then stopped for a split second (the loudness and pitch of the whining sound leveled off at this point) and then moved quickly on a perfectly straight horizontal course for about twenty-four feet. As it moved, the pitch and loudness of its noise remained the same. Saplings located directly under the object's flight path swayed as if the downward air blast were still continuing. The witness saw and felt nothing that would indicate a *sidewards* propulsion blast. At this point, the object again stopped and swung around clockwise in midair for about ninety degrees before accelerating straight up and out of sight behind tree branches. He described the speed as being as fast as a solid fuel ground-to-air missile. Simultaneously with its final ascent was a great increase in the pitch and loudness of the whining sound. He heard the sound from above die down as if the object continued to recede away vertically. On-site witness reenactment of this final vertical-horizontal-vertical maneuver from start to stop (before final ascent) took only 2.5 seconds. This is important, as it seems as if the sound associated with this maneuver was what was heard by the witness's mother and sister, who were at a distance of about eight hundred feet away.

Witness reaction. Upon the object's departure, the boy immediately turned and ran home, shouting for his mother as he went! An on-site timed reenactment of his run along the identical route took just about two minutes.

Audio witnesses. During the boy's encounter with the UFO, his mother had opened a window and was talking to her daughter, who was skating on some ice about seventy-five feet from the house. This window was facing in the general direction of the sighting area but was in under trees that blocked a clear view of the sky. Suddenly, both mother and daughter heard a strange *whining sound* fill the air! They told me that it sounded like "an elevator which started up, stopped at the second floor to pick up a passenger, and then restarted and moved nonstop all the way to the top floor." Their description corresponded with the sound associated with the final maneuver of the UFO. Then, they told me, they could hear the son's voice yelling from up in the woods. He arrived out of breath and so excited that he could hardly talk. His mother told me that when he finally blurted out what he had seen, she warily followed him back to the sighting area.

Witnesses of physical traces. Upon arriving at the place where the object had been, they found a circular impression seemingly blown out of the heavily matted area of pine needles. It was about two feet in diameter, about four to six inches deep at the center, and shaped somewhat like a large shallow bowl. Elongated impressions were visible around and outside of the depression's circumference. The witness's mother told me that they resembled the impressions that a ruler might make if laid flat on the pine needles and pressed down about one inch. They then returned to the house, where she asked her son to draw a sketch and write out a description of what he had seen. She said his hands were literally shaking as he sat down at the kitchen table with pencil and paper. The witness's father arrived home from work soon thereafter and found his son still at the table forty-five minutes after the sighting. After being briefed on what had happened, he grabbed a Kodak Instamatic camera with flash attachment and went up to the site with his son and daughter. He took three photographs, which turned out to be very poor.

The witness's father made the following observations about the physical traces and sighting area: (1) The center depression was perfectly smooth and rounded and had to be "mechanically made." (2) He saw no traces of foreign substances or scorching. (3) He *sniffed* around the markings but did not smell anything. (4) The round impression appeared to have been smoothly blown out of four inches of pine needles and two inches of earth. (5) He found a freshly broken twig about two feet long and about the diameter of a pen on the ground under the horizontal flight path of the object. (6) The object had been sitting under a near-solid canopy of white pine. It could not have come down from the sky through them but would have to have been intelligently guided down through, in and under these pines, in just the reverse of the way it had left the area. (7) He expressed some dismay as to how an object of that size and corresponding weight could be lifted up by a reaction-type engine. There was no residue or scorched area and no violent markings such as would have been made by a jet engine.

Four days after the sighting occurred, the family's Saturday handyman was shown the markings. During my investigation, I questioned him. He confirmed the markings and told me that nothing grew in the disturbed area for about two years.

Sighting aftermath. After the father had interrogated his son, he phoned a friend of his who was acquainted with a state policeman in order to find out what the procedure was for reporting UFOs. The state police officer told his friend that they had been ordered to relay all such UFO reports directly to Pease Air Force Base and then drop the matter. He advised against reporting the incident because the Air Force might ridicule the witness and the newspapers might somehow get hold of the story. He warned that any publicity would attract all kinds of publicity seekers to his property. That was enough for the witness's father! He never officially reported the bizarre episode.

During my investigation of the "UFO in the woods," I researched NICAP files to ascertain if there were similar reports on record. I found only one other sighting description that was somewhat akin to it.

Young Michael J. Bizon had gone outside his home in Hubbard, Oregon, to let the cow out of her stall. His mother, Mrs. Leonard M. Bizon, was inside the house. The time was about 7:30 A.M., May 19, 1964.

"I went to put the cow in the field," Mike said. "Usually she can't wait to get out there. . . . She was crosswise in the stanchion and seemed very nervous. . . . She was bucking all the way."

Then he saw a square object about four feet high. The silver colored UFO was sitting in the middle of a wheat field. It had four shiny legs.

"It started with a soft beep and started to go up," the boy told Marion County Deputy Sheriff Shirlie H. Davidson, who sent his official report to NICAP. "It went up slow until it got to about the height of a telephone pole. Then it shot up just like a rocket. . . ."

Mike said the UFO emitted a smell like gas fumes as it rose. He then ran into the house. Mrs. Bizon said her son "had been very frightened and half crying when he had made the report to her."

At about this time, Ray Mortenson, the Bizons' carpenter,

arrived on the scene. He went with the boy to the wheat field, and they found a spot where the wheat had been flattened out.

"I would say the area was between three and four feet across," the carpenter stated, "with the wheat being pushed out in a flower-shaped pattern."

After being notified of the incident, Officer Davidson also arrived on the scene and saw the flattened area.

"The grain appeared to have been pushed down by some object," Davidson wrote in his report. "Three particular spots were noted. These were spaced about thirty-six inches apart...."

Later, an officer from Adair Air Force Base also inspected the site....[9]

The similarities between the two sightings are striking. In both cases the witness was a young boy; the UFO was shaped like a box with a domelike protrusion; the sightings took place in a rural area; the "blown-out" area included three impressions made by the object's legs, and, both departed straight up like a rocket! It is possible that the differences in description were a result of witness error. The Oregon sighting did not take place at close range. It is perhaps significant that although Michael Bizon reported seeing four legs, only three depressions were found around the blown-out area at Hubbard, Oregon.

And Goes Out like a Lion!

The following day, March 30, brought still another series of low-level UFO sightings. The setting this time was along the Massachusetts and Rhode Island border at Rehobeth, Massachusetts. I was alerted to the incidents by a newscaster who saw the reports come in over the state police teletype. Ernest Reid, a detective and member of the subcommittee, was sent to conduct an enquiry into the matter.[10]

GROUP 1

The first group consisted of two young couples driving west on Cedar Street at about 8:20 P.M. Suddenly, a dark object carrying horizontal bright pulsating red lights passed over the road just ahead of them. It barely cleared the telephone poles. Startled, they slowed the car and stared at the object, which abruptly stopped, hovered, and then slowly descended toward a wooded area. They watched incredulously as the pattern of lights moved slowly from a *horizontal* position to a *vertical* position, brightened, and then dimmed to nothing. The alarmed witnesses received the impression that it had landed in the woods. They drove immediately to the state police barracks to report what they had seen. The police, in turn, phoned Otis Air Force Base. Later, the young couples were questioned by Air Force Captain Paul McManus.

GROUP 2

In the meantime, during the same time frame, five other persons were returning home from choir practice along Route 118. As they rounded a bend, they sighted a group of very bright red lights hovering about five hundred feet over the road just ahead of them. The dim outline of a reflecting metallic oval object could be discerned behind the lights. As the car closed on the object, it suddenly accelerated to a terrific speed from a dead standstill and disappeared behind trees!

GROUP 3

Later on during that same evening, the Rehobeth postmaster was watching television when his wife called him to the window to see some strange lights approaching in the sky. He got up, took a quick look and ran out to the backyard. The bright red pulsating lights lay in a horizontal plane and appeared to be attached to one object. As the object passed by at about one thousand feet away, he heard a strange *whistling* or *humming* sound. The lights were too brilliant to be able to see the actual shape of the craft. As he watched, it swung around in a broad arc into the southwest and disappeared behind a hill about a quarter of a mile away.

THE INVESTIGATION

Investigator Reid arrived in Rehobeth just three days after the sighting. A detective and Civil Defense radiological monitor,

Ernie had proven to be a great asset to the subcommittee. He probed about the estimated landing area with a Geiger counter but obtained negative results. Later, as I examined his report, one cryptic remark leaped out at me from the page. I read:

An interesting and perhaps significant fact uncovered was that there is a large concentration of high tension electrical power coming into a substation in the area of the UFO sighting.

Looking back in retrospect, it seemed as if the three groups of witnesses had all sighted the same or very similar objects within a radius of several miles. The characteristic intensely bright red pulsating lights, oval configuration, ability to hover and dart away from a standstill, and the reported *humming* or *whistling* sound were all reported characteristics of a host of other UFO reports. This particular group of sightings at Rehoboth was nearly identical to the type of sightings just reported along the Massachusetts-New Hampshire-Maine borders! The pattern of power lines at the sighting locale was becoming a very familiar aspect of UFO sightings.

March may have come in and gone out like the proverbial lion, but the dam burst in April! There were more than "April showers" on tap for the following month. It was to be a torrential downpour!

April Cloudburst!

In April 1966 the sky literally burst from the weight of UFO sighting reports. The man on the street, reading the Boston and other big city newspapers, had no inkling about what was going on. Radio and television newscasts were silent. A friend of mine, employed at a Boston radio station, told me that during this hectic period, his supervisor would not allow him to include UFO reports arriving via teletype on the newscast. Contacts within the FAA told me that during this period of 1966, they were relaying radar contact UFO reports to the Air Force Foreign Technology Division at Hanscom Field, Bedford, Massachusetts. The only public media reporting this deluge of UFO sightings were the *local* newspapers. I was receiving large brown envelopes literally crammed with local clippings from the New England Newsclip Agency. It soon became apparent that there were just too many sightings for the subcommtitee to handle. We concentrated on those that seemed the most significant. In the meantime, our sister subcommittee in New Hampshire, barely organized and undermanned, was also overwhelmed by a flood of reports in that state. Even as I write, researchers are still trying to pick up all the pieces from this particular deluge of UFO sightings.

I shall not attempt to describe all of the April 1966 UFO sightings that we investigated within the confines of this chapter. (The interested reader can refer to the Appendix for a listing of 160 local "unknowns" investigated between 1963 and 1973.) Instead, I shall concentrate mainly upon two of the best UFO sightings that took place during this fantastic month. The first to be discussed occurred on April 18/19 at Sharon, Massachusetts. Perhaps the best place to start would be the following transcript taken from the blotter of the Sharon Police Department. Two officers had been dispatched to investigate some strange lights in the sky at about 11:30 P.M. on April 18.

The Sharon Saucer

OFFICER'S REPORT

As the result of a telephone call received from Mr. and Mrs. May, 7 Holly Lane, reporting strange objects in the sky, Officer Jones and I responded to Holly Lane. On arrival, we found Officer Testa and Sgt. Donovan observing distant lights in the sky with Mr. and Mrs. May and May's sister. About 12:10 A.M., Sgt. Donovan and Officer Testa left and Officer Jones and myself watched these distant lights with the Mays. One of these objects was in a northwesterly direction, similar to a star, only brighter. It appeared to be rotating and changing colors from red to white to green. There were two other objects of the same description in a southwesterly direction. While we were observing these distant lights, Mrs. May said, "Here it comes," or "There it is," and we all looked in an easterly direction. The object appeared to be a falling star at a great distance, only three times the size of a star, and brighter. Within a matter of two or three seconds the object appeared over the tree line on the easterly side of the field in front of the Mays' house. It was about two hundred to three hundred yards away from us and approximately five hundred feet up. When the object was hovering over the tree line, it appeared as a very bright, large mass of white light with a ballish appearance. The object made no noise whatsoever and did not cast any light onto the tree line or ground below. The object stopped and hovered over the tree line for approximately two or three minutes. While the object hovered, a plane passed over in a northerly direction. When the plane moved off, the object started to move across the field in front of us in a southwesterly direction. As the object passed in front of us, I viewed a red light in front and a red light to the rear that remained on (not flashing), and a wide section of white light extending from red light to red light which appeared to be inside lights. I concentrated on trying to see inside of the object for any figures or movements but failed to detect any sign of life or figures. I feel as if I did see inside the object. The object disappeared as it went over the tree line in a southwesterly direction.[11]

I assigned investigators Jack O'Neill and Ernest Reid to this case. Their report stated that all of the witnesses agreed that the UFO was about the size of an automobile. Sergeant Coffee, who had written the report up in the blotter, told them:

I could see the curvature of these lights which would indicate that the object was oval. The curvature of lights appeared to be like windows.[12]

Our investigation took place on April 20. We had beaten Air Force investigators to the site by just a few days. Officers from Hanscom Field conducted an official enquiry on April 22. Ernie Reid had found this fact out when he returned a week later to obtain additional information from the police. The policeman at the desk told him that the Air Force had instructed the Sharon police chief to say no more concerning this or any future incidents. The police were instructed to maintain a separate nonpublic log on further UFO reports in the area!

The officer soon found out that he had told this to the wrong person. Ernie knew his rights under the law. He headed a detective agency and was studying for his doctorate in criminology.

He informed the police officer that the blotter was within the public domain and threatened to phone a complaint in to the district attorney's office. The policeman, a bit shaken at this turn of events, put in a phone call to the chief at his home. The chief decided that he would rather face the Air Force than the D. A. and Ernie was given the requested data; During the course of the investigation, we discovered a number of other sightings that had occurred on the same date.

OTHER SIGHTINGS THAT NIGHT

Several minutes after the *Sharon Saucer* had buzzed the startled witnesses at the Mays' field, others in the area reported sighting a similar object. Mr. and Mrs. Keeling were driving along Wallamalapoag Street in Sharon, about one-half mile from the May home. Suddenly, a "white beacon-like light with smaller red lights at either end" was seen moving slowly, less than a thousand feet above the ground.[13] Simultaneously, Mr. David Clapp, who was driving along South Main Street, a mile away from the May home, saw a bright white light "like a locomotive headlight" moving along about five hundred feet above the ground. In a split second, it abruptly reversed its direction and accelerated into the distance and out of view. Unknown to the UFO observers in Sharon was the fact that similar UFOs had been seen at Bellingham at 10:00 P.M.,[14] Peabody at 10:45 P.M.[15] and at Quincy, just prior to midnight.[16] Five aircraft and a helicopter circled a nearly landed UFO at Bellingham! Then, just three days later on Friday, April 22, a similar UFO sighting took place practically in my own back yard, at Beverly, during the mid-evening hours. It too involved civilians and investigating police officers observing a UFO at close range![17]

The Beverly Affair

PRELUDE

This part of the Beverly Affair has never been told. The evening of the twenty-second found me busily preparing final reports on a number of UFO sightings. The phone rang. It was the Beverly police. They informed me that phone calls were being received concerning a fiery green object. I ran out to the car and set off for the area where the object had been seen. The car radio was playing, and as I neared my destination a news bulletin interrupted the program. The announcer stated that the object which had just startled New Englanders was a huge meteor—a fireball! Disgusted, I started to look for a place to turn the car around when my eye caught a red light moving in the sky. I stopped the car and got out to observe it. Puzzled, I wondered why I could not see any red and green identification lights as it slowly approached my position. Thinking that the glowing red mass must be a strangely lighted helicopter, I strained to hear the usually noisy sound of its engine. It passed almost directly over me, moving very slowly, but all I heard was a faint indistinct sound. Excited, I got back in the car and was able to actually get ahead of the object once again by maneuvering down some back roads. I got out of the car again and walked into a large field along Route 22 in Wenham just as the red glowing blob again passed overhead. I flashed my flashlight at it half in fun but without effect. Just as it was moving over the distant tree line, it suddenly swung in an arc as if it were attached to the end of an unseen body and descended behind the trees. I stood there for a few minutes thinking about the matter and decided that it must have been a helicopter. It was about 7:00 p.m. as I headed back home to work on the ever-increasing pile of UFO reports. Little did I know that in just a few hours Beverly would be visited by something more substantial than a red light. Had I realized then what was about to occur, I would have paid more attention to what I had observed. Now, I'll always wonder if it really was a helicopter and what I might have seen if I had stayed out observing the sky on that fateful night.

On Saturday morning I received the news. Mrs. Claire Modugno phoned to tell me that many persons had seen three UFOs over the Beverly High School last night. I started to dismiss the sighting as the fireball but stopped when she interrupted to tell me that their sighting had taken place much later. I was about to suggest Jupiter as an alternative, when I realized she was trying to describe a close-encounter UFO sighting to me. When she further told me that the Beverly police had been involved, I was very skeptical because I felt sure that they would have reported such a thing to me. I told her this and mentioned that they had phoned me earlier about the fireball. She agreed that this was strange and related to me that she had phoned the police just prior to calling me to ask about the sighting but that no one at the station would admit any involvement at all. She sounded serious, so I decided to drop everything and check this one out personally.

THE INVESTIGATION

I phoned the police and was told that there was no such report on the blotter except an earlier report on the fireball. I asked who was on duty during the sighting period and obtained the names of two pairs of officers who were on patrol at that time. I phoned and eliminated the first pair, which narrowed it down to Officers Bossie and Mahon. When I called them, they hedged my questions at first but finally admitted that they had seen something and agreed to be interviewed.

On the following day, Sunday, April 24, 1966, I interviewed all the civilian witnesses and had each fill out and sign standard questionnaires. I then proceeded to Beverly Police Headquarters. At the station, I was again given the runaround. However, after pointing out that other police departments had cooperated with me and that both Officers Bossie and Mahon had agreed to be interviewed, the officer in charge ordered the desk sergeant to summon the witnesses to the station by radio. Upon their arrival, they were told to tell me exactly what they had witnessed. We were ushered to a private room, and I interrogated them for about an hour. They filled out and signed UFO report forms and signed brief statements regarding the sighting.

THE SIGHTING ACCOUNT

The UFO sighting started about nine o'clock in the evening when Nancy Modugno, age eleven, noticed a blinking light shining through her bedroom window. She looked out the window and saw a football-shaped object about the size of an automobile. It was flashing blue, green, red, and soft white lights as it passed along Sohier Road, seemingly only forty feet away! A soft "whizzing" sound came from the strange craft as it passed behind nearby trees heading toward a large open field behind the Beverly High School. The lights could still be seen through the trees, and it appeared as if the object was landing in the field.

Nancy was terrified and ran downstairs to tell her father about what she had seen. Angelo Modugno was watching television at the time and was experiencing difficulty in reception as Nancy came tearing down the stairs. His wife, Claire Modugno, was in the adjoining apartment visiting neighbors Barbara Smith and Brenda Maria. Barbara and Brenda left Claire and walked into the Modugno home to use the telephone to order some pizza. When they entered, the found Nancy in an hysterical condition and her father Angelo attempting to calm her down. They tried to comfort Nancy by telling her that what she saw was probably just an airplane. They looked out the window towards the field and saw some flashing lights. Then they told Nancy that they would walk down to the field and prove that it was an airplane in order to reassure her.

Barbara and Brenda went next door and got Claire. The three of them then walked down Sohier Road to Herrick Street and then down a slight hill onto the high school field. Puzzled, they sighted three brilliantly lighted objects flying in circular patterns. They would circle and hover and then proceed to circle again. One object was directly over the high school. The others were in the distance, seemingly over Route 128 and the Bomac Research buildings. The witnesses told me that the strange vehicles looked as if they were "playing tag"!

Brenda, half in fun, began waving her arms and motioned as if she wanted them to come closer. At this point, while the closest object was completing a circle over the school, it started to move directly towards them! Barbara and Claire took one look at the strange wingless craft bearing down on them and turned and began running back up the rise onto Herrick Street. Brenda, momentarily unaware that her companions were no longer standing behind her, was shouting that it was going to pass right over them. In the meantime, Barbara and Claire stopped running and looked back to see if Brenda was coming. They gasped at the frightening sight they saw. The object was hovering only twenty feet over Brenda, who was screaming and covering her head with her hands. She told me that she felt that the object was going to squash her! Barbara and Claire shouted at Brenda to run, and she broke into a run as the object moved back toward the high school in a semicircular pattern. As the trio ran home along Herrick Street, they could see it again maneuvering over the school.

Three very excited women burst into the Modugno home and phoned neighbors to come out and see the UFOs. Mrs. Theresa Scanzani could not leave her yard but could see one of the objects from her vantage point. Mr. and Mrs. Bob Lessor came right over and joined Barbara, Brenda, and the whole Modugno family. They all ran down to the corner of Herrick Street and Salem Road to a fence overlooking the field. Two objects, exhibiting the same changing colors, could be seen hovering at a high altitude in the distance. They apeared a little larger than stars and were very brilliant. One object was hovering directly over the high school about six hundred feet from them. It appeared to be only thirty feet above the roof! It was oval shaped and was flashing a very bright red light along with dimmer green and white lights. This was enough for Bob Lessor. He tore back up the street and phoned the police.

Police officers Bossie and Mahon had been parked less than a mile away when the phone message was relayed to them via radio. They arrived on the scene shortly and jokingly enquired of the witnesses gathered at the fence, "Where's the airplane?" The group excitedly pointed the object out to them as it circled the school. Both officers were visibly shaken. They got out of the cruiser and watched for a few moments and then jumped back in and sped down Salem Road into the school parking lot. They stopped and started to get out of the cruiser as the object began moving away from them. They took up chase but lost sight of it. Meanwhile, police headquarters had notified the Air Force. Not too long after the sighting, both civilians and police saw and heard two airplanes and a helicopter circling the general area. They may have been sent to investigate. It is significant to note that the witnesses immediately recognized these craft as being conventional. Their running lights were nothing like the lights they had observed on the UFOs. In fact, one of the things that amazed all of the observers was that, except for the initial sighting made by Nancy, the objects had been completely silent. Brenda said that even when the UFO was directly over her head, she hadn't heard a thing—not even a stirring of the air!

SAMPLE DESCRIPTIONS

The following descriptive statements by some of the witnesses are typical of many other observers who have attempted to describe close encounters with UFOs. One immediately senses the utter *strangeness* of the witnesses' experience as they painstakingly grasp for the proper words to describe the *indescribable!*

Nancy Modugno: The object had four lights: red, blue-green, and a lamp color. It looked like a football but was the size of a car. On the top, it had no windows. The front was pointed. I was terrified.[18]

Barbara Smith: While watching one that was completing a circle, it started to come toward us. I started to run. Then a friend called, "Look up, it is directly over us," so I looked up and stood still in surprise. I saw a large round object at rooftop level. It was just like looking at the bottom of a plate. It was solid. I saw no flashing lights as I did when they were farther away, but I did see a halo-like light that went across the front. The color of the object was a grayish white. I heard no sound at all but I felt this thing was going to come down on top of me. It was like a giant mushroom. I was fascinated, stunned, unable to think and automatically found myself running away from it.[19]

Brenda Maria: This object appeared larger and larger as it came closer. The lights appeared to be all around and turning. The colors were very bright. When overhead, all I could see above my head was a blurry atmosphere and brightly lit-up lights flashing slowly around. I was very, very excited—not scared— very curious. I would not have run at all except for the fact that the object got too close and I thought it might crash on my head.[20]

Claire Modugno: It came right toward me. It looked brilliant. It was grayish, seemed very smooth, and seemed to take on the red and also the green from the very brilliant lights. I was terribly scared.[21]

Officer Bossie: I saw an oval red object just ahead of me. The lights were bright and were blinking all the time. I heard no noise and the object seemed to stay at the same height and just move away very smoothly.[22]

Officer Mahon: On arrival, I observed what seemed to me to be like a large plate hovering over the school. It had three lights —red, green and white—but no noise was heard to indicate it to be a plane. This object hovered over the school.[23]

FROM HIGH SCHOOL TO COLLEGE

While the *Beverly Affair* was underway, it would apear that perhaps one of the two similarly colored objects seen in the distance had buzzed the campus of Gordon College in my own hometown of Wenham![24]

Vivian Russell and Patricia Wells had just left the Gordon College Student Union. Suddenly, Vivian called Patricia's attention to a bright yellow-orange light, larger and brighter than a star, which was approaching the campus from the south. As it got closer, it took on a rough circular or squashed rectangular shape, which was divided by a dark center line. Patricia dashed back into a coffee shop and alerted Diane Hopkins, while Vivian remained observing the slowly approaching object. They watched it come within an estimated six hundred feet of them at an altitude of about a one hundred feet, when it abruptly stopped. Then, almost instantaneously, it suddenly executed a smooth ninety-degree turn and darted at terrific speed into the west over the tree line! As it turned, its shape changed to an upright sliver of light and then to a larger, glowing, flattened oval. Almost immediately afterward, a small aircraft flew over the campus. The witnesses compared it with the strange object. The airplane's noise and configuration was easily identifiable, whereas the weird, silent, glowing object was unlike anything they had ever seen before.

During the month of April 1966, I received a total of twenty-two reports that were evaluated as being in the "unknown" category! Six of these reports involved UFOs hovering over or around *school buildings.* The similarity of the sightings at Beverly and Wenham is striking. Both featured a large grassy quadrangle, a school, and adjoining reservoirs of water. March and April 1966, both locally and elsewhere throughout the world, truly were *the incredible months!*

NOTES

1. Personal Files, UFO Report No. 66-2.
2. Personal Files, UFO Report No. 66-3.
3. Personal Files, UFO Report No. 66-10A.
4. *Ibid.*
5. Personal Files, UFO Report No. 66-2A.
6. Personal Files, UFO Report No. 66-2B.
7. Personal Files, UFO Report No. 66-2C.
8. Personal Files, UFO Report No. 66-3A.
9. NICAP, *Strange Effects from UFOs*, pp. 53, 54.
10. Personal Files, UFO Report No. 66-4.
11. Personal Files, UFO Report No. 66-24.
12. *Ibid.*
13. *Ibid.*
14. Personal Files, UFO Report No. 66-21.
15. Personal Files, UFO Report No. 66-17.
16. Personal Files, UFO Report No. 66-23.
17. Personal Files, UFO Report No. 66-26 A/B.
18. *Ibid.*
19. *Ibid.*
20. *Ibid.*
21. *Ibid.*
22. *Ibid.*
23. *Ibid.*
24. *Ibid.*

10

ASSIGNMENT: COLORADO PROJECT

Both Norm and I consider the accumulation of sightings in Massachusetts about as impressive as the UFO business offers. . . . . and have concluded you must be working more than full time on the UFO question.

> DR. ROY CRAIG
> Colorado Project Investigator[1]
> Letter of September 14, 1967

Close Encounter at Methuen

During the months that followed, local UFO reports dropped sharply from a high of twenty-two unknowns in April to an average of about two unknowns per month for the remainder of 1966. Several months after the open congressional hearings on UFOs, held on April 5, the Air Force announced that it would contract the University of Colorado to conduct an independent scientific study of UFOs. Needless to say, I was highly pleased about this prospect and was grateful that my report on the Exeter incident had figured so prominently in these hearings. As the new year dawned, I had high hopes that research conducted by the Colorado Project would finally result in the scientific recognition of a new species—the UFO.

In the meantime, UFO reports were on the increase again. The sighting rate had taken a noticeable swing upwards in November and continued to climb throughout the month of January. One of these sightings took place on the evening of January 20, 1967, along a dark country road at Methuen, Massachusetts.[2] The witnesses, enroute to a basketball game, experienced a close encounter with a UFO concurrent with a complete disruption of their automobile's ignition system!

I heard about the sighting less than three hours after it occurred. Shortly before nine o'clock on that Friday night, the telephone rang. It was a former company associate, Roger Bulmer, calling me from Methuen. He had just returned from a local high school basketball game and had overheard three young ladies discussing a strange object that had approached their car while they were enroute to the game. His neighbor also had mentioned seeing something similar while driving his daughter and friend to the game. Remembering that I was interested in such things, Roger phoned me about it. After he hung up, I placed a phone call to the witnesses and arranged an interview and a visit to the sighting area on the following day. Their intriguing account follows.

GROUP 1

Miss Kimberly (Kim) Lodge was driving friends to the local basketball game. She had already picked up Ellen Kenney and Janice Shafer and was proceeding northeast on Washington Street to Juan Sierpina's house. The lonely street was bordered by woods, fields, and very few houses. Reaching the top of a hill, they were shocked to see a string of nine to ten bright glowing red lights up ahead that were moving over a field just off the road to their left.

"What's that?" Janice said.

"It must be a helicopter," Ellen replied.

Kim laughed. "It must be a UFO or a flying saucer!"

During my interview with the witnesses, Ellen remarked to me that at this point "all of a sudden, it wasn't funny anymore."

The object stopped moving and they were closing on it rapidly. Kim slowed the car. Simultaneously, the object seemed to swing around as if it were "spinning on its axis" and revealed lights of a different color and configuration. At this point, Ellen told me,

> Kim pulled over. They wanted to get out of the car but I didn't. Janice said, "Let's go look at the helicopter." All of a sudden,

the car stalled and the radio and the lights went off. Then nobody wanted to get out of the car. Truthfully, I was too scared to carefully observe the object.[3]

Kim told me that during this juncture in the sighting, she had opened her side window in order to get a better look at the object. She stated:

> The lights and our radio all went off at the same time. After this, I tried to start the car twice while the object remained stationary. Thinking that the lights and radio would be drawing too much power from the battery of the car, I shut the light switch and the radio off. Then I tried to start the car again. It did not start.[4]

Kim had observed the object through an open side window. The others were too afraid to put down the larger windows. Ellen was so terrified that she was crouching in the back seat! However, Kim and Janice did look out and described what they had seen to me. It was hovering about one hundred to three hundred feet away from the car near or over a darkened house. Four glowing lights formed a perfect trapezoid. Two red lights formed the top and two white lights formed the base. Janice thought she saw a dimmer white light just above the two red lights. Kim felt that the red lights were blinking slightly. She compared them to the color and brightness of a hot electric stove burner. The center of the trapezoid pattern seemed to be dark and nonreflecting. However, around the lights, a metallic glow of reflecting metal could be seen. It was "like the color and texture of erector-set material" and formed an inverted bowl shape around the lights. All were impressed with its size and compared it with the size of the darkened house that was about one hundred feet away. Kim felt it was "as wide as the house but not as tall." Janice said she thought it was one-half as large as the house, whereas Ellen estimated it to be just as large as the house.

I questioned Kim thoroughly about the car ignition failure. She told me that it just made a "moaning sound" when she pressed the starter. She did note, however, that the generator panel lamp was dimly pulsating off and on. This may be significant. They observed the strange craft for one to two minutes before it started moving very slowly at first, but then it shot away at terrific speed back along its original flight path. Kim then was able to start the car with no trouble at all and turned on the lights, which worked perfectly. The trio continued nervously along the road to pick up Juan and turned the radio back on; it worked fine. When they reached Juan's house, Kim rushed in and phoned her father about what had just happened. Kim's father, a foreman at the Lawrence Gas Company, signed a statement to the effect that:

> I was watching Walter Cronkite on Channel 5, approximately between 6:30 and 7:00 P.M., when I received a call from my daughter stating that she and two friends saw a flying saucer on Washington Street, Methuen, while on the way to pick up a friend who lives in this area. The car stalled, lights went out, and radio went dead. My daughter said it was heading this way. . . . I did go outside . . . and looked at the sky. Nothing out of the ordinary was observed by me.[5]

GROUP 2

Interestingly enough, another group in a car less than three miles away sighted "a big square-shaped pattern of red, blue, green and yellow lights moving in the sky at about 7:00 P.M. Mr. Arthur ——, the driver, was bringing his daughter Nancy and her friend Peggy to the same basketball game. Nancy saw the unconventional grouping of lights and called out to everybody to look. He told me that he slowed and got a glimpse of seven to eight bright lights flying only three to four hundred feet above the ground about a half mile away from them. He had dismissed them as probably lights on a low-flying airplane and even thought he heard the muffled sound of an aircraft engine. None of them could actually see what was carrying the lights, and his daughter and girl friend felt that it was not an airplane. The sighting time estimated by the Group 2 witnesses was just before seven o'clock. The flight path of the departing object described by Group 1 would have intersected the route of Group 2, who were proceeding northeast along Lowell Street. Lowell Street would parallel Washington Street if it were extended. I concluded that it was highly probable that both groups had observed the same object.

ADDITIONAL WITNESS CHECK

A spot check of seven residences in the Group 1 sighting area revealed that three families had been out shopping and that four families were inside their houses during the sighting period. No homes experienced problems with radio, television or electricity. The three girls had noted that street lights along the road had remained on. Only the car was affected. The weather had been clear with an unlimited ceiling.

ATTEMPT AT IDENTIFICATION

Astronomical phenomena were checked and ruled out. Wind direction and speed ruled out a lighted balloon because the object would have to have moved directly into the wind when it departed. I talked to Mr. Kirkman, manager of the Lawrence Airport, which is located three miles southeast of the Group 1 sighting area. He told me that he knew of nothing flying out of his field on that night or any other night that would display the reported lights, colors, and hovering attitude. He furthermore stated that the sighting area was not on the landing and takeoff approach to the airfield. He stressed that planes entering and leaving the airport would be away from the sighting area. Another check revealed that the infamous Sky-Lite advertising plane was grounded and had been under repair since the first of the year.

WITNESS BACKGROUND (Group 1)

The girls were straightforward and very mature. All were seniors at the Tenney High School in Methuen. Kim, age seventeen, was a member of the National Honors Society, the editor-in-chief of the school newspaper, assistant editor of the yearbook, member of the math and physics clubs, secretary of the French and college clubs, a majorette, and a member of the Rainbow

Girls. Janice, age seventeen, and Ellen, age sixteen, had much the same type of background. Dr. James E. McDonald and Dr. J. Allen Hynek, who made enquiries into this case at a later date, were both equally impressed with the girls' sincerity and maturity.

THE AUTOMOBILE

The affected automobile was a 1961 Rambler four-door sedan. It had a six-cylinder engine and standard transmission. Three weeks prior to the UFO incident, it had been given a general winter check-up and a new battery. No one had experienced any problems with it prior to or after the sighting. I checked to see if the car had an electric clock or if the witnesses had been wearing watches. A strong electromagnetic field might have affected a clock's solenoid or magnetized wrist watches. The car did not have a clock and the girls had not been wearing watches. The ignition switch was *on* during the electric failure, which lasted about three minutes.

EVALUATION

With all due respect for Mr. Nicholson's (Group 2) belief that the object he saw was a normal aircraft, I nevertheless evaluated this sighting as being in the "unknown" category. The overall data collected and examined concerning this UFO report had no conventional explanation.

The UFO sighting rate continued to climb, with six "unknowns" catalogued for the month of February and seven for the month of March. Early in March, a close-encounter event similar to the Methuen case took place at Leominster, Massachusetts. This time, however, the UFO affected more than just the car ignition, lights and radio. It struck out at one of the witnesses! News of the episode came to me through a resident of Leominster who sent me a tiny newsclip about it from the local paper.[6] Our newsclip service had missed it completely! After talking to the witnesses by phone and performing cross-checks on their story, I assigned assistant chairman Frank Pechulis to investigate their weird experience.

A UFO Attacks

According to the U.S. Weather Service, it was a clear cool night during the early morning hours of March 8. The skies were crystal clear and visibility was twelve miles. In Boston, the thermometers read twenty-eight degrees Fahrenheit. A recent snowstorm had left a beautiful blanket of white velvet draped over the fields and trees. The new-fallen snow was so beautiful that Mr. and Mrs. William Wallace of Leominster got a sudden inspiration to go for a late night scenic drive through the countryside. After driving about for an hour and a half, they started home. It was about 1:00 A.M. when they entered the town of Leominster and encountered something very strange at St. Leo's cemetery on Lancaster Street. Mrs. Wallace told investigator Frank Pechulis, "We suddenly came across a very thick fog and had to slow our car to a real low speed for safety reasons." Mr. Wallace continued:

THE UFO

As we passed the cemetery, I noticed what looked like a large light to my left. I asked my wife if she saw anything and she said no. I was certain that I had and decided I would look again.[7]

Mr. Wallace turned his car around and drove back into the fog. He thought that the light might be a fire and that the fog was smoke. This time both of them saw the light. The glow was not from a fire. It was something glowing in the air directly over the cemetery! Mr. Walace told Frank that at this point "I then lowered our windows and came back again. I got excited and told my wife, 'I think we have something here!' " He then stated that he had driven his car off the road so that it was broadside to the glowing object. For a moment, they just sat there gaping at the thing. Hovering about two hundred yards away and several hundred feet above the cemetery was an object shaped like a flattened egg. It was making a whirring sound like a dynamo. "It put me in mind of an acetylene torch," he said.

THE ATTACK

Against his wife's wishes, William got out of the car. He raised his hand and excitedly pointed at the blazing object. Simultaneously with this quick movement, several events occurred:

    1. The automobile lights, radio and engine ceased functioning.
    2. He felt an electrical shock and his body became numb and immobilized.
    3. The arm that he pointed with was pulled against the roof of the car by an unseen force. It hit the roof so hard that it left an imprint in the ice and snow.

Mr. Wallace told Frank:

I was unable to move. My wife was in a panic. My mind was not at all affected. I just could not move, and it felt like a shock or numbness.[8]

Mrs. Wallace interjected that "When the car went dead, I was yelling for Bill to get back in the car, but he did not move!"

When Mr. Wallace did not respond to her screams, she slid across the seat and tugged at his jacket through the open window. Mr. Wallace could hear his wife begging him to come back into the car but he could not move a muscle. He was totally paralyzed from head to foot! He explained, "I was there thirty to forty seconds before the object moved away. It moved quickly at an increasing speed, not instantly." Then, abruptly, the lights and radio came back on! The humming object, which had been "rocking back and forth," accelerated upward and out of sight above the fog patch. After this, Mr. Wallace related, "I was able to move again. My reactions were slow and sluggish." He climbed slowly back into the car and turned the ignition key. The car started without any trouble and he headed for home. The Wallace's driveway is on a downgrade, and his reflexes were so slow that he failed to brake in time. The car hit the garage door!

Dazed and "feeling heavy all over," Mr. Walace followed his wife inside the house, where they sat down to collect their senses about this bizarre experience. Both felt strongly that they had to tell someone about it. Having no phone, they went out and phoned William's mother, who resided in Vermont. Mrs. Wallace also phoned her own mother, who lived locally. She insisted that they both come to her home at once and phone the police department.

During the course of his probe into the incident, Investigator Pechulis interviewed the police officer who had responded to the witnesses' phone call. In his report, Frank wrote the following remarks:

> I talked with Lieutenant Matteo Ciccone of the Leominster Police Department. He showed me the record of the police investigation. The lieutenant knows Wallace pretty well and feels that he was telling the truth. It appears that Mr. Wallace is a rather fearless character who does not scare easily.[9]

When I also checked with the police, they told me that the Wallaces were badly shaken when they arrived to investigate. During my cross-checking of their story, I phoned the mothers of both Mr. and Mrs. Wallace.

Mrs. Wallace's mother told me that she and her husband were awakened by the telephone ringing at 1:30 A.M. that fateful morning. She told me, "My daughter sounded so upset that I told her to come right over." She explained to me how she persuaded them to let her call the police. The police interrogation lasted until 4:30 A.M. Her account of what her daughter and son-in-law told her checked out perfectly with the account that they had given Frank. She emphasized that neither were under the influence of liquor and said, "I have never seen my son-in-law so thoroughly shaken up." Then, obtaining Mr. Wallace's mother's telephone number from her, I placed an immediate call to Vermont.

Mr. Wallace's mother further confirmed the sighting account. She said that she was roused out of bed at 1:45 A.M. to answer her son's telephone call. She told me that "He was so upset and excited that he could hardly talk at first!" She further explained that "It must have been something to upset my son, as he's the type that isn't afraid of anything." According to her, the paralysis seemed to be the major cause of his being so upset.

The sighting data was carefully checked and cross-checked. Frank even checked the garage door and found two fresh marks where the car had hit it shortly after the sighting. Thoroughly convinced of the validity of the Wallace's account, I labeled this report as being in the *significant* "unknown" category.

AUTOMOBILE INFORMATION

The affected automobile was a 1955 eight-cylinder Cadillac sedan with a twelve-volt system. Just prior to the reported effects, the car engine was running in neutral gear, the emergency brake was activated, and the lights and radio were on. The automobile started easily just moments after the UFO had left the area. A check on its condition on April 1 revealed that the car had operated perfectly since the incident.

SIGHTING LOCALE

Although the object was situated directly above a cemetery, it was interesting to note that two chemical companies were located nearby. The Solar Chemical Company is positioned directly across the street from the cemetery and the Dupont Chemical Company was just three hundred yards down the street.

EFFECTS

The rocking motion, bright glow, humming sound, electrical ignition failure, and temporary paralysis are all consistent characteristics of other UFO sightings throughout the world. Of particular interest are the following possible *cause and effect* aspects of the event:

1. The mist or fog seemed to have been directly connected with the presence of the UFO. When the Wallaces left their home to use a telephone, they had to drive past the cemetery. As they went by, there was no trace of the fog. This means that the

fog had dissipated within about ten to fifteen minutes after the object had left the area. Coupled with these curious facts are the *localized* nature of the fog on an otherwise perfectly clear night and the fact that *no moisture* from the fog had accumulated on the car's windshield.

2. The electrical failure and paralysis occurred simultaneously with Mr. Wallace's *pointing at the object with his arm.* It was *only* his arm that was thrown back and pinned to the car roof. He actually *felt* it "being pulled" to the roof.

3. No effects were noticed when the Wallaces drove back and forth several times before driving off the road for a closer look. The *effects* started only when Mr. Wallace left the car and pointed. The effects lasted only as long as the UFO hovered there. When it left, the effects simultaneously ceased, except for the reported physiological aftereffects, which lasted for fifteen to twenty minutes.

One wonders what would have happened at Methuen if any one of the girls had left the car and approached the object. My mind thought back to similar cases on file where witnesses attempting to approach UFOs at close range were rendered immobile until the object left. Observational evidence in such cases seem to indicate that the paralysis and electrical interference associated with UFO events are *directed* rather than just being a nonvolitional by-product of UFOs. It is personally encouraging to me that such effects are usually temporary and do not cause physical harm to the witness. This in itself is rather remarkable. It would seem that the intelligence or force that directs the effects knows the limitations and endurance of the human body very well!

The number of unexplained UFO reports again peaked in April and took a sharp drop in May, when an average of only one or two "unknowns" per month continued through the year. Nonetheless, some of these sightings and the events directly associated with them were highly significant and aided towards reaching my goal of UFO recognition by science.

Early Warning Coordinator

A SURPRISE INVITATION

It was Friday, spring was at its height, and I was glad to be home from a busy week of work. The smell of cooking and the familiar chattering of children's voices greeted me as I opened the door. Margaret's mother and father, visiting from England, were giving her some help with the dinner as I greeted them all in the kitchen.

"Any interesting mail for me?" I asked.

"There's something from the University of Colorado on your desk," she said. "But don't get too involved. Supper is just about ready."

"The University of Colorado? That *does* sound interesting," I thought, as I began sorting out the stack of mail on the desk. This particular university had been selected by the Air Force to conduct a civilian scientific study of UFOs. I was most interested, as the Colorado Project was a direct outcome of the previous year's congressional hearings on UFOs in which I had had a personal part to play. I anxiously tore open the envelope and read the letter. It was from the *principal investigator* of the project, Dr. David R. Saunders. Pertinent excerpts follow.

> Beginning in early June, the CU UFO Study expects to have enough staff to permit the conduct of one or more on-the-scene investigations per week. . . . I hope that this is where you come in. . . . The involvement of persons like yourself is highly desirable . . . because your prior familiarity with the UFO problem can facilitate your preliminary screening of these events. . . . If you feel that you might volunteer . . . to undertake to keep us currently informed of UFO sightings in your area, I will be pleased to supply you with telephone numbers (willing to accept collect calls) and guidelines as to which sightings we most want to hear about in a hurry.

I must admit that my reaction to this letter was a paradoxical mixture of enthusiasm and suspicion. The Colorado Project was financed by the Air Force. On the one hand, I did not want to get mixed up in just another whitewash attempt to further debunk UFOs. On the other hand, I did not want to sidestep an opportunity to give personal assistance to a scientific study of UFOs. The latter possibility, coupled with NICAP's pledge to aid the Colorado Project, caused me to accept this surprise invitation.

Shortly thereafter, I became an Early Warning coordinator for the Colorado Project. I was issued special reporting instructions and a set of toll-free numbers to use, in the event certain types of UFO sightings came to my attention. Two months later, I relayed two such UFO sightings via the Early Warning system. The first was of special significance because it directly involved one of my own investigators with *signals from a UFO!*

Signals from a UFO

"WHEN THE CAT'S AWAY . . .

I had just returned home from an extraordinary vacation. Imagine, if you will, a compact station wagon straining along containing two parents, three children, piles of luggage, and my two visiting in-laws riding shotgun! At one point during our journey, several jars of raspberry syrup broke and oozed out the back of the wagon! Passersby gaped in horror when we parked to clean up the "blood" that was flowing profusely onto the sidewalk in downtown Syracuse! We then blazed a trail through the scenic wonders of New York State to Niagara Falls before backtracking and depositing my wife's parents with friends in Vermont. Then, off we headed for Maine to visit my parents near Bar Harbor. We finally arrived home on July 28. I glanced bleary-eyed at the lawn, which looked like a field, and began stoically unpacking the car. Then, after helping Margaret feed and bed down three excited kids, I promptly collapsed in an easy chair for the duration of the evening. UFOs were the farthest thing from my thoughts. This state of mind was short-lived, however, for on the following morning, I was "back in the saddle again"!

. . .THE MICE WILL PLAY!"

On Saturday morning, I received a phone call from a very excited investigator—Gary Storey. He told me that he had sighted a UFO on Wednesday night while visiting his sister and brother-in-law at Newton, New Hampshire. They had observed it through both binoculars and a telescope. It had answered patterned flashlight signals with exact responses!

Then, on Sunday, I received a call from Paul Munier, superintendant of the New England Military School at Byfield, Massachusetts. Paul had not *seen* anything on Wednesday night but he had undergone a very unusual *auditory* experience. On Monday, upon returning to work, I was told by friends that radio stations and police departments had received many calls about weird *humming* sounds. Those calling in had heard those unconventional noises late on Wednesday night and during the early morning hours of Thursday. On Tuesday, the *Haverhill Gazette* briefly mentioned that someone had observed an orange glowing object emitting a *humming* sound on this same night at Rowley, Massachusetts.

I dispatched investigator Herb Eismann to look into the Rowley sighting. My brother Richard and I investigated the Byfield and Newton incidents. After our investigation, I used the hot-line to the Colorado Project and relayed the data to project investigator Dr. Roy Craig for possible reinvestigation. In the meantime, our own investigations confirmed that some very strange *happenings* had been reported during the night of July 26 and the early morning hours of July 27, 1967.

STRANGE SOUNDS IN THE NIGHT

At 11:15 P.M., Mr. and Mrs. Ricker of Rowley, Massachusetts, were startled by a "loud, whining, whirring sound."[10] Mrs. Ricker got out of bed and looked out of a window. There she saw an orange glowing object in the sky. Others living in the neighborhood also heard and saw the object. Its northwesterly flight path coincided with a set of *power lines* that stretched between Ipswich and Groveland, Massachusetts.

Byfield, Massachusetts, located several miles northwest of Rowley, lay along the general flight path of the humming UFO. At Byfield, Paul Munier, superintendent of the New England Military School, was about to retire for the night. All at once, a loud, intermittent "whistling sound" filled the air. It sounded as if something was landing on the school grounds! Rushing outside to investigate, he heard the sound all around him, as if something was hovering directly overhead. Scanning the sky in all directions, he saw nothing. Then, abruptly as it had started, the sound died down and there was complete silence. He told me that the sound was not like that of a helicopter or airplane. "I've never heard anything like it before," he said.[11]

Meanwhile, at Newton, New Hampshire, just several miles farther to the northwest, subcommittee member Gary Storey was about to experience one of the weirdest experiences in his life.

"IT FLASHED BACK!"

Gary had set up his telescope around eleven o'clock to observe the moon, which had just started to rise in the east. He was visiting his sister Evelyn and his brother-in-law, Francis. At about 1:00 A.M. Francis, who had earlier noticed an apparent bright star in the north, suddenly saw the "star" turn bright orange-red and start to move! He yelled to Gary and they both called Evelyn, who was in the house making coffee. Gary related to me that

> As it moved eastward, it changed to a steady red light with two steady white lights on either side and below it. I shifted my telescope from the moon, changed from a 350X to a 75X eyepiece, and focused on the object. Through the telescope, I saw a row of lights flashing in a sequence of 1-2-3-4-5-4-3-2-1. They appeared to be along the length of an elongated object which had a bright white light on each end. A red light was on top. It passed by us and over Gale Village road. Fran blinked his flashlight three times at the object. It immediately reversed direction without benefit of a turn.[12]

At this point, some very interesting things began to happen. Turning to Francis's report narrative, we read that

> It returned three flashes with its lights! It did this by dimming its lights until they were barely perceptible and then returned them to their previous luminosity.[13]

As the object moved in a back-and-forth flight path, Francis continued to signal with the flashlight. It would respond about midway between its flight path terminal points.

> *Fran:* I flashed the light four to five times, using three flashes. Each time, it would answer in like mannner.
> *Gary:* Then we heard a jet, which directly approached the object. The object extinguished all its lights until the jet passed beyond where it was. We thought it had left. Suddenly, in the same location, the object appeared as a brilliant, oval-shaped white object!
> *Fran:* The object flared bright—at least ten to fifteen times brighter. Then it went back to the two white lights with a red one above. I then changed the light flash to one long and one short flash. The object answered in kind. It made nine to ten passes, and I varied the signal to two flashes, one flash, and finally four flashes. After answering the four flash signal, the object flashed its lights and then disappeared into the darkness behind trees.[14]

THE WITNESSES

Both Gary and Fran have technical backgrounds and are considered good observers. Gary was a former Air Force radar operator and is an electronics technician. Francis had been a Navy radar operator during World War II and the Korean conflict. He had attended several Navy schools for sonar, gunnery, and radar. He was employed as an environmental laboratory technician. The local minister vouched for the good character of Francis and Evelyn. He said they were good churchgoing people and not the type who would lie or seek publicity. Evelyn held the positions of sexton and organist at the church.

EVALUATION

A check was made regarding astronautical, aeronautical, and satellite data in relation to the sighting, but no conventional explanation for the observed phenomenon was forthcoming. Acoustics in this large, open field at Newton are such that traffic can actually be heard from the New Hampshire Turnpike, which lies several miles away. The jet aircraft was easily heard by the witnesses. They are thoroughly familiar with the sight and sound of aircraft flying in and out of Pease Air Force Base. The silent UFO and its strange lights and maneuvers were totally outside of their realm of experience. I evaluated the sighting as a significant "unknown." Further investigation by several scientists and official investigators failed to identify the extraordinary object.

COINCIDENCE OR CONTACT?

I often run into some rather bizarre circumstances during the course of investigating "flying saucers." So it was with the Newton event. Unknown to myself and all principals involved was the fact that on the same night a scientist, a physician, an author, and Mr. and Mrs. Barney Hill were conducting an experiment to contact a UFO in a field just several miles from Newton. The Hills, you recall, had been allegedly kidnapped by a UFO in the fall of 1961 and given a physical examination. They appeared to have been released with an induced memory block, which was broken through by the use of hypnotic regression during treatment by a well-qualified pyschiatrist. Mrs. Hill had felt strongly that she could somehow mentally communicate with a UFO on the night in question. She pleaded with those who had been intimately involved with their case to accompany her and her husband to a field where she hoped to contact a UFO. Several responded out of curiosity and a strong personal interest in the couple. No UFO was seen and the nighttime vigil seemingly had ended in failure.

I found out about this experiment a few months after the Newton sighting. Dr. James E. McDonald mentioned the Newton sighting while appearing on a local Boston talk show. During the show, I received a call from the Hills, who wanted to know what date the Newton incident had taken place. When I told them, they were astonished. The signaling UFO had appeared on the same night as their experiment. To be quite frank, I was highly suspicious about their story. It seemed fantastic to me at the time. I went out of my way to personally check it out with a scientist who had been indirectly involved with the attempted contact. He told me that he had been unable to personally attend and had sent a trusted scientist friend to participate in his stead. Needless to say, my publication of the Newton, New Hampshire, report caused much excitement among those experimenting with the Hills. The obvious question arose—"Was the *signaling UFO* incident on that same night at nearby Newton a *coincidence* or an attempted *contact* by the UFO with the wrong people in the incorrect field?"

Mystery over Cape Ann

No sooner had I relayed data on the Newton sighting to the University of Colorado and begun my own investigation than another spectacular sighting was brought to my attention. The initial input was a telephone call from William Cooper of the *Gloucester Times.* He informed me that on August 2, at 9:30 P.M., many persons had been frightened by a bright flashing UFO that seemingly came in over the sea and made a low pass over Cape Ann. A check with the Sky-Lite Advertising Company revealed that their illuminated aircraft was in a holding pattern over Fenway Park in Boston during the sighting period. It came nowhere near the sighting area. I located seventeen independent groups of people who claimed to have seen the UFO. Most had only seen a string of brilliant yellowish lights flashing on and off in sequence. However, two sets of witnesses along Good Harbor beach at Gloucester claimed to have seen an object close at hand carrying these bright flashing lights.

One witness, Miss Carol Chisholm, told me:

We were all at the Good Harbor parking lot. There were six

of us talking. All of a sudden, Dana Knowlton said, "What's in
the sky?" We all looked. It seemed to be a plane crashing, because there were two bright lights. It seemed to stop and almost
revolve, and we saw about six or seven of the same lights.[15]

Miss Paula Scola continued:

The object was solid. It had two discs with seven orange lights
between the two. It moved at tremendous speed and made no
noise at all. As it vanished, the lights went off, one by one.
It headed in the direction of Rockport.[16]

A very distinguished woman, driving along Bass Avenue
towards Good Harbor Beach, told me:

All of a sudden, my eyes were attracted by a very unusual sight
through the left side of my windshield. I was shocked. It looked
like an inverted bowl on an upright bowl with three orange
lights on a rim between the bowls.[17]

This was enough for me! On August 7, I again contacted the
Colorado UFO Project via the Early Warning phone procedure.
This time I got some reaction. On the following day, I received
two calls from Dr. Norman LeVine, a field investigator and research scientist for the Colorado Project. Both he and Dr. Roy
Craig were being sent to further investigate the Newton, New
Hampshire, and Cape Ann, Massachusetts, UFO sightings. They
also expressed a desire to reinvestigate certain other cases that
I had submitted to Project Bluebook in the past. I arranged for
a coordination dinner meeting at my home on August 9 and began
making preparations for their arrival.

A VISIT FROM MUTT AND JEFF

A knock came at the front door in the midst of frantic preparations. My wife was busy in the kitchen feeding the children
ahead of time. My visiting in-laws from England, somewhat over-
awed by UFOs, investigations, and visiting scientists, were helping
set the dining-room table. I answered the door and found myself

trying to look *up* and *down* at the same time! Smiling *down* at me was Dr. Roy Craig. Roy literally towered over Dr. Norman LeVine, who was smiling *up* at me. They reminded me of the Mutt and Jeff cartoon characters! My wife jokingly told me later that she half wondered if they were *aliens* from another planet!

After introductions, we soon sat down on the living-room floor to examine a large map of Cape Ann, upon which I had noted the position of each group of witnesses in relation to the UFO. We discussed the event and I gave them the names, addresses, and telephone numbers of the witnesses. Our meeting was then interrupted by a call to come for dinner.

The conversation at the table centered around the general subject of UFOs and what the University of Colorado planned to do about them. I was surprised to hear both of them openly speculating about the possibility that UFOs were products of extraterrestrial intelligence (ETI). Both agreed that no defense was possible if such proved to be the case. Someone said, "Let's hope they are not hostile," to which Dr. Craig replied, "They probably are."

I enjoyed working with Norm and Roy. They spent much time on their own checking out both the current and older cases. They were particularly interested in the Beverly case (covered in chapter nine). We went to Newton, New Hampshire, together to reinterview the witnesses. It was most interesting for me to compare my investigating methodology with theirs. Before they left Massachusetts, on August 13, I had the distinct impression that both scientists had concluded that the Newton and Cape Ann sightings were unexplainable in conventional terms. Their check with both military and FAA installations indicated that no conventional aircraft were in the sighting areas when the UFOs were reported. It was not until about a month later that I uncovered new evidence which served to deepen the "mystery over Cape Ann."

THE MYSTERY DEEPENS

Considerable excitement was caused by a new sighting from Southbridge, Massachusetts. Other communities, more along the shore of Connecticut, Rhode Island and Cape Cod, also spotted a UFO during the same general time span. The reported phenomenon consisted of a string of bright lights that appeared and disappeared in perfect sequence. The Air Force told the press that the strange lights were caused by a B-52 bomber dropping high-intensity flares along the coastline. Since this sighting was extremely similar to the Cape Ann event, I decided to reopen this case and check out the possibility that flares had been seen in this incident also.

My first move was to place a phone call to Headquarters 8th Air Force (SAC), Westover Air Force Base, Chicopee Falls, Massachusetts. I was connected with Captain William J. Ballee, Assistant Chief, Operations Division, Directorate of Information. In one of those uncanny coincidences that happen so often in my UFO investigations, Captain Ballee had just finished reading the book *Incident at Exeter* and thus was familiar and sympathetic with my work in the area. He cooperated fully with my request for Air Force flare-drop information and wired the following message to all Strategic Air Command bases:

1. THIS HQ RECEIVED AN INQUIRY REGARDING FLARE DROPS FROM MASSACHUSETTS INVESTIGATING COMMITTEE ON AERIAL PHENOMENA

2. THE INVESTIGATION IS FOR THE PERIOD 1 JULY 67 TO 13 SEP 67. THE INFORMATION REQUIRED FOR EACH FLARE DROP IS AS FOLLOWS:
  A. DATE
  B. TIME (ZULU)
  C. COORDINATES AT START OF DROP
  D. NUMBER OF FLARES DISPENSED
  E. ACFT HEADING
  F. NUMBER OF ACFT

3. REQUEST REQUIRED INFORMATION TO REACH THIS HQ (DOTTA) NLT 6 OCT 67.[18]

Secondly, I contacted the Public Affairs Director of the First Naval District in Boston to recheck the possibility of a Naval flare-dropping mission near Cape Ann on August 2. The Colorado Project team had informed me that they had already checked this possibility out because the Navy had control of the area off Cape Ann and would know of any military activity in the area. Then I sat back and waited.

Before the end of October, I had received the desired information from both the Air Force and the Navy. Captain Ballee sent me photostats of wires he had received from every pertinent Air Force Strategic Air Command base.[19] Scanning them quickly, I found a flare drop indeed had occurred on August 2 and that the time and coordinates coincided exactly with the phenomenon sighted at Cape Ann!

Date	Time	Location	Heading	Dispensed[20]
3 Aug.*	1:25Z†	4300N 7025W	091°	16

---
*2 Aug.

---
†9:25 P.M. EDT.

Then I received a puzzling letter from the Navy, which controlled the area in question. Commander E. G. Shepherd stated in this correspondence that

> This office contacted Naval Air Station, Quonset Point, Rhode Island; Naval Air Station, South Weymouth; and, Coast Guard Headquarters in Boston. All requests received replies in the negative.[21]

I was confused. Why didn't the scientists from Colorado University find out about the flares? Why didn't the Navy know about the Air Force flare drop within an area strictly under their control? These project scientists were traveling under *military orders* and such data would have been easily accessible to them. A number of thoughts raced through my mind. Could it be that they had found out but were keeping quiet until the final report? If this were the case, it would put NICAP in a bad light. I had

assumed that they were on the level and that they had made all
the necessary checks with government installations during their
investigation. Then other thoughts struck me. Was the flare drop
intentional to test public reaction? Was it a cover-up explanation
specifically prepared by the Air Force to explain away a real UFO
sighting? I pondered such thoughts as I prepared a supplemental
report for all recipients of the original Cape Ann report, which
had already grown to an inch thick! I felt very thankful that it
was I who had discovered the "flares" answer. One thing was
sure as far as I was concerned: in any future dealings with the
Colorado Project, I would always conduct a *complete* parallel
investigation. I could not afford to rely upon them anymore.

"WHO TIPPED YOU OFF?"

Several days after I had mailed out the *solution* to the Cape
Ann case, I received a telephone call from Dr. LeVine. The Colorado Project had received the new data. LeVine sounded extremely upset and his first words to me were, "Who tipped you
off about the flares?" I replied that no one had tipped me off
about anything. I explained that I merely had seen a similarity
between the Southbridge and Cape Ann sightings. Since the
Southbridge sightings had involved flares, I had checked out the
flare answer for the Cape Ann incident. He retorted that his
official contacts had insisted there were no aircraft in the sighting
area regardless of what the Air Force told me. In the end, however, the Colorado Project conceded their error and gave me full
credit for solving the *Mystery over Cape Ann*. The final Project
Report states:

> A series of sightings around Cape Ann, Mass. (Case 29)
> offered testimony of numerous witnesses as evidence of the
> presence of a strange object. . . . The investigating team was
> convinced, after interviewing several of the witnesses, that they
> had indeed seen something in the sky. The team was not able,
> at the time, to identify what had been seen. The Chairman of
> the NICAP Massachusetts Subcommittee, Mr. Raymond E.
> Fowler, continued the investigation and subsequently learned
> that an aircrew from the 99th Bomb Wing, Westover AFB, had

dropped 16 white flares while on a practice mission about 30 miles NE of Cape Ann. The flare drop coincided in time and direction with the observed "UFO." As Mr. Fowler suggested, the "object" enclosing the string of lights must have been constructed by imagination.[22]

Concerning other cases investigated, the Colorado Project report goes on to state:

> On the other hand, some cases involve testimony which, if taken at face value, describes experiences which can be explained only in terms of strange vehicles (See for example, Case 6—Beverly, Massachusetts).[23]

To some, the Cape Ann UFO still remains a mystery. Dr. Saunders, principal investigator for the Colorado Project, continued to treat the report in the *unknown* category in his book *UFOs—Yes![24]* The witnesses themselves remain suspicious of the *flares* answer. Personally, I do not know what the answer is for sure. There are open questions. However, until someone is able to provide good documentation to demonstrate otherwise, my solution to the "Mystery over Cape Ann" must remain—Air Force *flares*.

The Project Report

The final report prepared by scientists who conducted the University of Colorado UFO study was printed in January 1969 amidst a storm of controversy. Contention about the reality of UFOs was so high between the field investigators and project heads Dr. Edward U. Condon and Dr. Robert Low that mass resignation almost became a reality at one point of time.[25]

Prior to the writing of the final report, several significant events occurred. NICAP broke off relations with the Colorado Project because of project head Condon's repeated statements to the press that were nonobjective and negative. Such statements gave the impression that his mind was already made up about the UFO question before the project had finished its study. Another disruption took place when Dr. Norman LeVine and Dr. David Saunders were fired for publicly revealing a memo from

Project files. The memo, written by assistant project director Dr.
Robert Low stated in part:

> The trick would be, I think, to describe the project so that, to
> the public, it would appear a totally objective study but, to the
> scientific community, would present the image of a group of
> nonbelievers trying their best to be objective but having an
> almost zero expectation of finding a (flying) saucer.[26]

Norm LeVine and Dave Saunders sent copies of the above
memo to NICAP and Dr. James E. McDonald. Subsequently,
John Fuller, author of *Incident at Exeter,* wrote an exposé for
Look magazine entitled "Flying Saucer Fiasco." *Look* published
the contents of the Low memo and a blow-by-blow account of
the disunity that existed among the Colorado staff. In the midst
of the turmoil that followed the dismissal of LeVine and Saunders, Dr. Condon's long-time administrative assistant quit in dis-
gust over the way Condon and Low were directing the project.
Some pertinent quotes from her letter of resignation provide excellent insight into the goings-on within this controversial project.

> I think there is an almost unanimous "lack of confidence" in
> him (Low) as the project coordinator. . . . Bob's attitude from
> the beginning has been one of negativism. . . . To me, too much
> of his time has been spent in worrying about what kinds of
> "language" should be used in the final report so as to most
> cleverly avoid having anything to say definitive about the UFO
> problem. . . . Why is it that Craig, Saunders, LeVine, Wadsworth,
> Ahrens and others [field investigators] have all arrived at such
> radically different conclusions from Bob's? It is not my im-
> pression that they came into the project with any particular
> bias concerning the UFO problem. I think that there is fairly
> good consensus among the team members that there is enough
> data in the UFO question to warrant further study.[27]

The Low memo and subsequent *Look* exposé also had a number of repercussions within the Congress. Dr. James E. McDonald
met with Congressmen J. Edward Roush (Ind), William F. Ryan
(NY), Emilio Q. Daddario (Conn) and Morris K. Udall (Ariz).
All appeared disturbed by the unfortunate attitude at Colorado

University. On both April 30 and May 1, Representative Roush made speeches on the House floor calling for a congressional investigation of UFOs. He said, in essence:

> The story in *Look* magazine raises grave doubts as to the scientific profundity and objectivity of the project. . . . This article will cast in doubt the results of that project in the minds of the American public . . . [and] the scientific community. We are poorer—$500,000 later—not richer in information about UFOs. . . . I am not satisfied; the American public will not be satisfied. . . . I am recommending that we launch a congressional investigation.[28]

Although the report was endorsed by the National Academy of Science, many scientists who were intimately acquainted with the UFO problem were highly critical of its contents as well as of Dr. Edward Condon's conclusion:

> We place very little value for scientific purposes on the past accumulation of anecdotal records . . . we have recommended against the mounting of a major effort for continuing UFO study for scientific reasons.[29]

Dr. J. Allen Hynek, former Air Force scientific consultant on UFOs, was one of the dissenters. In his review of the project report within the pages of the *Bulletin of the Atomic Scientists*, he stated:

> The *Scientific Study of Unidentified Flying Objects* is a strange sort of scientific paper and does not fulfill the promise of its title. . . . While devoted in the large part to exposing hoaxes or revealing many UFOs as misidentifications of common occurrences, the book leaves the same strange, inexplicable residue of unknowns, which has plagued the U.S. Air Force investigation for 20 years. In fact, the percentage of unknowns in the Condon report appears to be even higher than in the Air Force investigation. . . . Over the last 20 years, some of the most baffling cases are those involving radar contacts with as well as visual sightings of the same object. The Condon report does not resolve this long-standing problem. . . . On the basis of many years' experience with the UFO phenomenon, I would

have deleted nearly two-thirds of the cases included in the report as potentially profitless for the avowed purposes of the project.[30]

The prestigious American Institute of Astronautics and Aeronautics (AIAA) organized its own UFO Study Committee to examine the Colorado Project report in light of the overall available evidence on UFOs. The AIAA committee, concluded after a year's review:

> We find it difficult to ignore the small residue of well-documented but unexplainable cases that form the hard core of the UFO controversy.[31]

A 1971 poll taken by a national research journal indicated that eighty percent of those subscribers who responded believed that "The Colorado University Study was not definitive."[32] Even as I type this particular chapter, the controversy has still not died down concerning the Colorado Project report. One of our nation's pioneers in aviation recently called the Condon Report "one of the most deliberate cover-ups ever perpetrated on the public."[33] John Northrop, eighty-year-old founder of Northrop Aircraft Company and cofounder of the Lockheed Corporation, told an audience at the California Institute of Technology that "The twenty-first century will die laughing at the Condon Report."[34] As I bring this chapter to a close, my mind goes back to a word of warning given me by the late Congressman William H. Bates. It was Congressman Bates, if you will remember, who introduced my report on the Exeter UFO sighting into the minutes of the first *open* congressional hearings on UFOs. The Colorado Project was one of the results of these hearings. When the Air Force told Congress that *it would contract* a scientific panel to study the unexplained phenomena, Congressman Bates wrote me that

> I think it would be good to get *another* [italics mine] group of scientists to take a look at this matter so we can be more certain of the decisions which are being made.[35]

I believe that he was right!

NOTES

1. Personal correspondence to the author from Dr. Roy Craig, Colorado Project investigator, dated September 14, 1967.
2. Personal Files, UFO Report No. 67-5.
3. *Ibid.*
4. *Ibid.*
5. *Ibid.*
6. Personal Files, UFO Report No. 67-18.
7. *Ibid.*
8. *Ibid.*
9. *Ibid.*
10. Personal Files, UFO Report No. 67-44B.
11. Personal Files, Supplement to UFO Report No. 67-44A.
12. Personal Files, UFO Report No. 67-44A.
13. *Ibid.*
14. *Ibid.*
15. Personal Files, UFO Report No. 67-45.
16. *Ibid.*
17. *Ibid.*
18. *Ibid.*
19. *Ibid.*
20. *Ibid.*
21. *Ibid.*
22. Edward U. Condon, *Scientific Study of Unidentified Flying Objects*, pp. 61, 62.
23. *Ibid.*, p. 62.
24. David R. Saunders, *UFOs—Yes!* pp. 122, 123.
25. *Ibid.*, pp. 145-147.
26. *Look* magazine, May 14, 1968, and Personal Files.
27. J. Allen Hynek, *The UFO Experience*, pp. 243-250.
28. On file at NICAP.
29. Condon, *op. cit.*, p. 48.
30. "The Condon Report and UFOs," *Bulletin of the Atomic Scientists*, April 1969.
31. "UFO, An Appraisal of the Problem," *Astronautics and Aeronautics*, November 1970.
32. Opinion Poll, *Industrial Research*, April 1971.
33. "UFO Theory Gets Support," *Star News*, Pasadena, California, January 30, 1973.
34. *Ibid.*
35. Personal correspondence to the author from the Honorable William H. Bates, 6th District, Massachusetts, April 5, 1966.

11

THE WAVES SUBSIDE—
TEMPORARILY

UFO waves are sudden peaks of the number of sightings that come as an addition to a constant phenomena of low intensity.

JACQUES VALLÉE[1]

The year 1967 had proved to be an interesting one. Curiously enough, the number of UFO reports received rose and fell with the approach of the planet Mars. The number of sightings had peaked in April, which coincided with the opposition of Mars on April 15. Other researchers, using international data, have found this same pattern exists for other years as well as a smaller peak at mid-opposition, when Mars reaches its farthest position from earth. Even as this book is in its final stage of editing, the opposition of the planet Mars in October of 1973 has coincided with a huge UFO wave which has thrust the subject of UFOs into the national news again!

In any event, except for a brief rise in the number of local sightings in April of 1968, the huge prolonged UFO sighting waves had at last subsided. During this general lull in UFO activity, I nonetheless experienced some very interesting encounters with national personalities involved with the UFO problem. In addition to this, the UFOs themselves were not entirely inactive, as we shall soon see. The first encounter was my first face-to-face meeting with Dr. J. Allen Hynek.

"Dr. Hynek, I Presume?"

The letter was dated June 2, 1969, and it read, in part:

166

Dear Mr. Fowler:

It so happens that I shall be in Boston from late June 12 to early June 14, and on June 13 my son gets his Ph.D. at MIT, and we are all coming to watch the proceedings. It occurs to me that it might be a good time, at long last, for us to meet and have a good chat. . . . There are a number of things I should like to ask you, for I certainly have been an admirer of your highly systematic and businesslike way of approaching the UFO problem and its investigation. . . .[2]

It was from no other than Dr. Hynek himself! Needless to say, I was very excited over the prospect of finally meeting him in person and quickly fired off a reply containing arrangements for visiting with him.

THE PARKER HOUSE RENDEZVOUS

It was a sweltering summer day. I drove into Boston and left my car at the Boston Common underground parking lot. A blast of hot air hit me as I came up the stairs onto the Common. I stopped briefly to glance at a map before striking out across the Common toward the Parker House Hotel. Boston Common was typical that day. Students and "hippies" sprawled out on the green. The elderly were sitting on wooden benches under the shade of the trees reading and watching the world go by. I was nervous and my clothes were sticking to my skin as I entered the air-conditioned lobby of the Parker House. Glancing about, I quickly recognized Dr. Hynek from pictures I had seen of him. Walking up behind him, I extended my hand and said, "Dr. Hynek, I presume?"

Dr. Hynek turned around and I found myself staring at the smiling bearded scientist who then and even now is somewhat of an enigma to me. After exchanging greetings, he suggested we step into the hotel restaurant for something cold to drink. We went in and ordered some iced tea. He then looked me straight in the eyes and said: "I want to make something perfectly clear before we get underway. There are some things we shall talk about that must be kept in complete confidence. If they are not, we cannot have anything further to do with each other." I agreed and we got down to talking about UFOs from A to Z. Later, we retired to his room for further discussion.

Hynek told me that the Air Force was about to discontinue Project Bluebook upon the recommendation of the Colorado UFO study. Future UFO reports would be processed through normal Air Force Intelligence channels. He informed me that his consultant job with Bluebook had been terminated; thus he would be more of a free agent in matters relating to UFOs. I then proceeded to ask him whether or not it was true that his personal activities were being monitored by the government. Specifically, I queried him about a U.S. Intelligence report given to the late Dr. Olavo Fontes by the Brazilian government.[3] Fontes, a leading surgeon and UFO researcher in Brazil, had received courtesy copies of UFO reports from his government from time to time. One such report sent to the Brazilian government by U.S. officials concerned the monitoring of Hynek's visit to the Aerial Phenomena Research Organization headquartered at Tucson, Arizona. Hynek nodded that this was correct and that he had seen the report himself.

"Do you mean someone might be keeping tabs on us right now?" I asked.

His eyes twinkled and he smiled. "That's right," he said!

Shortly thereafter, Mrs. Hynek arrived. It was time to break up our meeting as they had to get ready to go out somewhere. As Dr. Hynek and I headed for the elevator, he asked, "Would you be interested in working full-time on a UFO Project?"

Taken somewhat aback by his statement, I said, "I certainly would!"

He then assured me that if he were ever to direct such a project, I would certainly be offered a key position! I thanked him very much and said goodbye to him at the lobby door.

It was still hot as I stepped out of the air-conditioned hotel and was hit by the smothering city air. I headed straight for the parking garage. Walking parallel with me was a gentleman with his head buried in a newspaper taking odd glances in my direction.

"Is this just my imagination?" I thought to myself, "or is that guy watching me?"

The whole experience was soon left behind as I drove out of Boston onto Route 128. Hynek's last minute comments about working full-time on a UFO project kept drifting through my mind. I had never expected such an invitation, and only then was the impact of his question beginning to strike home.

My wife and I talked much about the prospects of Hynek's proposal. She was quite agreeable to the idea providing that such a UFO project showed promise of job security and longevity. However, preparations for our forthcoming vacation in England kept us both too busy to think much further about it.

OFF TO ENGLAND!

Apart from an emergency landing at Shannon, Ireland, with one engine afire, we enjoyed our stay in merry old England with Margaret's parents! One of the high spots of our trip was a personal tour of the Tower of London arranged by friends of her parents. No less than the Deputy Governor of the Tower himself showed us the crown jewels *before* regular visiting hours. Later on that evening, he arranged for us to observe the famous Ceremony of the Keys. Visits with old friends, going to historical places, and returning to our old *courting* grounds kept my mind off UFOs for a full month! The subject came back in full force, however, while we were flying home over the Atlantic.

My daughter and a passenger on the other side of the aircraft sighted several strange objects from their windows. At the time, I had a baby on my lap who was sound asleep and was vainly trying to see the objects out of my window. Finally, in desperation, I was just about to hand the baby to my wife, when the pilot's voice broke in over the intercom. "Ladies and Gentleman. We are encountering air turbulence. Please fasten your seat belts!" Frustrated, I listened to my daughter and her seat companion trying to describe what they were seeing. I gaped out the window on my side and several minutes later finally saw three white *blobs* in the distance behind us outlined against the ocean below. I took a photograph. Whether or not they were what the others were observing at a closer range I'll never know. The photograph merely shows three white, shiny point sources, which could very well have been clouds reflecting the bright sunlight. My daughter and the woman beside her told me that the objects looked something like *box kites*.

I wondered about the incident's coinciding with the pilot's seat belt warning. The plane did not behave as if we were encountering air turbulence. Was there a connection? Several years later, after doing a TV show on UFOs, a gentleman called the station who identified himself as a commercial airline pilot. He stated that the standard procedure followed by airline pilots when encountering UFOs at close range was to warn the passengers to fasten their seat belts because of air turbulence!

COINCIDENCE OR SABOTAGE?

Reams of mail awaited us when we finally arrived home from England and got settled. Among the letters was one from Dr. Hynek. He was puzzled about the fact that no public announcement had been forthcoming regarding the termination of the Air Force UFO Project Bluebook. Another letter from Hynek arrived in October with the news that the prestigious American Association for the Advancement of Science (AAAS) was going to hold a symposium on UFOs at their annual meeting in Boston during the month of December. Both he and Dr. McDonald were among a number of scientists who had been invited to deliver papers. This was a real breakthrough! Hitherto, the AAAS had publicly ignored the UFO phenomena. A summary of this symposium will be found in the next chapter.

December 1969 finally arrived, and with it two big UFO stories hit the newspapers. One announced the AAAS UFO symposium. The other was the long overdue announcement from the Air Force that UFOs did not exist and that Project Bluebook was officially closed as of December 17, 1969. The announcement could not have been timed better for a negative effect. It appeared to be a deliberate attempt to undermine the AAAS Scientific Sym-

posium on UFOs. My suspicions were confirmed shortly thereafter during a telephone call concerning the symposium with Dr.
Donald Menzel. Menzel admitted to me that the Air Force
announcement at this time was more than a coincidence and
coyly suggested that he had been involved in the decision to
release it at this time as an Air Force consultant. Menzel was
not the only scientist out to denigrate the symposium. Dr. Edward
U. Condon, former director of the University of Colorado Scientific Study of UFOs, was working hard behind the scenes to
convince the AAAS to cancel the UFO meetings! He wrote to
each board member pleading with him to boycott the meetings.
His attempts proved futile, however, and the symposium went on
as scheduled.

My meeting with Dr. Hynek at the symposium was brief, and
it would be almost two years before we would meet again. During
this time, correspondence between us continued, and then one
evening I received a telephone call. It was Dr. Hynek, who told
me that he was in the process of writing a book on UFOs. He
wanted permission to use and quote from a number of my UFO
investigation reports! After our conversation, I just sat at my
desk dumbfounded. My mind went back to the year 1966 when
I had appeared on a television show with Dr. Gerald Hawkins.[4]
Hawkins, at that time, was the head of the Department of Astronomy at Boston University and has become internationally famous
for his study of the ruins of Stonehenge in England. Dr. Hawkins
had stated on this television program, "When J. Allen Hynek
informs the scientific community that the UFO problem bears
looking into, then the scientific community will sit up and take
notice." Was my goal of scientific recognition of a *new species*
(the UFO) finally going to be realized? I wondered.

DR. HYNEK COMES TO DINNER

An air of excitement prevailed at the Fowler home. Dr. Hynek
was coming to dinner! It was August 1, 1971, and the summer
heat was almost unbearable as I left for Boston to pick him up
at the now-familiar Parker House. Our first meeting had been

on such a hot day, and while driving into Boston I thought back over our growing relationship. His visit on this day was for the purpose of allowing me to read the galleys of his book, especially where my name and reports were used. Hynek's concern for accuracy and fair play impressed me, and I appreciated having been asked to proofread the material. Parking, as usual, was practically impossible near the hotel, but I managed to find a place in a nearby vacant courtyard about two blocks away. Allen met me in the hotel lobby, and forty-five minutes later we were pulling into my driveway at Wenham. After introducing him to my family, we sat out in the backyard on lawn chairs and discussed the book. It was very rewarding to see many of the cases I had personally investigated being used and fully credited in a book written by such a respected scientist.

After dinner, investigator and scientist Nat Gold and an associate, John Oswald, arrived to meet with us. John had designed a simple yet ingenious electromagnetic detector device for a survey of the area around Exeter, New Hampshire. The survey was based upon the premise that UFOs create or disturb a magnetic field in their vicinity. Several years prior, he had left a good job to come east to set up and monitor a number of these detectors. Hynek seemed quite impressed with both the device and John's research. Since then, I have worked closely with John in the preparation of a full report on his twenty-month survey. Although geomagnetic storms on the sun accounted for many detector alarms, there still remain a number of unexplained alarms. Some of these coincide with known UFO sightings in the area. (A schematic diagram of John's device can be found in the Appendix section of this book.) NICAP has published summary data relating to this UFO detector study conducted at Exeter. Hynek's book, of course, has since been published and has already gone through several printings in this country and abroad.[5] It has received favorable reviews in a number of scientific and popular periodicals.

Menzel Versus Fowler

Dr. Donald Menzel stands out as a striking contrast to Dr. Jr. Allen Hynek. There are marked similarities relating to professional backgrounds. Menzel is a respected astronomer and directed the prestigious Harvard Observatory for a number of years. Hynek is a respected astronomer and is director of the Dearborn Observatory and the Lindheimer Astronomical Research Center at Northwestern University. Both have served as scientific consultants to the Air Force on the UFO problem. Both have written books on UFOs.[6] One would think that they would have similar views on UFOs, but this is hardly the case. Their views seem to be unequivocally and diametrically opposed to each other. In the eyes of UFO buffs, Menzel is the archdemon and Hynek the archangel of UFOlogy! Thus, when I was contacted by the "For Women Today" television show in Boston to debate on the subject of UFOs, I naturally suggested Dr. Menzel to be my worthy opponent.

Ever since my run-in with him a number of years back on the radio "Night-Line" show, Menzel intrigued me. His attitude on UFOs seemed *too* negative. I wondered if he were just part of an overall governmental policy to debunk UFOs publicly. As early as January 1953, the C.I.A. had ordered the Air Force to actually carry out an extensive debunking program. (This is fully discussed later in chapter thirteen of this book.) Was Menzel part of this program, or was he really ultranegative and emotional about the question of UFOs? One way to help size him up would be for me to have a face-to-face encounter with him, and so I did during the taping of "For Women Today" on June 18, 1970.

I arrived at television station WBZ in Boston around eight o'clock in the morning. Menzel had not arrived, and I was ushered into a conference room to discuss my part in the debate with the host and hostess, Jack Cole and Sonya Hamlin. We first went over a set of 35mm slides to be used in my discussion of the famous Socorro, New Mexico, landing and other photographic material. Jack and Sonya were very interested in the subject. I showed them the infamous *Low memo,* which, as previously mentioned, was released to the public by two scientists later fired from the University of Colorado UFO study for this very act. It was just about at this point that the door opened behind me and in strode Menzel. As he passed by me, he glanced at one of the UFO photographs I had brought along and remarked, "That photograph is a fake!" and promptly sat down. Since the University of Colorado UFO study could not explain this particular photograph, I challenged this offhand remark and quoted from the analysis performed by Dr. William K. Hartmann, photographic analyst for the Colorado Project:

> This is one of the few UFO reports in which all factors investigated, geometric, psychological, and physical appear to be consistent with the assertion that an extraordinary flying object, silvery, metallic, disk-shaped, tens of meters in diameter, and evidently artificial, flew within sight of two witnesses . . . the accuracy of certain photometric measures of the original negatives . . . argue against a fabrication.[7]

Then I turned to Jack and Sonya and said: "Dr. Menzel is well known for making such nondocumented statements concerning UFOs on programs like this. If I were you, I'd ask him to document what he says. My material is thoroughly documented." Menzel just glared at me and let out a "hummpf" as we all proceeded to discuss the show's format. Just before we left for the studio, Jack Cole showed Menzel my copy of the *Low memo* and asked him if he would care to discuss it on the show. Menzel's face became visibly reddened and he jumped to his feet and shouted, "If that memo is going to be discussed, I shall refuse to appear on this show!" Jack, somewhat taken aback by this tirade, retorted, "I was only asking."

Funnily enough, just prior to going on the air, Jack whispered to me that he was going to use it. However, for better or for worse, he missed the cue card concerning it and it never was brought up. It was just as well. I am sure it would have created an unpleasant scene.

During the show, I stressed the significance of cases like the April 24, 1964, UFO landing at Socorro, New Mexico. The witness, a policeman, had heard and watched a white, car-sized, egg-shaped object descend from the sky into a deserted gully. During his investigation, he saw two child-sized figures in white coveralls standing near the object. As he maneuvered the police cruiser to a better vantage point, he lost sight of the weird object and figures momentarily. After parking the cruiser on a small hillock overlooking the gully where the object was sitting, Officer Zamora was able to advance to within 100 feet of the object, which sat on four stilts. Suddenly a loud roaring sound and a burst of blue flame erupted from the object. Thinking that it was about to explode, Zamora turned and ran toward the cruiser, instinctively hitting the dirt along the way. Looking up from where he lay on the ground, he was amazed to see that the object was now several feet off the ground and just hovering. The blue flame shrank to nothing. It then emitted a whining sound before moving silently off with a strange, unconventional *up-and-down motion*. His radio would not function until the object had disappeared from view. Meanwhile, back at the police station, telephone calls had been coming in that reported a blue flame of light in the area. Shortly thereafter, the state police arrived and found strange markings and a smoldering area. Dr. Hynek, who arrived later to investigate the sighting for the Air Force, stated that he found no evidence of a hoax. The object was unidentified.

When Menzel was given his opportunity for rebuttal, he offered a unique explanation for the Socorro UFO:

> In 1966, I was in Peru to observe an eclipse of the sun. I was driving along a road with a native driver, and all of a sudden, in front of me, I saw an object that looked almost identical with what they described—the little legs, the two little men in white around it—and I was fascinated and surprised. I recognized it immediately from the Socorro case, and, ah, my driver did not stop at all! And this thing moved across the road, and then as we went past it, I saw it take off and go up into the atmosphere. . . . It was what we call a *dust devil* (little whirlwind) of a very sharply-defined character. And dust devils are very frequent out in this area of Socorro, and I think that could have been what he saw.[8]

Jack then asked Menzel, "Did the dust devil bring down the two little men in the white suits?" Menzel even had an answer for *them!*

> The two little men in the white suits were just part of the dust devil around the bottom of it, where you are looking through the edges of the places where the dust was being picked up from the dusty road. . . .[9]

Later Jack challenged this explanation. I had shown a photograph of one of four clearly defined depressions and a diagram drawn of their arrangements in relation to the burned areas. Dr. William Powers, assistant to Dr. Hynek, had drawn this diagram to illustrate that the UFO's center of gravity was directly over a burn mark that had heat applied in a *straight down* direction. This indicated an equal distribution of weight on the four stilts. The four depressions were rectangular and each measured twelve inches long, six inches wide and three to four inches deep. Powers stated that the force creating these impressions was equivalent to gentle settling of at least a ton on each mark. He added that this fact, coupled with the equal distribution of weight, strongly argued against a hoax.

Menzel totally ignored this significant supplementary evidence that supported Officer Zamora's verbal testimony. He appeared to completely overlook the fact that this data was the product of investigation by capable scientists operating in an official capacity!

Menzel: There was absolutely no proof connecting . . . what Zamora was reported to have seen with the burned area. There are burned areas all over the country, and the fact that they found this burned area does not prove there was a connection.

Fowler: Excuse me! Zamora . . . saw the object sitting on four stilts. There were four depressions. He described the object as lifting off with the blue flame right smack in the middle of these four stilts, where the blue flame supposedly left a burned area. . . . I find it very hard to believe that a whirlwind could have given the illusion that Dr. Menzel alludes to. The roaring sound—perhaps. The blue flame, the depressions, the high-pitched to a low-pitched whine—no. He even saw an insignia on this white object.

Menzel: . . . He lost his glasses somehow around the middle of this story. He had dropped them while he was frightened and didn't get them until after the whole thing was over. It turned out that his vision was something like 20-100 and, therefore, after he had lost his glasses, anything he saw was pretty much guesswork.

Fowler: The point he lost his glasses, he had walked within a hundred feet of an object sitting there in front of him. When the roar started from the object . . . he ran back to the cruiser and hit the dust. That's when the glasses fell off!

Jack: Let's wait. We only have a few minutes more and I want to refine this as much as we can.

Menzel: Well, I don't think that this is that important a case. I think it may very well be a hoax.[10]

I just sat there in front of the cameras shaking my head slowly in utter dismay at this man's closed mind. However, Menzel did have a funny side to him, in spite of his negativism on the subject. At one point in the show, when the host and hostess were discussing the prospects of the existence of Martians, Menzel made a startling revelation!

Menzel: I paint Martians. That's one of my hobbies.

Everybody: (Laughter)

Jack: What do they look like?

Menzel: Oh, they are very friendly creatures and very colorful!

Jack: Little men in white suits?

Menzel: No. They're all different colors but you can always tell the females![11]

After the show, I shook hands with Dr. Menzel and told him that I had enjoyed debating with him very much.

Menzel's negative attitude and incredulous remarks concerning UFOs still remain a mystery to me. Is he sincere or are there ulterior motives involved? Dr. Menzl knows; I can only speculate. Later, as I reviewed the show in my mind, a thought suddenly struck me concerning the Socorro, New Mexico, sighting. I had forgotten to mention that the state police found the grass still smoldering upon arrival at the scene! How I could have overlooked this important facet of the sighting I'll never know. Menzel knew, too, but he wasn't about to bring it up. He was finding it tough enough to debunk the sighting with the facts that had already been presented!

Here They Come Again!

The year 1971 heralded an upswing in the frequency of UFO sightings reported throughout the world. Throughout October and November, newspapers across the length of the British Isles were reporting well-witnessed sightings of unidentified cylindrical and oval-shaped objects. In Brazil, for example, during the weekend of September 24-26, two men, driving independently near Rio de Janeiro, had to be treated for shock after being followed by a low-flying object carrying a blinding light. Both men reported to the police that their vehicles would not respond when they tried to speed away from the object.

In Australia, on September 30, more than a dozen witnesses observed a whitish grey, *hat-shaped* object descend and hover at flagpole level over a bowling club at Kemble Heights. It shone two lights onto the parking lot before moving off and disappearing behind trees. Investigating police could find no explanation.

Newspaper reports of UFOs in this country continued to follow a now well-established pattern. News of sightings were usually confined to just local papers covering the area in which the events took place. National press releases and big city newspaper stories concerning UFO sightings were practically nonexistent. Many reports never reached newspapers at all. Records kept at NICAP headquarters indicated that the increase in UFO reports had started in April and May of 1971. New England was not bypassed during this period. I investigated two low-altitude UFO sightings in the month of May. The first incident took place during the predawn hours of May 29 at Oxford, Massachusetts.[12]

Besieged by a UFO

UFOs were the farthest thing from Warren MacCarthy's mind as he woke up his two teen-aged sons, Mark and Michael, to go fishing. After picking up Ray Beaudry, a teen-aged friend of his sons, they headed for Buffumville reservoir and arrived there at 3:00 A.M. Echoes of their car door slamming and the rattling of fishing equipment pierced the early morning solitude as they walked along Buffum beach. Stars sparkled overhead and an eerie mist hung over the calm water. One by one they cast their lines into the two hundred-foot stretch of water that joined two large ponds. The temperature stood at only fifty-three degrees, and a fire was soon set on the beach to warm their hands. An hour later, it happened!

Raymond was the first to notice it. A bright, erratically moving light came slowly toward them from the western horizon.

"What's that, Mr. MacCarthy?"

Warren and his sons glanced up to where Raymond was pointing. Dumbfounded, they watched a bright bluish white light bobbing up and down and moving from side to side. As it approached, it took on the shape of a glowing rectangle, which seemed to be attached to the top of a dark object with a shiny surface. Initially more curious than frightened, their fascination suddenly turned to shock. The silent object, about three hundred feet away at treetop level, abruptly flipped up on edge "like a pancake," revealing a round bottom with seven to eight diffuse white lights spaced evenly around its perimeter. Then, almost instantaneously, it backed off at terrific speed and was soon lost to sight! Excited, and not knowing what to do, they nervously discussed what had happened.

Several minutes later, it again appeared, moving erratically toward them. Spellbound, they watched it approach, and before they even had time to react the object streaked right at them, stopping two hundred feet short of them right over the opposite shoreline. Instinctively, the fishermen ducked. Mr. MacCarthy stated that he actually could see its "ports" reflected on the water's surface. It hovered momentarily and an uneasiness crept over them. They felt as if they were being watched! Then, in a split second, it streaked away from them at a "speed too fast to estimate." This was enough for the witnesses! They doused the fire and returned home. Warren, after discussing the episode with his wife, phoned the Worcester *Telegram* to see if anybody else had reported seeing the object. No one else had, but the paper ran an article on their sighting that soon was brought to my notice. Shortly thereafter, I questioned the witnesses by telephone and later sent investigators Charles Valentine and Frank Pechulis to perform an on-site investigation.

Checks were made with local police departments, the Worcester airport and other agencies, but no other reports of the early morning *visitor* had been made. Someone from nearby East Brookfield had phoned Warren MacCarthy shortly after the newspaper article appeared on the newsstand. He said that he had seen a strange object hovering over nearby Howe Pond at 5:25 A.M., about an hour after the original sighting. We were unable to locate this caller.

A check of astronomical data indicated that Venus had risen in the east *behind* the observers at 4:12 A.M. Jupiter was setting in the direction that the observers were observing the UFO and did set at 4:32 A.M. Trees would have effectively blocked the observers' view of either of these bright planets, as the beach was located down in a hollow. In any event, the close-encounter aspects of this sighting hardly fit the description of either planet! In addition, Jupiter would not have been very prominent in the lightened near-dawn sky. The sun rose at 5:12 A.M., less than forty five minutes after the object was last observed. If one takes the witnesses' description at face value (and I found no reason not to), the incident adds up to four people sighting an unconventional, noiseless lighted object at very close range. Its reported shape, performance, flight path and motion are typical of other UFO reports. I classified this sighting in the category of "unknown" and sent detailed reports to NICAP and other interested parties.

The second low-altitude UFO sighting followed the Oxford affair just two days later at Newmarket, New Hampshire.[13] Since the witnesses have requested that their names be kept confidential, I have not employed real names or identified the exact location of the sighting in the account that follows.

The Priest and the Saucer

The fragrance and sounds of late spring filled the air. Studies and exams now seemed far away to Paul. The last four years had found him busily studying for the Roman Catholic priesthood thousands of miles away from the beautiful southern New Hampshire homestead. And now he was home again. He would spend the summer helping his brother Joseph work the farm before returning to final graduate studies and assignment by the Church.

It was Monday—Memorial Day. Attending the local parade and ceremonies brought back many childhood memories to Paul's mind. Afterwards, Paul set out with Joseph in a pickup truck to check on some equipment left in a rented field on the day before. It was just after one o'clock. The skies were gray and threatening. The field was surrounded by trees and swampland. The truck wound its way along the heavily shaded dirt road that led to the isolated field. Bursting out from under the canopy of trees into the large open field, their eyes were suddenly confronted with an incredible sight! There, plainly outlined in front of trees at the lower edge of the field and hovering about three feet off the ground, was a strange aerial object.

"Like a Squashed Pear!"

Joseph slammed on the brakes! As the truck skidded to a halt, the object began to rise, slowly at first, but steadily picking up speed. Paul stuck his head out of the side window while his brother pressed his face against the windshield. The whitish gray object was about the size of a car and shaped "like a squashed pear without a neck." A horizontal series of indentations could be barely seen around its upper circumference. It continued to pick up speed as it gained altitude and accelerated straight up until it was barely seen against the clouds. Abruptly, it arced over and sped quickly away, disappearing into the distance.

Stunned, they just sat there staring where the object had just been. The wind blew dust across the newly plowed field. Impulsively, Joseph swung the truck onto the field and started a slow topsy-turvey ride downhill to where the object had hovered. Jumping out of the truck, the brothers thoroughly examined the area but saw no one and nothing unusual. No traces, no odor—just some deer tracks besides a little pool filled with tadpoles.

Raindrops began splashing the windshield as Joseph drove laboriously back up through the plowed field to the road. After checking on the equipment, they jointly decided that it would be best not to tell anyone of their strange experience. However, after reaching home, they decided to at least phone nearby Pease Air Force Base located at Portsmouth, New Hampshire. The Air Force questioned them over the phone and stated that they would be contacted later.

It was inevitable that such an experience could not be kept completely confidential. Joseph felt that he had to tell his wife about it. He told her that he was beginning to wonder if he were "seeing things" because of all the recent hard work and stress, except for the fact that Paul had also seen it. Joseph's wife (you guessed it!) couldn't keep a secret and told her father, who in turn told his boss. That very evening, his boss told an employee on the night shift. Coincidentally, the employee was none other than my friend and associate investigator, John Paul Oswald! John phoned me about it on the following day, and I asked him to initiate an investigation immediately.

THE INVESTIGATION

Paul and Joseph were two very surprised individuals when they stepped out into the usually deserted farmyard in the early morning hours of Wednesday, June 22. There stood John Oswald armed with a tape recorder, notebook, compass, camera, a set of topographic maps and a friendly, disarming smile! John persuaded them to be interviewed by promising them anonymity. They took him to the sighting area and went over every aspect of the incident with John. Both were reluctant to fill out and sign forms because they felt that the observed craft might have been a government secret. John then arranged a meeting with me at my home to discuss the matter.

John arrived on Friday evening shortly after seven o'clock. Shortly thereafter, NICAP special adviser Walter Webb and investigator Herb Eismann arrived. We listened to the taped interview and went over John's notes with great interest. The sighting sounded impressive and we unanimously concluded that it was worthy of further investigation.

My first step was to telephone the brothers. I managed to catch Paul at home on Sunday and asked him pertinent questions as a double check on already accumulated data. Telephone calls were also made to police departments in Dover, Durham, Exeter, and Newmarket, New Hampshire, to see if others had reported seeing the object. No one had. I then phoned John and made ar-

rangements to meet with him early on Monday evening to personally visit the sighting area and meet with the witnesses. In the
meantime, I decided to check out aircraft and balloon activity
in the area during the day.

Pease Air Force Base Air Weather Service and Lt. Joseph
Benton, Public Information Officer, checked on the local weather
conditions, aircraft, and balloon launch schedules for me. I found
that no balloons had been launched from Pease AFB and that
there was no aircraft activity on Memorial Day. I was told that
the airbase was essentially dead except for a holiday skeleton
crew. The weather data matched the witnesses' description of
conditions that day, and the wind direction and speed ruled out
a balloon. A balloon would have had to take off vertically and
fly almost directly into the wind. A further check with the Atlantic
Weather Project indicated that no balloons had been launched
from their weather ships An official working on this project told
me quite emphatically that a *downed* balloon could not do what
the described object was reported to have done. Logan Airport,
about sixty miles down the coast from the sighting locale, had
launched a small weather balloon just ten minutes prior to the
UFO sighting but distance, time, size and wind direction ruled
this possibility out completely.

I then phoned the administration headquarters of the Federal
Aviation Administration at Burlington, Massachusetts, and talked
with Assistant Chief Stone. He paved the way for my telephoning
the Radar Operations Center at Nashua, New Hampshire. There
I was able to question the deputy chief of operations, Mr. Waldo
Aldrich, regarding the UFO sighting. Mr. Aldrich made a personal
check of the FAA radar watch logs for the date, time, and sector
of the sighting. He said that he had "two possibilities" but wanted
to "check on something first." He returned to the phone several
minutes later to inform me that he had "found nothing unusual
on the log." Puzzled by his previous remarks, I asked him point
blank what procedure he would follow if he knew of something
"unusual" on the log. He told me that "unexplainable radar targets
are relayed to the military." I had no recourse but to accept what
he said. Returning home from work, I then grabbed a quick bite to

eat and drove into southern New Hampshire to meet John Oswald.

John and I arrived at the field shortly after seven o'clock that Monday evening. We took further compass readings, rechecked the area with a topographical map, drew sketches, and took more photographs and measurements. The objects had hovered over a small grassy patch near a shallow pool of water filled with tadpoles. It was located in front of nearby trees so that the witnesses' estimate of its size could be mathematically worked out. The derived size matched their previous estimate. It was about the size of an automobile. Railroad tracks passed within two hundred feet of this spot. They were located on an elevated mound which separated the field from more woods and a vast saltwater marsh. We walked along the tracks and criss-crossed the field but found no evidence that an object had actually landed. Finally, dusk and hordes of IFOs (mosquitoes!) sent us scurrying back to the car and to the witnesses' farm.

The brothers were both still hard at work when we pulled into the farmyard. I questioned them at length. They explained to me that their initial reaction had been that a balloon had come down over the field or that someone was launching a balloon from the field. Within a moment, they both realized that its movements ruled out a balloon. "It moved rigidly and mechanically, like it was attached to something solid but invisible," they said. Both were very impressed with this nonwavering, straight-up movement, as if it were *under control*. I then proceeded to ask them what they thought about UFOs. Both laughed and said they hadn't read much on the subject. They seemed to think that the object was an experimental military aircraft. I was very impressed with their sincerity and cautiousness in reporting just what they had seen without embellishment.

On the following day, I phoned the basic data on this sighting to Stuart Nixon, executive director of NICAP. I told him that my next step was to do some character checking and further field investigation before I would be sending NICAP a final written report.

On Wednesday, I telephoned Dominican College at Racine,

Wisconsin, and chatted with Father Barry McCabe, vice-president of academic affairs. He told me that

> Paul was a good student. I have known him for three years. He was a veteran and older than most other students, thus providing a mature influence on the other students. He has a solid, stable character. I would give him the highest recommendation.

When I proceeded to tell Father McCabe, in confidence, what Paul had reported seeing, he stated to me, "If Paul said he saw, he saw it." He confirmed to me that Paul had just graduated with a degree in Human Relations. He added that Paul would be attending seminary in the fall and would eventually serve as a priest in Kentucky.

On Thursday evening, I drove up to the sighting area again and performed a house-to-house check along the main road from which the dirt road to the field egressed. Although I could not find any other witnesses, I did come across an older report that involved a brightly lit UFO circling the area during the incredible spring of 1966. The woman told me that the local police had chased it in their cruisers. A relative working at the police station had phoned her to enquire if she could see it. She told me that both she and her husband rushed out to the front yard and saw an erratically moving object carrying changing, multicolored lights. I put in a phone call to the police from her home to confirm her account and had John Oswald look into the matter, but that's another story. As far as the Newmarket sighting was concerned, it was placed in the "significant unknown" category and a detailed report was sent to NICAP and interested researchers.

The Chicken Coop Caper

Another interesting low-altitude UFO sighting took place just a year later at Canterbury, New Hampshire.[14] On the evening of Sunday, May 14, 1972, I received a phone call from John Oswald. He, in turn, had just received a call from a contact employed at the Air Force-sponsored Satellite Tracking Station at New Boston, New Hampshire. He gave John the name and telephone number of a Mr. James Lilley, who had just reported a UFO sighting to the station. John told me that he had already conducted an initial telephone interview with the witnesses and related the following account to me.

Mr. James Lilley of Canterbury, New Hampshire, told John that shortly after 9:30 P.M. on May 13, he had accompanied his two sons and two friends to a partially constructed *chicken coop* where they were going to camp out. He had left them for only ten minutes, when they ran up from the field and burst into the house like scared rabbits! They claimed that a strange-shaped buzzing object with fiery exhaust had flown over the open chicken coop and shined a light on them. Mr. and Mrs. Lilley left their TV program and hurried outside to look. Flying away from them in the distance, low over a swamp, was a lighted object. It made a sound similar to but not exactly like a jet. Thinking it must have been a helicopter, he told the boys to go back down to the coop and go to sleep. They refused to go and insisted that it had not been a helicopter. Taking the two oldest boys aside, Mr. Lilley asked them to draw separate and independent drawings of the object. To his surprise, both sketches were consistent and showed a very unconventional looking craft! This fact, coupled with the unfamiliar noise and lights that he and his wife had seen, prompted him to phone the Air Force Tracking Station to report it.

On Monday, I phoned the Canterbury Police to see if anyone else had reported a UFO on May 13. No one had, but Police Chief Harold Streeter gave Mr. Lilley an excellent character rating as both a good citizen and friend. Tuesday brought a letter from John Oswald stating that Mr. Lilley had sent him photostats of the boys' initial sketches. On Friday, I phoned Mrs. Lilley to find out if her sons had access to or an interest in UFOs. She stated that none of the boys involved had shown any prior interest in the subject. She said that she would be agreeable to a NICAP investigation if her husband approved.

On Saturday, I drove up to see John to take a look at his notes and the boys' sketches. By Monday, I decided to conduct a detailed investigation and set up an appointment with the Lilleys for Wednesday evening. I then phoned the Air Force Tracking Station on Tuesday to see if any anomalous radar targets had appeared on their screens during the sighting period. The crew that had been on duty on that date were not available and I was asked to call back later. A call to the FAA Air Traffic Control Center initiated a check of the radar operators' logs for the sighting time and place. Again, I was asked to call back later for the desired information.

On Wednesday, I contacted the FAA Control Tower at the Manchester, New Hampshire, airport. I wanted to check on possible helicopter flights that might have instigated the Canterbury UFO report. I was told that there were no helicopters at the Manchester airport but that fifteen National Guard helicopters were located at the Concord, New Hampshire, airport and that they flew regularly over the Canterbury area! At this point, I could envision cancelling my appointment to interview the witnesses. A military helicopter combined with some imaginative youngsters seemed to provide an easy answer. To be quite truthful, I wasn't too keen on driving eighty miles to Canterbury on a wild-goose chase after a day of work. Nevertheless, I phoned the FAA Flight Service at Concord Airport to check out the whereabouts of these military helicopters during the sighting time frame.

To my surprise, the Flight Service informed me that their logs showed no aircraft in the Canterbury area at that time. Their logs indicated that the last two National Guard helicopters had landed between five and six o'clock on that evening, four hours prior to the reported UFO sighting! I decided to double-check their records and put in a call to the National Guard. They confirmed what the Flight Service had told me. The FAA had also informed me that the only other helicopter that flew over that area on occasion originated out of Wiggans Airways, Norwood, Massachusetts. It would operate out of Concord Airport to perform a periodic check of power lines in the area. But, the FAA official told me, it had not been in the area for a long time. A personal call to Wiggans Airways confirmed this. The official did tell me of another possibility. He said that an Air Force search mission had been conducted for a lost private plane earlier in the month. This had consisted of a series of low-level flights by C-130 Hercules aircraft across Canterbury and other areas of New Hampshire. The downed plane was reported missing on May 2. He said that he doubted the search was still going on as late as May 13 but that it was worth looking into. I agreed and made a note to check this possibility out before leaving work and heading north up Route 93 to Canterbury.

I arrived within town limits at about 5:30 P.M. and parked just off the road beside some power lines to eat a typical flying saucer investigator's supper—dry sandwiches! While munching away and glancing up the road, I saw a man staring at me from the porch of a distant house. Soon he began walking down the country road toward me. Then, one of the coincidences I encounter so many times during investigations occurred again.

"Hi!" he said, "Are you in trouble? Saw your car off the road and wondered if you need any help."

"No, just eating my supper," I replied. "You might be able to help me out on something else, though. I'm going to be visiting a Mr. James Lilley. According to his directions, I can't be too far away from his home."

The man looked very surprised. "Why, Jim Lilley works for me!" he said. "I'm Arthur Stavros."

We shook hands and I introduced myself.

"You must be the fellow who is interested in the flying object," he said.

"Yes, that's me. What do you know about it?"

"Well, only what Jim told me at work last week. Strangely enough, I saw a bright red light flying north right over these power lines earlier on that same night from my backyard down there. I thought it must have been a helicopter and never gave it a second thought until Jim told me what was seen up at his place. His house is just a few miles from here."

Before he returned home, I asked him what he thought about Jim Lilley.

"Well, he's honest and hard-working. Not the type to create a hoax."

I thanked him, gulped down the rest of some cold coffee, and drive to the Lilley home, which was located on "Sno-Shoe Hill." I arrived there to find the Lilley family, their sons' two friends, and the local school science teacher waiting for me. I felt that my first step was to get the four boys away from the adults and down to the now-completed chicken coop where the object was initially observed. We went down to the coop. After a detailed cross-examination, I took compass readings and some photographs of the area before returning to the house to interview the boys' parents. The boys' story is as follows.

GROUP 1

It was about 9:30 P.M. when Jim Lilley said goodnight to his sons (Jimmy and Scott) and their two friends, Tommy and Peter. Their sleeping bags were spread on the floor of the nearly completed chicken coop located beside the barn. The coop was still without one wall, and this particular side opened onto a very large field facing the west. According to the U.S. Weather Service, the skies were clear and visibility was unlimited. Just before their father left, they asked him what the bright star was that was setting in the west. He didn't know, so they called it the "North Star"! In actuality, it was the planet Venus.

About a quarter of an hour later, Scott, who was still looking out at the so-called North Star shouted to the others, "Hey, there are two North Stars out there and one's on fire and coming this way!"

The older boys sat up and saw a very bright light source erratically descending toward the open field "like a falling floating balloon" from the WSW. They all jumped up and went outside onto the grass. The object had leveled out and was rapidly approaching them. Jimmy, who had taken his father's large flashlight out with them, turned it on and pointed it at what they thought was an oncoming helicopter. (Jimmy's father had once flashed a light at a military helicopter and it had responded by coming overhead with its landing lights on.) The object abruptly slowed when the flashlight was turned on. A loud grinding, buzzing sound filled the air as the lighted object passed directly over the boys' heads. It was just in these last few seconds that they saw the object was neither helicopter nor conventional aircraft. Shocked by what they saw, four very terrified young boys made a beeline for the Lilley house!

The boys described the object as a decahedron or perhaps toplike in shape. It was flying with its forward moving side tilted ahead at a forty-five degree angle. It had four pipelike legs with round pads affixed to their ends. A bright white light on its forward moving side lit up the coop and the surrounding area. A flashing red light ("like the color of a heat lamp in the coop") was noted on the objects's trailing side. A fiery ten-foot exhaust poured down from the object's underside, which alternately changed colors as if they were *switched from one to another*. All the boys caught a fleeting glance at a number of silver U-shaped cablelike things sticking into and around the top of the object. Tommy thought he saw some boxlike protrusions attached to the object's sides.

The strange buzzing craft appeared to have passed at only 150 feet above their heads. Its real size was estimated to have been one-to-two car lengths long and high. A dog slept undisturbed in the coop, but their cat "took off like a bullet" as the object bore down on them.

GROUP 2

Mr. and Mrs. Lilley were watching television when the four boys came tumbling through the front door yelling about a *strange object* outside. The Lilleys went outside and were just in time to see the lights on a slow moving object moving away from them low over a swamp across the road from their house. An unfamiliar sound somewhat like a jet but different came from the direction of the receding object.

SUPPORTING WITNESSES

A house-to-house check in the area revealed others who saw or heard the object. Marilyn——, who lives nearby, told me that around nine o'clock on that night, she heard a very loud sound "like a jet" and opened her bathroom window to see what it was. She saw nothing but said that the noise was unusual. "It suddenly died from a loud roar to nothing. It didn't gradually fade away as jet aircraft usually do."

During the same time frame, Peter and Tommy's grandparents, also neighbors, heard "a loud roar like a low-flying, throttled-back jet bomber." The grandfather quickly stepped outside to see what it was. He observed a bright moving light shining downwards. The old gentleman told me that he was skeptical about his grandsons' description of the object and that it had probably just been a jet bomber with lights shining down through an open bomb bay.

Another resident, Mr. Alfred———,told me that he had seen strange lights between the power lines and the Lilleys' home during that week but could not remember if it had been on the same date. Other than Arthur Stavros's earlier sighting of a red light over nearby power lines, I could find only one more group who saw strange lights in the area around the same time as the principal sighting. Two ladies reported seeing a "strange horizontal set of little square white lights" from the Sky High Drive-In Theater at nearby Boscowen.

THE INVESTIGATION CONTINUES

During the course of my investigation, I contacted the Air Force Public Information Officers at both Hanscom Field and Pease Air Force Base to ascertain whether any low-level military flights could have provided the stimuli for the reports. They checked and phoned back. The last low-level mission in the Canterbury area had been performed by an Air Search and Rescue unit stationed at Pease Air Force Base on May 2. It had been in connection with an air search for the downed private plane mentioned previously by the FAA.

Later, the FAA Control Center at Nashua, New Hampshire, phoned back to tell me that their radar did not cover the Canterbury area. They did add that nothing unusual was noted in those sectors of New Hampshire covered by radar. Having gone as far as I could, regarding the presence of conventional aircraft in the area that night, I decided to check out the character of the boys through their schoolteachers and minister.

One of the boys' teachers told me that Jimmy and Tommy told her about the incident when they returned to school on the Monday after the sighting. She said that she gave them a good cross-examination and was personally convinced that the boys were accurately describing what they had observed. She added that both boys had scored high on special "observe and report" tests that she administers from time to time. In her estimation, both boys were top students and not the type to fabricate or exaggerate such a story.

The pastor of the local church said much the same thing. He told me that he had overheard Jim Lilley talking about the incident after the Sunday morning service. This was just a day after the sighting. He was most curious and decided to pay a visit to the Lilley family on that very afternoon. After talking with the boys, he too was convinced that they were telling the truth. He told me that he found no evidence of a hoax. The pastor had been the first to personally interview the Lilley family.

THE "CANTERBURY TALES" ANALYZED

After analyzing this sighting thoroughly, I found myself in agreement with the schoolteacher and pastor. Evidence seemed to be in the boys' favor that something strange was indeed observed. My checks with civil, FAA, and Air Force authorities seemed to preclude any conventional aircraft flying low over this rural area. Also, the boys were very familiar with the sight and the sound of the National Guard helicopters that flew regularly over their neighborhood. Several minutes before the sighting, they had seen and recognized a high-flying commercial airliner. The reported shape, sound, exhaust, padded legs, maneuvers, and very low altitude of the strange object would imply the grossest of misinterpretations. I found such a possibility hard to accept under the overall circumstances. The only bright astronomical object in the sky was the planet Venus. However, the witnesses had both Venus and the object in sight at the same time. The description and movements ruled out astronomical phenomena. A research balloon was also ruled out for the same reasons, as well as the fact that its movement was incompatible with wind direction. A hoax seemed highly improbable in light of the good character references obtained on the witnesses and the fact that there were supporting witnesses. Visibility was unlimited and allowed for excellent seeing conditions. The sideways zigzag descent or *falling-leaf* motion is a consistent flight characteristic of UFOs. The boys, not well-read on the UFO subject, described this maneuver in such a way that it obviously did not presuppose prior knowledge of this peculiar characteristic.

It is highly probable that Marilyn——*heard* the object as it transited the fringe of the neighborhood. Likewise, the flight path and description of the object seen at a distance by Peter and Tommy's grandfather appears to fit that of the same object seen at close range by the boys. The sudden cutoff of engine noise reported by Marilyn and the inability of the grandfather and the Lilleys to differentiate the sound as being either a jet or prop-driven aircraft adds to the *strangeness* of the event. It is interesting to note that both Marilyn and the grandfather were familiar with normal aircraft but that both immediately tried to see what was causing the noise. Marilyn had opened a window to look out and the grandfather had rushed outside to investigate. The strange lights seen over the area by Arthur Stavros and Mr. Alfred——add to the intrigue.

What *would* be flying low over the area that night? The falling-leaf descent over the field was unconventional and certainly could not be duplicated by any known aircraft. On the other hand, the description of the reported object did not fit the typical oval or cylindrical UFOs usually reported. It is possible that in actuality the object was shaped like a top or upright egg. These configurations have been reported in the past. My evaluation of the Canterbury sighting placed it in the "unknown" category. Again, I had noticed a familiar and recurring pattern: 115-kilovolt power lines ran parallel to the chicken coop about three thousand feet to the west of the observers. Another set of 230-kilovolt power lines lay parallel to these, about four miles to the west. The object descended in the vicinity of these power lines!

"Hello, This Is the 'Dick Cavett Show' "

The voice on the phone was that of Michael Zannella. I was busy at my desk at my place of employment and, to be quite truthful, was not even familiar with the "Dick Cavett Show."

"What can I do for you?" I asked.

"We would like to schedule you to appear on the 'Dick Cavett Show' on October 26 to discuss UFOs." Michael replied.

Thinking that he represented some local TV show in Boston, I replied, "I'm sorry, my schedule is just too busy at the present time."

"But, Mr. Fowler, Dr. Hynek suggested you to appear in his place. He's traveling abroad that week to promote his new book."

"Well," I said, "if Dr. Hynek is involved, I may be able to swing it. What TV station carries this show?"

"Mr. Fowler! Aren't you acquainted with the Cavett show? We're carried nationally out of the Dick Cavett Theater in New York!"

Sheepishly, I answered, "New York! I thought you were in Boston."

"Do you mean you've never seen our show? That's hard to believe. We're one of the leading late evening talk shows!"

Then the significance of all this suddenly dawned on me. It was no longer a matter of my being too busy to appear on this show. I was scared stiff of appearing on this show!

"Give me time to think it over, Mr. Zannella. I'll have to look at my schedule and obtain permission for time off from my company. I assume that my expenses will be paid."

"Of course, Mr. Fowler! You'll be reimbursed for travel and be given an honorarium for making the appearance. But we've got to know by tomorrow whether you are coming or not."

"Well," I replied, "I can suggest others if I can't make it."

"No, that won't do. We will only act on Dr. Hynek's recommendation. If you are unable to come, we'll have to cancel a show on UFOs."

I thanked him and said that I would let him know my decision on the following day.

My heart was literally pounding with excitement and nervousness when I returned home and told Margaret about it. We both felt that it was an opportunity not to be passed up, regardless of my busy schedule and nervousness. It was not that I had not appeared on TV shows before. I had been on quite a few shows in Boston. The trip to New York and the idea of being televised *live* in a Broadway theater, as a substitute for Dr. Hynek himself, shook me to the very core! However, on the following day I obtained my company's go-ahead and placed a phone call to New York to accept the invitation. I was told that the drum player and comedian, Buddy Rich, would be hosting the show and that Helen Gurley Brown, editor of *Cosmopolitan* magazine, would be among the guests. At the time, her name and the magazine meant nothing to me. However, I soon was informed by my friends at work that she had written a popular book entitled *Sex and the Single Girl!* Needless to say, my associates began to give me a hard time about my appearing on the show with her. In addition, a constant comment met me wherever I went: "Buddy Rich? Uh-oh, you've had it now. He's unmerciful to his guests!" I'll tell you, I was one mighty apprehensive fellow as I boarded the plane at Boston on that sunny day of October 26, 1972!

I arrived at New York City in good time and hailed a taxi to the Cavett Theater at 1790 Broadway. People were already lining up at the doors as the taxi pulled up to the theater entrance. I informed the doorman who I was, and he escorted me to a small dark room where a number of people were sitting, watching the show's rehearsal on a monitor TV set. A few were other guests and others were members of Buddy Rich's troupe. I introduced myself and soon a preshow, spirited discussion on UFOs was underway.

"Buddy wants you to tell us about the *alien bodies* from a crashed saucer that the Air Force has at Edwards Air Force Base," one of them said.

"That's just a rumor," I said. "I just want to talk about facts."

"But Buddy told us that a general told him about it, so it must be true!"

"Maybe," I said, "but I can't document it. It will just have to be hearsay as far as I'm concerned."

Just then, the show's writer came in and asked me to sign a release.

"What do you have for visuals?" she asked.

I gave her a large blown-up picture of a UFO photographed at McMinnville, Oregon, on May 11, 1950. I used this particular photo often because the University of Colorado UFO study could find nothing negative about it after careful analysis. I was fortunate to have a copy made from the original negative. Subcommittee investigator Dave Webb had assisted Dr. William K. Hartmann in their analysis and made copies from the negatives. No sooner had I given the writer the photo, than a call came for me to report to the *makeup* girl.

Soon expert hands were daubing my face with powder, cream and eye-shadow! It was amazing to see what a little makeup can do when applied at the right places! I then returned to the waiting room to find that I would be the last guest to be interviewed on the show. Thus, until curtain time, I sat gazing at the monitor, feeling much like the proverbial lamb waiting to be led to the slaughter! Buddy Rich, true to what I had been told, was certainly raking his guests over the coals. In the meantime, the other guests kept leaving the waiting room, until I was the only one left. I continued to watch intently, and then a voice caused me to jump!

"Mr. Fowler, you're on! Please follow me."

I got up and followed the man to the darkened stage entrance and waited for the signal to walk on. Now I knew how a green parachutist felt when he was about to make his first jump! Then the band struck up a fanfare and I was announced.

"Here I go, Lord," I prayed. "Please be with me," and I strode out onto the stage.

The bright stage lights hit me with a blinding jolt, and I could barely see the audience as I shook hands with Buddy and his guests. Much to my relief, Buddy turned out to be most amiable and treated the subject seriously. For the better part of a half hour, we talked about all major aspects of the UFO problem, including the difficult position our government finds itself in regarding UFOs and security regulations governing national security. One of the highlights of the show was the overwhelming audience response to my statement regarding the hostility of human beings. Helen Gurley Brown had interjected at one point that extraterrestrial *aliens* would not harm us, as they would see that we were a peace-loving people! I retorted that if such aliens indeed existed, they probably considered us as dangerous lower life-forms in the light of the wars and crimes mankind has continually committed against one another. This brought a loud ovation from the audience. In summary, the show went off extremely well, and since it had been taped at the Cavett Theater between 6:00 and 7:30 P.M., I was able to catch a plane in time to arrive back home and watch the show myself at 11:30 P.M.[15]

"How did it go, Daddy?" my oldest daughter, Sharon, asked as I arrived home around 10:30 P.M. Her question was soon echoed by my wife, and I was soon sitting down with a cup of coffee telling them all about my adventures in New York! Later, as we watched the show, I could not help but think of the complex technology involved that not only produced the show but had brought me winging home from New York to watch it in just a matter of hours. Such a thing would have appeared to be *like magic* not too many years ago. Hence, what kind of a civilization might UFOs represent if they were extraterrestrial spacecraft? A technology capable of supporting interstellar space travel would seem *supernatural* to us. Would we be able to comprehend the by-products of such a society? I wonder.

NOTES

1. Jacques Vallée, *Anatomy of a Phenomenon*, p. 64.
2. Personal correspondence to the author from Dr. J. Allen Hynek, dated June 2, 1969.
3. Jim and Coral Lorenzen, *UFOs over the Americas*, p. 191.
4. "Dateline Boston," Channel 5, Boston, 1966.
5. J. Allen Hynek, *The UFO Experience*, Chicago: Henry Regnery Co., 1972.
6. Donald H. Menzel, *The World of Flying Saucers*, New York: Doubleday, 1963.

    7. Edward U. Condon, *Scientific Study of Unidentified Flying Objects,* p. 407.
    8. "For Women Today," Channel 4, Boston, July 3, 1970 (extracted from taped transcript).
    9. *Ibid.*
    10. *Ibid.*
    11. *Ibid.*
    12. Personal Files, UFO Report No. 71-10.
    13. Personal Files, UFO Report No. 71-11.
    14. Personal Files, UFO Report No. 72-5.
    15. "The Dick Cavett Show," October 26, 1972.

12

TIME TO TAKE INVENTORY

SUCCESS

If a man has a vision but no task,
he has a dream.
If he has a task but no vision,
he has drudgery.
But if he has both a vision and a task—
he has victory.

ANONYMOUS

A Decade of Fishing

In chapter three, entitled, *Examining the Catch,* a comparison of fourteen *local* unsolved UFO reports with global characteristics was initiated. The results of this initial "fishing expedition" showed definite signs that the "local pond" was indeed being infiltrated by the same "unknown species" being reported elsewhere throughout the world. However, in order to better ascertain this to be really the case, it was obvious that a larger local sample had to be collected, compared and tabulated. This chapter records such an analysis. It is based upon nearly a decade of personally supervised UFO investigations within the New England area, particularly in Massachusetts. I would like at this time to express my gratitude to those who have served as investigators and listening posts over these years. If it were not for their meeting the critical need for "more fishermen and better nets," it would have been impossible for me to collect and analyze the data presented here.

For the sake of practicality, only those UFO reports that have been evaluated in the "unknown" category will be employed. A total of 160 such *local* reports were recorded over the period of June 1963 through December 1972. (See Figure 3.) Sample

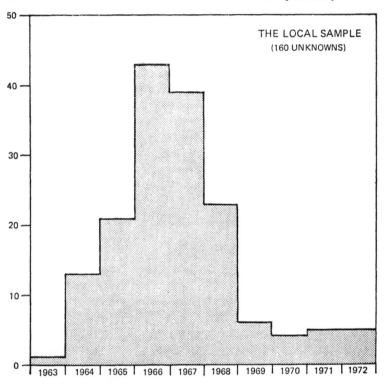

FIGURE 3

statistics relating to these strange local UFO reports having no
identification are listed in Appendix I as general information.

Will the Witnesses Please Take the Stand?

Before undertaking a descriptive analysis of the reported
UFOs, we should first address ourselves to the question "Who
were the UFO reporters?" The following chart indicates that 291,
or 63 percent of the 461 witnesses, were in the young and middle-
age adult category. Relatively few children or senior adults reported seeing UFOs.

Child (7-12)	Teen (13-19)	Young (20-30)	Middle (31-59)	Senior (60-__)
9%	25%	24%	39%	3%
(42)	(115)	(111)	(180)	(13)

Further statistics indicated that there was no evidence to support the popular notion that most people who report UFOs are irresponsible, uneducated, or mentally unbalanced. On the contrary, the data collected relating to the witnesses' education and occupation quickly dismissed such stereotypes. Most of the adults had at least a high school education and sixteen percent had undergone further schooling. Included within this percentage, twenty-one persons had at least a bachelor's degree and four had advanced degrees.

The 291 young and middle-adult witnesses represented a large variety of occupations, some of which are outlined as follows.

Scientist	Engineer	Technician	Teacher	Police	Other
2%	2%	3%	2%	8%	83%
(5)	(5)	(8)	(7)	(24)	(242)

The "other" category included the following types of occupations:

Doctor	Stewardess	Minister
Cabinetmaker	Mechanic	Horticulturist
Priest	Dental Assistant	Accountants
Nurses	Secretaries	Postmaster
Writer	News Reporter	Clerks
Truckdrivers	Administrators	Bus Driver
Firechief	Insurance Salesman	Farmer
Realtor	Sweeper	Machinist
News Editor	Bakers	Airport Manager
Taxidriver	Telephone Operator	Draftsman
Architect	College Students	Housewives

Many of the male adults had also attended a variety of military training schools. Eight were still qualified private or commercial pilots.

"Who were the UFO reporters?" The facts are inescapable. In this *local* sample, the people who initiated the UFO reports recorded in this book represent a broad cross-section of the public at large. This is exactly what one would expect if the reports involved the sighting of real physical objects. Let us now examine these reported phenomena. What did the witnesses say they saw?

Presenting the State's Evidence

It is now time to repeat the procedure previously employed in chapter three. We shall again compare "specimens" from our localized sample with a global baseline, in order to help ascertain whether or not the same type of objects are involved. In our initial sample, the results were relatively successful, but only fourteen specimens were involved. Since then, the number of reports in the "unknown" category has risen to 160. If the reports of a new "species" being seen in "ponds" throughout the world relate to real physical phenomena, one would think that our catch from the *local* pond would exhibit the exact same characteristics. Let us see if this is so. We shall first consider the physical appearance or *shape* of the reported objects.

CONFIGURATION
(Unknowns Only)
Comparison with Global Percentages

	Local Sample[1] (1963-1972)	NICAP[2] (1942-1963)	Air Force[3] (1947-1952)
Elliptical/Oval	59% (95)	60% (333)	61% (264)*
Cylindrical	8% (12)	9% (48)	7% (30)*
Balls of Light/Other	33% (53)	31% (175)	32% (140)*
Total(s)	160	556	434

Proportional assignment of 24% (no shape reported)

The above statistics dramatically illustrate that an astonishing similarity exists between the percentage of UFO configurations reported both locally and on a global scale. Again, we see that the elliptical or oval configuration was reported more than any other shape. In striking contrast, the cylindrical shape was *least* reported. This is significant, for if UFO reports were largely misidentifications of man-made aircraft, one would think that the opposite would be true! The reason for this is that other than a few short-range oval experimental hovercraft, all conventional aircraft have *cylindrical* fuselages. Yet, only 12 of the 160 local UFOs were cylindrical in shape, and their reported flight characteristics were for the most part highly unconventional. On the other hand, the elliptical or oval configuration is purely unconventional in terms of man-made aircraft. A total of 95 of the 160 local "unknowns" dealt with oval or elliptical objects. In 27 of these 95 cases (28 percent), a *central dome* was noted on the top of the object by the observer.

The remaining reports fall into the "balls of light" or "other" category. They involved, for the most part, *night-flying* objects carrying lights that did not correspond with the standard identification lights of conventional aircraft. In a number of these cases, the lights were so arranged that the witness received the impression they were attached to an elliptical or oval object. The few remaining reports in this category were strangely behaving singular light sources and a few very odd ones—like the box-shaped *UFO in the woods* discussed in chapter nine!

Figures 4A through 4D record the witnesses' *impressions* relating to the configuration of the 160 locally reported objects evaluated in the "unknown" category. I say they are impressions because it is important to realize at the outset that these crude sketches are not exact drawings of the observed UFOs. In all cases, the witnesses did not draw them until hours, sometimes days after their experience. Considered separately, without the benefit of an investigated sighting account, these sketches are of little apparent value. Some of them could just as well be drawings of the moon, balloons, or conventional aircraft obscured by running lights. However, if one examines these sketches as a whole, in parallel with a carefully recorded sighting account, the similarities between the reported objects—in both the local and global sense—is amazing, to say the least!

SKETCHES BY WITNESSES

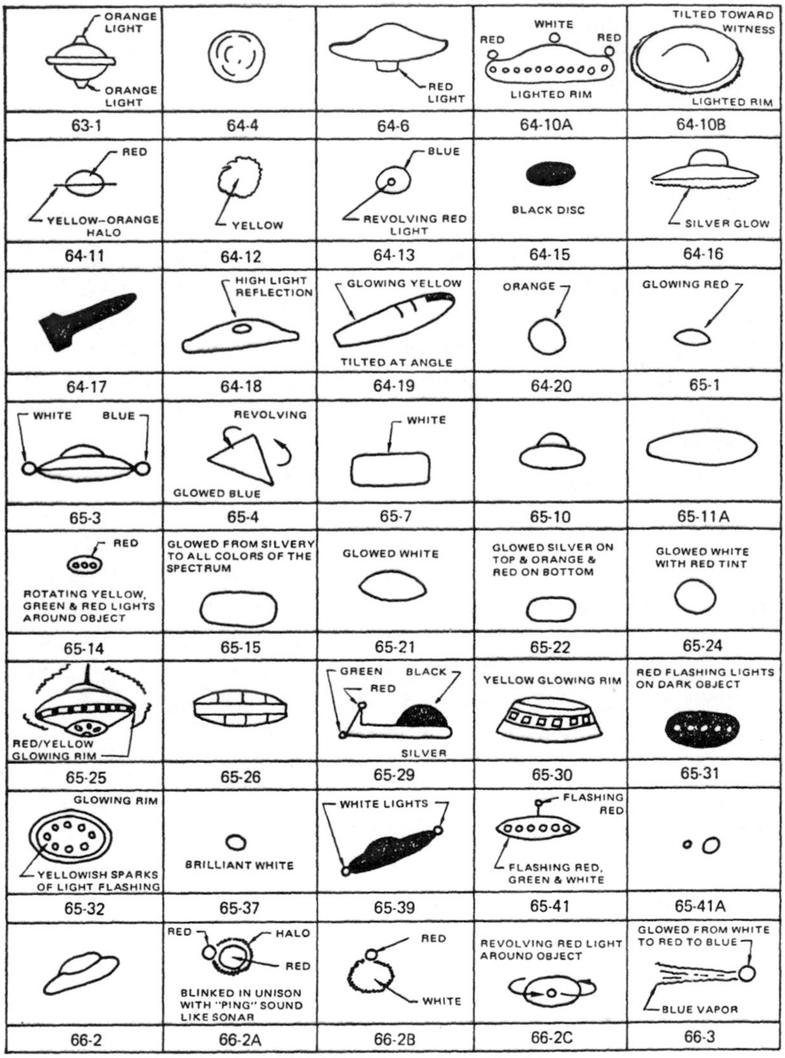

FIGURE 4A

SKETCHES BY WITNESSES

			BRIGHT WHITE PORTS	COLORED LIGHTS ON BOTTOM
	2 RED LIGHTS	GLOWED WHITE "RAYS"	SILVER	
66-3A	66-4	66-9	66-10 A	66-11
RED ORANGE LIGHTS	BLUE LIGHTS RED RED		ROTATING WHITE LIGHTS AROUND OBJECT	BRIGHT RED GLOWING OBJECT
66-12	66-13	66-14	66-16A	66-16B
RED GREEN WHITE BLUE	BLUE RED WHITE CHANGING COLORS	GREEN RED RED	BLUE GLOW ON SIDE RED/GREEN RED/GREEN	RED FLASHING LIGHTS AROUND OBJECT WHITE
66-16C	66-16D	66-16E	66-17	66-18
PURPLE	GREEN RED	RED	RED GREEN RED WHITE	3 DISCS FLASHED RED & WHITE LIGHTS
66-19	66-20	66-21	66-22	66-23
WHITE "WINDOWS" RED RED	BLUE GREEN RED WHITE	GLOWED YELLOW	WHITE LIGHTS AROUND OBJECT MULTI-COLORED LIGHTS ON BOTTOM	RED LIGHTS ON SPOKES
66-24	66-26A	66-26B	66-28	66-29
FLASHING RED, GREEN & WHITE	FLASHED WHITE TO YELLOW TO BLUE	LIGHTS VARIED FROM WHITE RED ORANGE-YELLOW GREEN	RED ORANGE WITH BLACK MARK	YELLOW OBJECTS GLOWED GOLDEN WHITE
66-30	66-33	66-36	66-38	66-49A
ROTATING WHITE LIGHTS & DARK GAPS	BLUE RED RED	WHITE FLICKERING LIGHTS ALONG SIDE	GRAY BRIGHT & SHIMMERED	FLASHING RED WHITE FIRE
66-45	66-45A	66-46	66-48	66-49A
RED RED	ORANGE-RED WITH HALO	GLOWED FROSTY WHITE WITH CENTRAL BRIGHT SPOT	GLOWED RED WITH WHITE RIM	WHITE RED RED GLOWED RED ORANGE
66-51	66-52	66-53	67-2	67-4

FIGURE 4B

SKETCHES BY WITNESSES

WHITE — WHITE BLINKING RED DARK TOP SECTION	WHITE — WHITE WHITE	WHITE RED RED	EJECTED RED OBJECT WHITE	RED REST ARE WHITE
67-5	67-7	67-8	67-9	67-11
REDDISH PURPLE LIGHTS ON RIM	RED — RED GLOWED WHITE	GLOWED WHITE WITH FUZZY TRAIL	GLOWED WHITE, THEN ORANGE WHEN MOVED AWAY	GLOWED WHITE WITH BRIGHT RIM
67-12	67-13	67-15	67-17	67-18
WHITE RED RED	GLOWED ORANGE RED	GLOWED FROM VIOLET TO ORANGE	GLOWED RED ON TOP BOTTOM GLOWED WHITE	MASS OF VERY BRIGHT WHITE LIGHTS
67-19	67-20	67-24	67-25	67-28
GLOWED WHITE REVOLVING RED LIGHT ON BOTTOM	RED WHITE WHITE	WHITE FLASHING RED	WHITE RED RED	YELLOW "PORTS" AQUA RED AQUA
67-29	67-30	67-31	67-32	67-33
WHITE LIGHT THROUGH "WINDOWS"	BRIGHT RED LIGHTS	2 FIGURES IN TRANSPARENT DOME ORANGE FLAMES IN RIM	OUTER – WHITE INNER – RED	HAD LEGS & RED LIGHTS AROUND IT
67-34	67-35	67-35B	67-36	67-37
GLOWING RED & WHITE RIM DARK	WHITE LIGHTS	GRAY VAPOROUS OUTLINE	ORANGE	RED — WHITE WHITE FLASHING WHITE
67-40	67-41	67-42	67-44B	67-44A
RED WHITE FLASHING LIGHTS ON RIM	BOTH SILVER	GREEN — WHITE RED	GLOWED AMBER WHITE LIGHTS ON RIM	REST ALL RED GREEN — WHITE
67-48	67-54	67-55	67-57	67-61
YELLOW	DARK 2 ROWS WHITE LIGHTS	STEADY WHITE ON TOP FLASHING RED & GREEN	BRIGHT WHITE LIGHTS	RED & WHITE FLASHING LIGHTS ON RIM
67-66B	67-66C	68-2	68-3	68-8

FIGURE 4C

SKETCHES BY WITNESSES

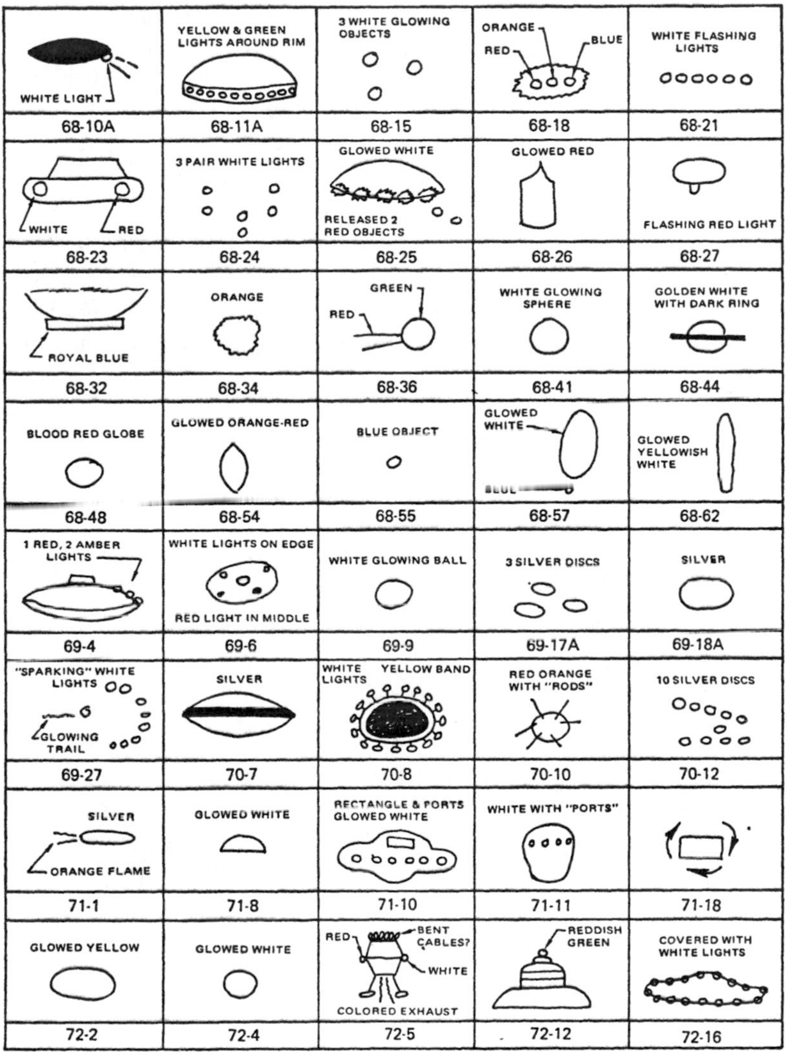

FIGURE 4D

UFO *configuration*, however, constitutes only a segment of the overall quality of *strangeness* that motivates a rational person to file a UFO report. Other such aspects relate to the strange *behavior* attributed to UFOs on a global scale. Chapter three, if you remember, contains a typical list of these characteristics that was extracted from Air Force statistics. These same characteristics are also inherent in thousands of UFO reports now on file at NICAP. If the UFOs are real physical phenomena, these same *strange* characteristics should also have manifested themselves within the *local* sample as well. Let us see if this is the case by employing the Vallée method of classifying UFO *behavior* as outlined in chapter three.

TYPES

A Type I UFO report involves the observation of an unusual object on the ground or at close range to a person, construction, or vehicle. A total of 57 reports, or 36 percent of the total 160 local incidents, fall into the Type I category! They break down into the following subdivisions.

Type	Definition	Number Reports	Percent
IA	Near the ground	32	20%
IB	Near the water	13	8%
IC	Intelligent signals	0	0%
ID	Scouts a vehicle	12	8%
	Total(s)	57	36%

Type II reports deal with the observation of a cylindrical object, often in a vertical position and associated with a surrounding diffuse cloud or vapor. A total of 5, or 3 percent of the total local sample, fall into this category and are broken down as follows:

Type	Definition	Number Reports	Percent
IIA	Erratic flight	2	1%
IIB	Assumes vertical position; sometimes ejects or absorbs smaller objects	3	2%
IIC	Flight with other smaller objects	0	0%
	Total(s)	5	3%

One of the local Type IIB reports took place at Ipswich, Massachusetts, on September 17, 1966.[4] Perhaps significantly, this particular sighting was one of the first that visiting scientists from the Air Force-sponsored University of Colorado UFO project enquired about shortly after their arrival at my home. Names have been changed in order to protect the witnesses' right to privacy.

The first inkling that something strange might be occurring in the area of eastern Massachusetts came from Brookline. Shortly after midnight, local police received two separate calls within just a few minutes of each other reporting a bluish green, egg-shaped object hovering over Anderson Park. It was estimated to be about fifteen feet in diameter and twenty five feet high. By the time the police responded, the reported object had left the area. Since the witnesses refused to identify themselves, no investigation was possible.

Several hours later, twenty-five miles north of Brookline, Mrs. David Rogers of Ipswich woke up at 4:45 A.M. with a coughing spell. On the way to get a drink of water, she noticed a light shining through a window that overlooked a lonely shoreline known as Crane's beach. The Ipswich River and the sea meet in this narrow bay bordered by the Plum Island reservation on one side and the huge, forested, vacated Castle Hill estate on the other. On a typical summer's day, this area swarms with boats, bathers and fishermen, but soon after Labor Day, the miles of sand dunes play host only to sea gulls, sandpipers and nature lovers. Mrs. Rogers glanced at the lighted window. "Hum-m-m, nothing should be out on the beach now," she thought. Curious, she walked over to the window to see where the light was coming from. She took one startled look and ran to wake up her husband to come and see. There, hovering at the water's edge over the beach, a bare half mile away, was a huge, elongated, cigar-shaped object standing on end! It glowed with a dim, golden, pulsating white light, which at times brightened enough so that the beach sand could be seen around its base. At times it would tilt slowly to about sixty degrees from the vertical and then move back to the upright position. Finding it hard to believe his eyes, David quickly stepped out onto an open-window porch to get a better look, with his wife trailing nervously behind him. It was no optical illusion. It was really there! The night was clear with no noticeable wind. A sound similar to *breaking surf* came from the object's direction. Suddenly, two small bright lights appeared moving just above the beach toward the glowing upright cylinder. Astonished, the couple watched them move "with a *skipping motion,* sometimes fast, sometimes slowly," and merge with the top of the cylinder! Almost instantly, three similar lights emerged from the top of the cylinder and sped off low over the ocean. One object appeared to be elliptical in shape and ringed with a yellowish glow as it momentarily approached within a quarter of a mile of them. Fascinated, they watched the smaller objects enter and leave the larger cigar-shaped object several times. Then, the larger object dimmed and just disappeared from sight.

Unfortunately, the witnesses did not report the incident to Coast Guard authorities until later on that morning. The Coast Guard told them that they were unaware of any operations going on in that area at that early hour of the morning! I checked out a number of remote possibilities but could find no satisfactory answer for the reported phenomena. My first thought was that perhaps someone had a searchlight directed skyward on the beach and that the smaller lights were from boats coming to and leaving the beach. However, the description given by the witnesses would conflict with such a theory. In fact, the tide was high at 1:24 A.M. EDT on that morning. The water was too low for any sizable boat to have been involved. It is improbable that the lights of fishermen or campers could have caused such a sight either, as this land area is closed to camping and fishing.

Another suspect was Venus, a typical stimulus for a UFO report. However, Venus did not rise until 5:14 A.M. EDT, well after the strange episode had terminated. A spot check of the witnesses' character indicated that they both were reliable and sensible citizens. No probable man-made or natural phenomena seemed to fill all the aspects of this sighting. On the other hand, *all* of the aspects of this sighting did fit similar descriptions given by people from all over the world. For example, let us compare this sighting with one that took place in the early morning hours of August 23, 1954, in the little town of Vernon, France.

Just before 1 A.M., M. Bernard Miserey, a businessman of Vernon, arrived home and put his car away. As he came out of the garage, on the south bank of the Seine [River], he was surprised to see a pale light illuminating the town, which had been in complete darkness a little while before. Looking at the sky, he saw a huge, silent, motionless, luminous mass, apparently suspended above the north bank of the river some three hundred yards away. It could have been compared to a gigantic cigar standing on end.

"I had been watching this amazing spectacle for a couple of minutes," M. Miserey later reported, "when suddenly from the bottom of the cigar came an object like a horizontal disk, which dropped at first in free fall, then slowed, and suddenly swayed and dived horizontally across the river toward me, becoming very luminous. For a very short time I could see the disk full-face; it was surrounded by a halo of brilliant light. A few minutes after it had disappeared behind me, going southwest at prodigious speed, a similar object came from the cigar and went through the same maneuvers. A third object came, then a fourth. There was then a longer interval, and finally a fifth disk detached itself from the cigar, which was still motionless. This last disk dropped much lower than the earlier ones, to the level of the new bridge, where it remained still for an instant, swaying slightly. At that time I could see very clearly its circular form . . . and the glowing halo surrounding it. After a few seconds' pause, it wobbled like the last four, and took off like a flash toward the north. . . . During this time the luminosity of the cigar had faded, and . . . had sunk into the darkness.

When M. Miserey described his nocturnal vision the next day, the police informed him that two policemen making their rounds at about 1:00 A.M. had also observed the phenomena, as had an army engineer who had been driving along Route N-181 southwest of Vernon.[5]

You will have noted the striking similarity that exists between these two reports. It is the overall consistency inherent in such reports that allows them to be categorized as specific *types* of UFO sightings. To the best of my knowledge, Mr. and Mrs. Rogers were totally unaware that they had unwittingly described a *Type IIB* sighting.

Type II sightings are not likely to be cases of mistaken aircraft. The lack of wings, vertical position, long hovering period, erratic maneuvers, and generation of smaller objects are utterly foreign to all known conventional aircraft.

Type III events concern the observation of a flying object that stops and hovers and exhibits peculiar flight characteristics. Analysis of our 160 local reports indicates that a total of 65, or 41 percent of the total, readily fall into one of the subdivisions of the Type III category.

Type	Definition	Number/Reports	Percent
IIIA	Flight discontinuity	18	11%
IIIB	Halts in flight	29	18%
IIIC	Absorbs/ejects objects	4	3%
IIID	Begins "dogfight" motion	0	0%
IIIE	Circles/changes course	14	9%
	Total(s)	65	41%

It is important to note that no common conventional aircraft, other than the noisy, easily recognizable, helicopter, is capable of abruptly halting in midair. Vertical takeoff aircraft and hovercraft are still largely in the experimental stages of development. None were operational in this country during the time span in which our local sample was taken. There are no experimental aircraft test ranges in the reporting area of the local sample. What is oval in shape, able to streak off at blurring speed from a standstill without a sonic boom, and capable of abruptly halting in mid-flight? What oval object bobs like a floating cork, swings back and forth like a pendulum, performs right-angle turns, or descends with a falling-leaf motion? The answer is simply that there is no man-made machine capable of executing these reported maneuvers! Balloons observed by a stationary observer rarely are described in this manner. In those few instances where erratic balloon flight is observed, it is always *with* the wind.

Again, so many observations have been made of machine-like objects consistently exhibiting these erratic maneuvers that reports of this nature have also become typified. The Type III object appears to be an oval-structured, metallic-appearing craft with a central dome or superstructure, which moves independently of not only the wind but also of the laws of physics as we presently understand them. What appears to have mass but no weight? A Type III UFO!

Type IV relates to reports of an unconventional appearing object in *continuous* flight which does not stop and hover. The local sample yielded 31 reports, or 19 percent of the total in this particular category.

Type	Definition	Number/Reports	Percent
IVA	Single object	25	16%
IVB	Affected by aircraft	4	2%
IVC	Formation of objects	2	1%
IVD	Zigzag motion	0	0%
	Total(s)	31	19%

Obviously, strange characteristics other than flight behavior usually trigger this type of UFO report because most aircraft travel in continuous flight. The exception, of course, is Type IVD. Some birds may fly with an up-and-down motion like a sine wave but no known aircraft does! Thus, in most cases, an *unusual configuration* provides the stimulus for a Type IV UFO report.

The Type V classification is perhaps the least interesting category. It involves the night observation of peculiar light sources in the sky. Most reports of this type can be explained as planets, stars, aircraft identification lights, landing lights, lighted balloons, searchlights and man-made satellites. A few, however, remain a puzzle to the investigator, such as the two cases shown in the following table, which comprise one percent of the total local sample.

Type	Definition	Number/Reports	Percent
VA	A moving light source	2	1%
VB	Starlike long hover	0	0%
VC	Erratic/fast flight	0	0%

Flying objects usually are evaluated as "unknowns" for additional qualities of strangeness other than those just outlined. For, in addition to the aspects of unconventional configuration and extraordinary flight characteristics, many UFO reports also exhibit some very unusual *effects.*

EFFECTS

People not only report *seeing* UFOs; in some instances they *hear, smell* and even *feel UFOs!* These and other *passive* effects usually seem just as foreign to the observer as the unusual configuration and flight of the object. They provide the witness with additional sensory reference points that further attest to the physical presence of the observed object. In chapter three, I listed a total of eleven often-reported effects reportedly associated with UFO sightings. Although they were extracted from an Air Force space science textbook, UFO reports on file at NICAP and other civilian organizations contain data that essentially agree with this list. In considering this attribute of the UFO phenomena, we shall make a differentiation between those effects that are *passive* and those that are *active* in nature. Out of the 160 local unknown category reports I have on file, the following *passive* effects were reported by the witnesses:

Light	Signal	Smell	Sound	Vapor
90%	1%	1%	23%	6%
(144)	(2)	(1)	(37)	(9)

A brief description for each of these effects follows.

1. *Light:* The objects displayed unconventional lights and/or glowed all over.
2. *Signal:* The objects flashed lights in exact response to varied sequenced flashlight signals from the observers.
3. *Vapor:* The objects issued a short vapor trail when accelerating away at great speed.
4. *Sound:* The object(s) hummed, buzzed, roared, whined, pinged, whirred, hissed or beeped.
5. *Smell:* The object left a smell like "burnt matches" behind in the air.

6. *Creatures:* The witness observed two humanoid figures in a transparent dome mounted on top of an oval object.

The first four of these passive effects have been adequately described in connection with a number of UFO sightings already recorded in this book. Items 5 and 6, however, have not yet been mentioned. Since only one local report involves *both* the sighting of *creatures* and the element of *smell,* we will briefly cover this case right now.[6] Because of the bizarre nature of the episode, the witness, a reputable businessman, did not want his real name associated with the event. I have complied with his wish to remain unknown by not using his real name in the following account.

Mr. Seaman owns a small airport alongside a major river in New England. It consists of one paved runway, some hangars and a dock to service pontooned planes using the river. He has flown since 1939 and spent four years flying for the United States Coast Guard. During the spring of 1967, he had a very unsettling experience that has been on his mind ever since.

"TWO HEADLIKE SILHOUETTES WATCHING ME!"

Shortly after two o'clock in the morning, Mrs. Seaman woke up with a start. A loud whirring sound permeated the house momentarily and stopped. Thinking that an aircraft might have made an emergency landing, she awoke her husband. Mr. Seaman reluctantly got up and turned on the yard lights. Sleepily, he put on his slippers and a jacket and stepped outside into the cool morning air. When he opened the back door, he stood transfixed with wonder at what he saw. Hovering just twenty-five feet over a small pond between the house and the airport was a strange, silent aircraft! It was not a helicopter. It looked like "two shallow metallic saucers, one inverted upon the other, with a transparent canopy situated on its topside." Elongated ventlike holes spaced evenly around the object's rim emitted soft orange flames. A softer, greener light illuminated the interior of the canopy, which revealed two headlike silhouettes that appeared to move and look at him!

Thinking that it was an experimental aircraft in trouble, he cautiously walked toward it yelling and waving his arms. Instantaneously, it moved smoothly and silently away from him and stopped over some gasoline pumps and aircraft at the edge of the runway. Mr. Seaman trotted around the pond and again headed toward the object, waving his hands at it as he went. Abruptly, a swishing and loud whirring sound came from the object and its orange lights began to spin faster and faster. Tilting back at an angle of about thirty degrees, it shot away into the dark morning sky at a fantastic rate of speed! Simultaneously, the yard light dimmed to practically nothing and then came back on as the object moved off into the distance. Mr. Seaman just stood and stared in disbelief. It was gone. All that was left behind was a smell like "burnt matches" lingering in the air.

The witness told me that he got a good look at the object, which reflected its own lights and the yard light. During his initial encounter with it, it was only one hundred feet away from him. It was about fifty feet in diameter and an estimated twenty-five feet thick if one included the upright dome or canopy. Its surface was smooth and metallic looking, "like dull brushed aluminum," with no signs of seams or rivets. The dome was constructed out of the clearest material he had ever seen.

In addition to the *passive* effects of *sight, smell* and *sound,* you will have also noticed an *active* effect. Concurrent with the object's noisy departure, the yard lights inexplicably dimmed to near nothingness. Electrical interference is one of several *active* effects often associated with UFO sightings. Temporary paralysis is another such effect, which we have already come across during the discussion of cases such as the Lynn[7] and Leominster[8] UFO reports. Analysis of the 160 local "unknowns" reveals that witnesses reported the same types of active effects associated with UFOs as those contained within the *global* sample.

Animal	Ground	Water	Power	Human
5%	1%	1%	6%	3%
(8)	(2)	(2)	(10)	(5)

A summary description of these effects is as follows:

1. *Animal:* Dogs howled, cat ran.
2. *Ground:* Smooth, blown-out oval depression.
3. *Water:* Splashed; steamed; made hole in ice.
4. *Power:* Car engine, lights, radio; area blackout; yard light dimmed.
5. *Human:* Temporary paralysis; hair stood up on end; internal organs vibrated; felt blast of moving air.

All of these aspects, except the active effects on water, have been noted within some of the UFO reports already covered in this book. Let us briefly examine the two *local* sightings that manifested an effect on water.

"LIKE A HORSE LANDING IN THE WATER!"

It was 7:30 A.M. on July 4, 1969. Ed Moore was in his element as he sat fishing from his boat. He was all alone and drinking in the solitude encompassing the quiet New Hampshire pond. The sun had just risen. The sky was clear with only a slight breeze blowing. Suddenly, there was a loud splash in the water behind him "like a horse landing in the water!" Swinging around, he saw an area of disturbed water about fifty-five feet away. Concurrently, something caused him to glance overhead. Startled, he saw a silver, oval-shaped object just several hundred feet above his head and rising vertically. At this point, he noticed a soft humming sound "like a motor shorting out." Amazed, he craned back his head and watched the object rise in a perfectly straight unwavering path and stop at several thousand feet. It just stayed there. Ed left the pond and returned by car to his cabin at nearby Ossipee Lake, where he awoke his wife. They both went outside and watched it hovering perfectly motionless. They went indoors and came out several times to check on the UFO. It remained there until they came out around 8:30 A.M. and it was nowhere to be seen.[9]

Mr. Moore told investigator David Webb (Walter's brother, a physicist) that his brother and family were staying in a nearby cabin but that they were reluctant to wake them about the object. Later, Mrs. Moore went over to tell them about it. The brother's wife said that she had just heard reports on the radio of a UFO hovering over North Moat Mountain, about twelve miles north of the sighting area. A question remains as to whether or not the UFO caused the splash. Nothing else was seen to account for it. The large size of the UFO itself negated it from either entering or leaving the water, which was only 12 feet deep. It is possible that a beaver or a muskrat startled by the UFO could have caused a splash, but not like a "horse falling in the water!" It is also conceivable that the UFO dropped something into the water. Due to the lack of skin-diver talent and a very muddy pond bottom, this aspect, unfortunately, was never checked out. Only two facts remain. First, that a UFO was reportedly observed at low level over Duck Pond, Ossipee, New Hampshire, within a few seconds of a loud splash. Secondly, the witnesses appeared to be above reproach.

The other local sighting in this category took place on Cape Cod two years later during the morning of January 7, 1971. It was investigated by the other Webb brother, Walter, who currently is assistant director of Hayden Planetarium in Boston.

"I SAW A HOLE IN THE ICE WITH STEAM!"

It was 7:10 A.M. John Brogan had just left his house to catch the school bus when his eyes caught sight of a strange object slowly descending in the southeastern sky. It was silvery, cigar-shaped, and a short orange flame issued from its rear. It seemed larger than an aircraft and disappeared behind the tree-lined ridge that bordered Scargo Lake. Thinking that the object would fall into the lake, John ran through the yard of Martha Koempel toward the ice-covered lake. At that moment, Martha came out of the house. Seeing her, John shouted "flying saucer!" Martha followed John to the Koempel's dock, about five hundred feet from her house. Martha's mother looked out the window just in time to see the two running toward the lake. Reaching the lake, they saw a large oblong hole in the ice. Steam could be seen rising from the water, which was in a state of agitation, as if something large had just fallen in.[10]

After about a minute's observation, they returned to Martha's house and met Robert Bottcher. He had seen John running and wondered what all the excitement was about. After a hasty explanation, both boys returned to the dock. Steam was still rising from the hole in the ice. They then ran to tell Robert's parents. Mr. Bottcher told Walter Webb that though the boys seemed genuinely excited, he had remained skeptical and insisted they go directly to the bus stop before they missed their ride to school. Mrs. Bottcher said that she was more receptive to the story. After the boys had left, she went down to the lake and saw the hole.

Another witness, Paul McCarthy, also saw the object as he left to catch the school bus that same morning. He first noticed it for about three minutes as it moved slowly in *horizontal* flight toward Scargo Lake.

"IT NOSED DOWN AND DROPPED"

Paul said that the object was elongated, solid-appearing, without wings or fins. He did not notice any flame coming from it. When it reached Scargo Lake, it nosed down and dropped out of sight behind the trees.[11]

When the witnesses reached school, neither the teachers nor the principal would believe their story. Finally, that afternoon, Mrs. Bottcher told Walter Webb that a neighbor had convinced her to report the incident to the newspaper. The newspaper, in turn, informed the police, who, after investigating and finding the hole, called the Air Force. I phoned Otis Air Force Base myself to enquire further into the incident on January 11. They denied any knowledge of the case, even though the local newspaper carried the story and the police insisted that they had indeed informed Otis Air Force Base. When I again phoned the police to tell them about the Air Force denial, they gave me a blow-by-blow account from a cruiser parked at the lake monitoring the efforts of a skin diver looking for a trace of the object. Due to the late hour, he had only spent fifteen minutes at the west end of the hole where the water had not completely frozen. *(See picture section.)*

Walter, arriving on the scene three days after the sighting, found the hole about one hundred feet from the southern shore of the lake. It measured approximately one hundred feet long by twenty-five feet wide. His immediate impression was that the hole had been formed abruptly by *melting* through three inches of ice! He found that the hole had not been there on the day prior to the sighting. Somehow, it had suddenly appeared overnight, according to people who lived around and skated on the lake. Walter's investigation negated underwater springs, a daytime fireball, or a jettisoned aircraft wing tank as having been the cause of the oblong hole. Using a topographical map of the area, he plotted the compass bearings taken from the vantage points of both sets of witnesses. Significantly, the lines of direction to the UFO from the viewing locations converged exactly over the hole in the lake!

Soon after, a cold spell set in and it wasn't until spring that a team of six divers searched the area where the hole had been. Almost twenty man-hours were expended but nothing of significance was found. The water was forty feet deep at this location and so murky that the steeply sloping bottom was visible only from a few feet away.

Again, we have a well-reported and investigated account of a UFO concurrent with an unexplained effect upon water. In this case, the water was frozen! As in the Duck Pond incident at Ossipee, New Hampshire, no one *saw* the UFO hit the water; but if the descending UFO didn't cause the hole, what did? The lake was completely frozen over with a three-inch crust of ice. The temperature at the time of the sighting was twenty-two degrees Fahrenheit, or ten degrees below freezing!

Up until this point we have discussed the *configuration, types,* and *effects* of reported unidentified flying objects. Another question we might ask is *where* the UFOs were seen? Is the *locale* of UFO sightings random, or do we find a pattern that indicates possible selectivity? Let us see.

LOCALE

An analysis of the 160 locale "unknowns" shows that 110—or 68 percent—of the sightings occurred in the country, whereas only 50—or 32 percent—were reported over a city. Further study of these cases revealed the following statistics with regard to what kind of *locale* the UFO either moved or hovered over.

Building	Field	Power Lines	Fresh Water
19%	21%	10%	14%
(31)	(33)	(17)	(23)

Thus, a total of 108—or 67 percent—of these cases show definite signs of selectivity. For example, let us see what kinds of buildings were involved:

(5) Power plants	(1) Parsonage
(6) Schools	(1) Oil company
(1) Ammunition depot	(1) Arsenal
(2) Apartment building	(1) Chemical Company
(3) Hospital	(11) Other

The *fields* included cemeteries, golf courses, swamps and airports, but sparsely-populated open-country situations were most prominent. A total of ten percent of the reports involved objects either seen hovering over or following *power lines*. A great number of sightings also were near but not directly over power lines. This is graphically illustrated by Figures 5A and 5B, which highlight those sightings that occurred in Massachusetts on an electrical power map. Again, this local pattern regarding UFOs and power lines is representative of a global pattern.

The same can be said of the large percentage of UFOs sighted over bodies of *fresh water*. What do these patterns mean? Does such selectivity indicate intelligent action or a remarkable coincidence? Power and water sources are the most essential commodities of our industrialized society. Without them, our highly mechanized social structure would grind to a halt. Chaos would result. If UFOs are extraterrestrial craft performing a surveillance of our planet, it is quite apparent that our power and water resources would be of great interest to their operators. The question is why? One would think that such a survey would be complete by now, and yet this pattern continues. Therefore, it is highly conceivable that this reported pattern reflects some type of practical *usage* of these sources by UFOs rather than just pure surveillance.

● - Local Unknowns (1963-72)

FIGURE 5A

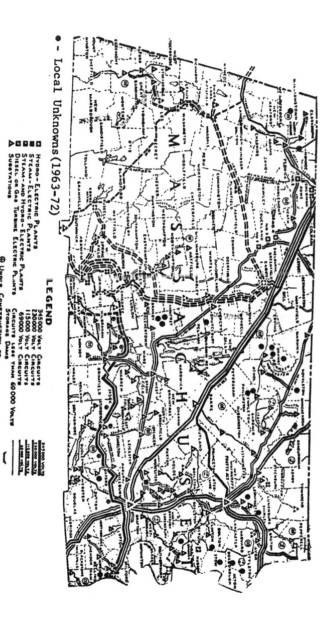

● – Local Unknowns (1963-72)

LEGEND

345000 Volt Circuits
230000 Volt Circuits
115000 Volt Circuits
69000 Volt Circuits
Circuits Less Than 69,000 Volts
Storage Dams

□ Hydro–Electric Plants
▣ Steam–Electric Plants
▨ Steam– and Hydro–Electric Plants
△ Diesel or Gas Turbine Electric Plants
▲ Substations

⊕ Under Construction or Scheduled For Construction

345,000 Volt
230,000 Volt
115,000 Volt
69,000 Volt

Principal Lines, Plants and Stations of New England Electric System Companies Shown by Solid Symbols
Lines, Plants and Stations not a part of New England Electric System Companies Shown by Broken Symbols

Scale of Miles

FIGURE 5B

Some people have the notion that many UFOs are seen under poor weather conditions, which in turn lead to misinterpretations of common phenomena by the observer. Nothing could be farther from the truth! Only a sparse handful of the 160 local sightings were made during poor weather conditions. For example, only four or three percent of the total reports evaluated as "unknowns" were seen during a rainstorm. One of these cases involved a UFO at treetop level hovering directly over the witness![12] Weather conditions pertaining to the 160 local UFO reports under consideration are outlined as follows:

WEATHER

Clear	Few Clouds	Overcast	Rain/Snow	Not Recorded
53%	24%	12%	3%	8%
(85)	(39)	(19)	(4)	(13)

Thus, the fact of the matter is that most of these sightings were made under excellent seeing conditions!

TIME

The Air Force Project Grudge Report of December 1949 concluded, on the basis of intelligence reports of UFOs: "The most numerous reports indicate *daytime* observation of metallic disc-like objects."[13] Since those early days, the situation has reversed. Most UFOs are now reported during the hours of darkness. Within our local sample, only twenty-four—or fifteen percent —of the UFOs reported were observed in broad daylight. It should be pointed out, however, that a good percentage of those UFOs reported at night were Type I close encounters. Some of these were reported at dusk or dawn, and the UFO configuration was clearly visible at close range. I mention this fact lest one get the impression that most UFOs observed at night are merely vague lights seen in the sky. A breakdown of the 160 local sightings in the unknown category by *local time* is as follows:

DAY		NIGHT	
AM	*PM*	*PM*	*AM*
(0600-1200)	(1200-1800)	(1800-2400)	(0000-0600)
6%	9%	66%	19%
(10)	(14)	(105)	(31)

Thus, most UFOs within our local sample were seen between six o'clock in the evening and midnight. This compares remarkably well with Air Force Project Bluebook Report No. 14 statistics (see fig. 6). For day of the week statistics, see figure 7.

The State Rests

Well, our inventory has been taken. What have we found? A total of 461 people representing a broad cross-section of society claim to have observed objects so strange that they were instigated to report them. The most commonly reported object was oval with a lighted rim. A central dome on top was noticed in many instances. In some cases, these objects were not only seen but also heard. In a few cases they were *felt*.[14] One close-encounter incident involved the witness's sight, smell and hearing. Significantly, this same report exhibited electrical interference and is the only reliable *occupant* report contained within the local sample. A comparative analysis of these 160 local "unknown" reports investigated over the last decade reveals the exact same characteristics being reported elsewhere throughout the world. The reported objects appeared to have been metallic and machine-like in appearance. They abruptly flew off when discovered or approached by a person. They flew in formation, chased automobiles and aircraft. The sighting locale in many cases seemed to have been very selective. In short, the mysterious unconventional appearing and behaving objects seemed in many instances to be under intelligent control. When faced with such overwhelming data, sometimes supported by photographs, radar, unexplainable physical traces and effects, most people would agree wholeheartedly with the following statement made by Dr. J. Allen Hynek:

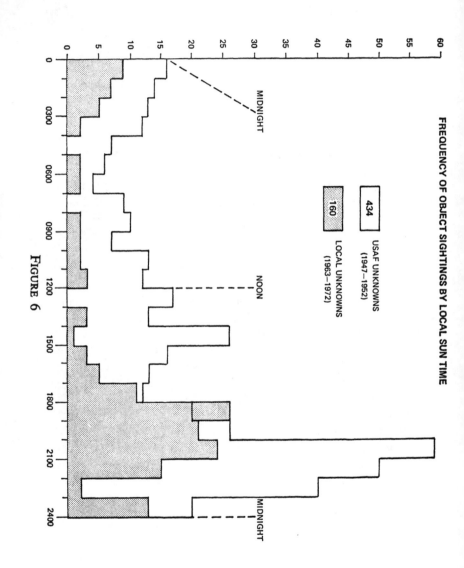

FIGURE 6

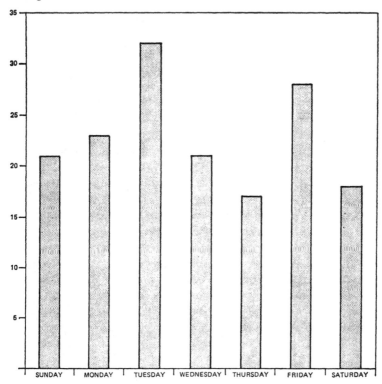

FIGURE 7

It would seem incredible that so many people would or could be fabricating the whole series of reported incidents. I have often said that it is paradoxical that the testimony of policemen, which in some cases might be sufficient to send a man to the chair, is in instances like this often totally disregarded.[15]

The sixty-four dollar question is, are they really being totally disregarded? I personally think not. It is my opinion that our government and other governments are seriously considering UFOs both scientifically and militarily as an unknown threat to international security. In a real sense, if UFOs are real, they have no choice but to do so. The remainder of this book is devoted to documenting this assertion as well as other important facets of the overall UFO problem. Suffice it to say at this point that the United States Air Force discovered that UFOs are *real* very early in UFO history. The following excerpts taken directly from a now declassified document make this quite clear. The subject of the memorandum is the Air Materiel Command's opinion concerning "Flying Discs." It is dated 23 September 1947 and is written to the Commanding General, Army Air Forces, Washington, 25, D.C., Attention: Brig. General George Schulgen.

As requested by AC/AS-2 there is presented below the considered opinion of this Command concerning the so-called "Flying Discs." This opinion is based on interrogation report data furnished by AC/AS-2 and preliminary studies by personnel of T-2 and Aircraft Laboratory, Engineering Division T-3. This opinion was arrived at in a conference between personnel from the Air Institute of Technology, Intelligence T-2, Office Chief of Engineering Division, and the Aircraft, Power Plant and Propeller Laboratories of Engineering Division T-3.

It is the opinion that the phenomenon is something real and not visionary or fictitious. There are objects probably approximating the shape of a disc, of such appreciable size as to appear to be as large as man-made aircraft. . . . The reported operating characteristics such as extreme rates of climb, maneuverability . . . and action which must be considered evasive when sighted or contacted by friendly aircraft and radar, lend belief to the possibility that some of the objects are controlled either manually, automatically or remotely. The apparent common description of the objects is as follows:

(1) Metallic or light reflecting surface.

(2) Absence of trail except in a few instances when the object apparently was operating under high performance conditions.

(3) Circular or elliptical in shape, flat on bottom and domed on top.

(4) Several reports of well kept formation flights varying from three to nine objects.

(5) Normally no associated sound, except in three instances a substantial rumbling roar was noted.

(6) Level flight speeds normally above 300 knots are estimated.

The above letter is signed by N. F. Twining, Lt. General, U.S.A., Commanding.[16]
Read this memorandum over again and think back over the local and global reports discussed thus far in this book. This memo could very well have been written to sumarize our local sample! Has our government changed its mind about the reality of UFOs since this significant memo from 1947? I think not. Ladies and gentlemen of the jury—*The State rests!*

NOTES

1. Personal Files.
2. NICAP, *The UFO Evidence,* Section XII (Patterns) p. 143.
3. Air Technical Intelligence Center, *Project Bluebook Special Report No. 14: Analysis of Reports of Unidentified Aerial Objects,* p. 28 (release date: 5 May 1955).
4. Personal Files, UFO Report No. 66-42.
5. Michel, Aime, *Flying Saucers and the Straight-Line Mystery,* pp. 19-21.
6. Personal Files, UFO Report No. 67-35B.
7. Personal Files, UFO Report No. 64-6.
8. Personal Files, UFO Report No. 67-18.
9. Personal Files, UFO Report No. 69-18A.
10. Personal Files, UFO Report No. 71-1.
11. *Ibid.*
12. Personal Files, UFO Report No. 65-32.
13. Project Sign, *AMC Technical Report No. F-TR-2274-IA: Unidentified Aerial Objects,* Appendix C, p. 19.
14. Personal Files, UFO Reports 65-30 and 68-32.
15. Personal Files.
16. E. U. Condon, *Scientific Study of UFOs,* pp. 894, 895.

PART III

AN ESTIMATE
OF THE SITUATION

In Intelligence, if you have something to say about some vital problem, you write a report that is known as an Estimate of the Situation. *A few days after the DC-3 was buzzed, the people at Air Technical Intelligence Center decided that the time had arrived to make an Estimate of the Situation. The situation was the UFOs; the estimate was that they were* interplanetary.

EDWARD J. RUPPELT, Chief
USAF Project Bluebook (1953)

13

THE SITUATION—UFOs

I know that neither Russia nor this country has anything even approaching such high speeds and maneuvers. Behind the scenes, high-ranking officers are soberly concerned about the UFOs, but through official secrecy and ridicule, many citizens are led to believe that the unknown flying objects are nonsense.[1]

ADMIRAL ROSCOE HILLENKOETTER
Former CIA Director and
NICAP Board Member

Military—Treated as a Threat

In this world of conflicting ideologies, wars and frantic arms races, it was only natural that the military, rather than the scientist, took an active interest in UFOs from the very outset. Although civilians were reporting UFOs in the early days, it was the military war machine that was first consistently confronted at close hand with the strange phenomena during World War II. Reports were prevalent among both Allied and Axis Air Forces of sharply defined luminous globes and silvery balls that paced their aircraft in perfect formations. Most of these early reports have come to NICAP directly from World War II pilots because very little public information was forthcoming during the war years. One exception was the following Associated Press release:

Paris, Dec. 13, 1944—As the Allied armies ground out new gains on the western front today, the Germans were disclosed to have thrown a new *device* into the war—mysterious silvery balls which float in the air. Pilots report seeing these objects both individually and in clusters, during forays. . . . It is possible that they represent a new anti-aircraft defense instrument or weapon. [This dispatch was heavily censored at supreme headquarters][2]

After the war, it was discovered that no such weapon existed in the enemy arsenal. Indeed, paradoxically enough, the German and Japanese command thought that they represented secret Allied weapons! To make matters more puzzling, reports indicated that the objects never showed hostility and were not harmed when fired upon. The *official* explanation for these strange objects and globes of light was that they were electrical phenomena known as *St. Elmo's fire*. Very few combat pilots would buy this explanation, but since authority had spoken little more could be said.

Recently, I talked to an airline pilot who had seen a number of these objects during World War II. He told me that on several occasions, his flight would encounter hovering formations of aluminum-colored balls while on the way to bomb targets within Germany. He said that many pilots were reporting them and assumed that they were some experimental device sent aloft by the Germans to confuse Allied radar.

Floyd Thompson, a personal friend and business associate, is an engineer and former World War II fighter-bomber pilot. He told me that his squadron was trailed by a whitish oval object during a bombing run over Italy. Floyd said that he had seen it following their formation and watched it hover as the squadron circled while waiting for a break in the clouds before making their bombing run. After the mission was completed, the aircraft regrouped and split into separate formations to evade possible interceptors. The object was still maneuvering in plain sight, seemingly observing their every move. No one reported seeing it during radio conversation. However, during the mission's intelligence debriefing, it was discussed. Floyd remarked that at first no one mentioned the object to G-2, but after awhile someone hesitatingly asked if anyone had seen something unusual during the mission. It was only then that quite a few pilots admitted sighting the strange device. No one wanted to be accused of hallucinating! These strange objects were dubbed "foo-fighters" from a maxim in the then well-known "Smokey Stover" comic strip: "Where there's foo, there's fire."

Over two thousand reports of strange, wingless objects originated in Scandinavian countries during 1946. Although foreign
newspapers in the sighting areas were regularly and prominently
reporting the sightings of these foreign objects, the press in the
United States was strangely silent. Typical newspaper accounts
are as follows:

> *Lindkoping, Sweden:* Late in the evening a rocket-like thing
> was observed by numerous people. At the rear one could see a
> line to which a copper-like sphere was fastened.[3]
> *Mjosa Lake, Norway:* . . . . they saw two rocket-like things
> that passed over their heads at such high speed and so low that
> they threw themselves to the ground. They could see the tree-
> tops swaying from the airpressure. . . . They fell simultaneously
> into the lake, throwing water several feet into the air.[4]
> *Norbotten, Sweden:* The Swedish army was searching for an
> object which fell into a lake. The thing had left a large hole in
> the mud at the bottom.[5]

The only indication of our government's interest was a brief statement in the foreign press.

> Other objects have been reported from Switzerland and, a few
> days ago, from Waterford, Ireland. . . . The American General
> James Doolittle has just arrived in Stockholm, officially on a
> business trip for the Shell Company. In reality he is to conduct
> an investigation along with the Swedish authorities.[6]

NICAP research has shown that similar sightings were being
reported in the United States but only by newspapers on the local
level.[7] It wasn't until June 24, 1947, that the well-known sighting
of nine discs by pilot Kenneth Arnold suddenly became the focal
point for national interest. The many sightings that had hitherto
been ignored by the wire services became national news overnight!
Silvery discs were being seen everywhere by people from all walks
of life, including close-up observations by military and civilian
pilots.[8]

"THE PHENOMENON IS REAL"

When the UFO dam burst in 1947, the Army Air Force was
going through the throes of a radical reorganization that would

involve becoming a separate service branch apart from the Army. Formerly classified documents reveal that UFOs caused panic within high military circles. Army Air Force Intelligence teams were dispatched all over the United States to interrogate civilian and military witnesses to UFO sightings. All data was funnelled to the Air Materiel Command (AMC) at Wright-Patterson Air Force Base near Dayton, Ohio. By the fall of 1947, AMC had completed its initial analysis and sent the results to the Commanding General of the Army Air Forces.

> The phenomenon reported is something real and not visionary or fictitious. . . . . The description is [of objects that are] metallic . . . circular or elliptical in shape, flat on bottom and domed on top.[9]

SIGN—GRUDGE—BLUEBOOK

Three months later, on December 30, 1947, the Commanding General of the Army Air Forces initiated Project Sign, assigned it a 2A priority and ordered it to thoroughly investigate the UFO phenomena. Fear prevailed that the objects were Russian in origin!

Responsibility for Sign fell into the hands of the Air Technical Intelligence Center (ATIC), an integral part of the new fledgling Air Force, which had hardly begun to try out its new wings. According to Edward J. Ruppelt, former chief of the Air Force UFO Project, ATIC concluded that the objects were not Russian but were interplanetary in origin. In August of 1948, a Top Secret report was prepared and sent up the chain of command for approval.[10] The startling report went as far as the Air Force Chief of Staff, General Hoyt S. Vandenberg, who rejected it for lack of proof and ordered it to be declassified and burned! The Pentagon denies that such a report ever existed. However, Major Dewey Fournet, former Pentagon monitor of the Air Force UFO project, now a NICAP board member, also has confirmed its existence. Shortly after this, on December 27, 1948, the Air Force made a public announcement to the effect that flying saucers did not exist and that it was terminating Project Sign.

The Air Force has discontinued its special project of investigating and evaluating reported flying saucers. The reports are the result of misinterpretation of various conventional objects, a mild form of mass hysteria, and hoaxes. Continuance of the project is unwarranted.[11]

Unknown to the public at that time, the project did not really close. It opened again *secretly* in February of 1949 under a new code name—Project Grudge! However, its existence surfaced publicly when 1952 ushered in a second worldwide UFO sighting wave with the resultant public pressure on the government to do something about the situation! Thus, in March of 1952 its code name was again changed to Project Bluebook. Edward J. Ruppelt, Bluebook chief at that time, has written that the rate of sightings in July of 1952 fluctuated between twenty to thirty reports per day![12] By December, Ruppelt stated, reports dropped down to the "normal average of thirty per month with about twenty percent falling into the *unknown* category."[13] Shortly after this, on January 12, 1953, the Central Intelligence Agency (CIA) convened what has now become known as the Robertson Panel because it was chaired by the late and renowned scientist, H. P. Robertson of the California Institute of Technology. The CIA asked the panel to examine and evaluate the UFO evidence. Ruppelt has presented a *veiled* account of these secret hearings in his book written in 1956. He writes that the panel was given three alternatives to choose from.[14]

1. All UFO reports are explainable as known objects or natural phenomena; therefore the investigation should be permanently discontinued.
2. The UFO reports do not contain enough data upon which to base a final conclusion. Project Blue Book should be continued in hopes of obtaining better data.
3. The UFOs are interplanetary spacecraft.

He continues:

The written verdict, the group was told, would be given to the National Security Council, a council made up of the directors of all U.S. intelligence agencies, and thence it would go to the President of the United States—if they should decide that UFOs were interplanetary spacecraft.[15]

Ruppelt writes that in addition to UFO movies and fifty selected top reports, the panel was asked to review a very hot and highly controversial study.

> The study was hot because it wasn't official and the reason it wasn't official was because it was so hot. It concluded that the UFOs were interplanetary spaceships. The report had circulated around high command levels of intelligence . . . but even though some officers at command levels just a notch below General Samford bought it, the space behind the words "Approved by" was blank—no one would stick his neck out and officially send it to the top.[16]

Ruppelt relates that the scientists chose the second of the three suggested alternatives and recommended that the Air Force quadruple its investigation capability. The panel also urged that all UFO data be made known to the public. I think that it is important to quote Ruppelt in some length on this point as he thus far has been the only person who has revealed what the Robertson Panel's *real* recommendations were.

> The panel didn't recommend that the activities of Blue Book be cut back, and they didn't recommend that it be dropped. They recommended that it be expanded. Too many of the reports had been made by credible observers, the report said, people who should know what they're looking at—people who think things out carefully. Data that was out of the circumstantial evidence class was badly needed. And the panel must have been at least partially convinced that an expanded effort would prove something interesting because the expansion they recommended would require a considerable sum of money. The investigative force of Project Blue Book should be quadrupled in size, they wrote, and it should be staffed by specially trained experts in the fields of electronics, meteorology, photography, physics, and other fields of science pertinent to UFO investigations.
>   Every effort should be made to set up instruments in locations where UFO sightings are frequent, so that data could be measured and recorded during a sighting. In other locations

around the country, military and civilian scientists should be alerted and instructed to use every piece of available equipment that could be used to track UFO's.

And lastly, they said that the American public should be told every detail of every phase of the UFO investigation—the details of the sightings, the official conclusions, and why the conclusions were made. This would serve a double purpose; it would dispel any of the mystery that security breeds and it would keep the Air Force on the ball—sloppy investigations and analyses would never occur.

When the panel's conclusions were made known in the government, they met with mixed reactions. Some people were satisfied, but others weren't. Even the opinions of a group of the country's top scientists couldn't overcome the controversy that had dogged the UFO for five years. Some of those who didn't like the decision had sat in on the UFO's trial as spectators and they felt that the "jury" was definitely prejudiced—afraid to stick their necks out. They could see no reason to continue to assume that the UFO's weren't interplanetary vehicles.[17]

However, the Central Intelligence Agency, who had organized the Robertson Panel in the first place, ordered the Air Force to initiate a debunking program to undermine public interest in UFOs. Since the panel's report remained classified for the next thirteen years, it was hard to judge the accuracy of Ruppelt's statements except for the obvious attitude of the United States Air Force, which indeed appeared to be debunking UFOs.

The Robertson Panel report was finally declassified and made public in an *edited* version during the summer of 1966. According to this version of the report, the panel had concluded briefly that there was no evidence for "any artifacts of a hostile power,"[18] and CIA representatives present recommended that there should be a *debunking* of the flying saucers.

The "debunking" aim would result in reduction in public interest in "flying saucers" which today evokes a strong psychological reaction. This education could be accomplished by mass media such as television, motion pictures, and popular articles. Basis of such education would be actual case histories which had been puzzling at first but later explained. As in the case of conjuring tricks, there is much less stimulation if the "secret" is known.[19]

Absolutely no reference was made in this sanitized version of the
Robertson Panel to the panel's recommendations as outlined by
former Bluebook Chief Ruppelt! This whole business is most curious. Why should such a report be classified *secret* for thirteen
years if it was so insignificant? Why do its contents *not agree*
with Ruppelt's statements?

The late Dr. James E. McDonald ran into some strange difficulties concerning this document even after it was declassified.
During the first of three subsequent visits to Project Bluebook in
the summer of 1966, he asked to see the *full* report of the Robertson Panel. Bluebook chief Major Hector Quintanilla, allowed him
to make notes from it. On June 20, 1966, McDonald again visited Bluebook and requested a personal copy. The response to his
request is most interesting. I'll let Jim tell you about this in his
own words:

> I requested a Xerox copy of the report. The copy was prepared
> for me, but not given to me because a superior officer suggested
> that since "another agency" was involved, they'd have to check
> before releasing it to me.[20]

McDonald was assured that he would receive a copy within a few
weeks but he did not.

> In fact, I never received it. The "other agency," the Central
> Intelligence Agency, ruled that this document did not come
> under the "12-year rule" and reclassified it. Although a so-called
> "sanitized version" was later released, the full document remains
> undisclosed.[21]

John Lear, science editor of the *Saturday Review,* published this
sanitized version in an interesting article.[22]

The Pentagon did not take long to put the CIA debunking
order into effect, and Bluebook was fairly successful at pacifying
the public until the huge waves of sightings took place between
1964 and 1967. Public interest in UFOs was aroused to the ex-
tent that it instigated the first *open* congressional hearings on
UFOs.

In a curious repeat of history, the Air Force again contracted a leading scientist to assist in the matter. This time, however, there was no secret panel meeting but an open announcement that the University of Colorado would conduct UFO studies in parallel with Project Bluebook. This study, as we have already seen, was headed by the renowned physicist, Dr. Edward U. Condon. Although thirty percent of the sightings investigated by the Colorado Project remained unexplained and many of the investigating scientists felt positively about the evidence uncovered, Project Director Condon wrote in the project's final report, published in January of 1969, that:

> Careful consideration of the record *as it is available to us* [italics mine] leads us to conclude that further extensive study of the UFOs probably cannot be justified in the expectation that science will be advanced thereby.[23]

On December 17, 1969, the Air Force *again* informed the public that it was closing down its UFO project on the basis of the negative conclusion reached by the University of Colorado UFO Study. Civilians were asked to report UFOs to their local police or to members of the scientific community. Looking back in retrospect, perhaps the Bluebook philosophy had proven to have done more harm than good to the public image of the United States Air Force. The *explanations* given to citizens regarding the objects they had reported to Bluebook sometimes bordered on being ludicrous! Thus, it was probably felt that since the best UFO data originated from within the military complex, further investigation of civilian reports would only cause continued embarrassment and undesired public pressure. This being the case, the Air Force decided to concentrate only on the government-controlled-source UFO reports in their continued but little publicized investigation of UFOs. Yes, *the Air Force is still investigating UFO reports!* I have in my possession a copy of correspondence between a NICAP associate, Mr. George Earley and the Department of the Air Force. It is dated May 26, 1970, and is a direct answer to Mr. Earley's enquiry about what government agency would now be responsible for investigating UFO sightings since the Air Force

had terminated Project Bluebook. In his answer, Colonel William
T. Coleman, Chief, Public Information Division, Office of the Secretary of the Air Force, stated the following fact:

> The Aerospace Defense Command (ADC) is responsible for
> unknown aerial phenomena reported in any manner, and the
> provisions of Joint Army-Navy-Air Force Publication [JANAP]
> -146 provides for the processing of reports.[24]

Now, just what does JANAP-146 stipulate and whom does it affect? I have managed to secure a copy of this hard-to-get document, so, let us see . . . .

SECRECY OR ELSE

MERINT 5126 N 1423OW 3 UNIDENTIFIED FLYING OB-
JECTS HEADED NW AT 17000 FEET CIGAR SHAPE 50
FEET TO SW AT 2 MILES VERIFIED BY NAVIGATOR
VISIBILITY UNLIMITED 211513Z JONES NKLN

The above cryptic message is given as an example of a UFO
report being reported under the auspices of JANAP-146.[25] If such
a report involves an airborne observation, it is called a CIRVIS
report. CIRVIS stands for COMMUNICATIONS INSTRUC-
TIONS FOR REPORTING VITAL INTELLIGENCE SIGHT-
INGS. The order originates from the Joint Chiefs of Staff Joint
Communications-Electronics Committee. In respect to *security,*
JANAP-146 issues the following warning:

SECTION III—SECURITY
210. MILITARY AND CIVILIAN

> a. All persons aware of the contents or existence of a CIR-
> VIS report are governed by the Communications Act of 1934 and
> amendments thereto, and Espionage Laws. CIRVIS reports con-
> tain information affecting the National Defense of the United
> States within the meaning of the Espionage Laws, 18 U.S. Code,
> 793 and 794. The unauthorized transmission or revelation of the
> contents of CIRVIS reports in any manner is prohibited.[26]

Those who can remember the early days of the UFO problem
will recall that airline pilots were then reporting UFOs regularly.

However, just one year after the CIA-sponsored Robertson Panel had convened, the Air Force imposed JANAP-146 on all airline pilots flying for major airlines. On February 17, 1954, a significant conference was held between the Air Force and representatives of airline companies. Jim Lucas, staff wrtier for Scripps-Howard, covered this meeting in the following press release:

> WASHINGTON, Feb. 13—Commercial airline pilots report between five and ten flying saucer sightings each night, it was learned today.
>
> Representatives of major airlines will meet Wednesday in Los Angeles with Military Air Transport Service intelligence officers to discuss speeding up saucer reporting procedures. The idea will be to "get the reports in the quickest possible way" so that the Air Force can send fast jet fighters to investigate.
>
> Heretofore, commercial pilots have landed and then reported to MATS through their companies. By that time, the trail is usually cold. Now, pilots are instructed to flash reports direct from the air to MATS intelligence in Washington or to the nearest Air Force base.
>
> *Airline pilots are asked not to discuss their sightings publicly or give them to newspapers* [italics mine].

Then, just one month after this significant meeting between the military and civilian airline companies, JANAP-146 was imposed on airline pilots. Revision C, dated March 1954, states that "Coordination has been effected with the Air Coordinating Committee, other governmental agencies and *commercial carriers*" [italics mine].

Now, it is one thing for the military to impose such an order within its own ranks, but this attempt to silence civilian airline pilots caused much consternation among some of them. During a period when NICAP was carrying on a well-publicized campaign for a full congressional enquiry on UFOs, a large number of airline pilots protested this imposition of JANAP-146 publicly. In an interview with the *Newark Star-Ledger*, first 50 then, later, 450 pilots signed a protest petition against being silenced by the military regarding UFOs. Pertinent excerpts from the news story covering this action are as follows:

A group of more than 50 top commercial airline pilots, all veterans of more than 15 years with major companies, yesterday blasted as "bordering on the absolute ridiculous" the Air Force policy of tight censorship, brush-off and denial in regard to unidentified flying objects—flying saucers.

One termed the Air Force policy "a lesson in lying, intrigue and the 'Big Brother' attitude carried to the ultimate extreme." Each of the pilots has sighted at least one UFO, the majority several. . . . "We are ordered to report all UFO sightings," one said, "but when we do, we are treated like incompetents and told to keep quiet. . . ." This pilot also pointed to a *Joint Chiefs of Staff order* [italics mine] giving top radio priority to UFO reports anywhere in the world and specifying that any pilot who fails to maintain absolute secrecy afterwards is subject to a maximum of 10 years in jail and a fine of $10,000. . . .[27]

JANAP-146 is reportedly only one of a number of military orders that forbid public disclosure of pertinent UFO information. Why have the United States and other major governments taken such a firm stand on the UFO problem? Militarily speaking, they have no other choice. Unidentified machine-like objects violating the air space of any country are automatically considered and treated as a threat to national security until proved otherwise. As we have already seen, military regulations governing UFO sightings state this quite specifically. It would seem that the questions relating to UFO origin, motivation and the ability to control the phenomena must be answered without any doubt before open studies and legitimate public information become a reality. If UFOs were or have been proved to be of extraterrestrial origin, it is highly debatable whether or not official admission would ever be forthcoming unless widespread overt contact with the aliens became a reality.

Information collected by our country's intelligence agencies concerning the performance and theorized power plant of UFOs would be considered vital data to our nation's security and would be jealously guarded from falling into the hands of an unfriendly power. As former Bluebook chief Edward J. Ruppelt so aptly put it, "Giving a final answer would require a serious decision— probably one of the most serious since the beginning of man."[28]

The implications of such a discovery will be discussed in chapter fifteen.

Science—Gaining Interest

GOODBYE BLUEBOOK

In the summer of 1969, I was told by Dr. Hynek that Project Bluebook was about to close. He felt then that such an announcement was imminent. However, the days, weeks and months went by and nothing happened. For some reason, the Air Force decided to delay the announcement. Why? I found out in December! Despite strong protests from Dr. Edward U. Condon, former director of the controversial University of Colorado UFO project, the prestigious American Association for the Advancement of Science (AAAS) announced that it would conduct a UFO symposium at the 134th annual meeting to be held in Boston, Massachusetts. The symposium was organized by a special four-man AAAS committee composed of Drs. Thornton Page (Wesleyan University), Philip Morrison (M.I.T.), Walter Orr Roberts (retiring AAAS president) and Carl Sagen (Cornell University). Perhaps significant was the interesting fact that Dr. Page had been one of the members of the aforementioned CIA-sponsored Robertson Panel.

This was a momentous occasion in the long twenty-two-year history of the UFO problem. Such an *open* meeting before the elite members of the scientific community had been impossible in the past. Then, just nine days before this well-advertised conference, the United States Air Force struck! The office of the Secretary of the Air Force announced on December 17, 1969, that Project Bluebook was closed! The widespread press release stated:

> In a memorandum to Air Force Chief of Staff General John D. Ryan, Secretary Seamans stated that "the continuance of Project Blue Book cannot be justified either on the ground of national security or in the interest of science," and concluded that the project does not merit future expenditures of resources.[29]

HELLO SCIENCE

The Air Force announcement was a well-timed effort to neutralize the effects of the AAAS UFO Symposium! The deliberate delay of the Air Force announcement to coincide with the planned scientific conference was admitted to me by none other than the Archdemon of Saucerdom himself during a rather heated telephone conversation I had with him several days before the symposium started! However, regardless of the attempts of Dr. Condon and the Air Force to downgrade the symposium, a total of fourteen papers were presented by qualified scientists during the course of three full-day sessions. They represented the fields of astronomy, physics, radar, meteorology, computer science, sociology, psychology and psychiatry. There appeared to be general agreement among the majority of the participants that no *firm* hypothesis yet explains the hard-core sightings in terms of known phenomena.

Dr. Robert Hall of the University of Illinois stated that scientists have historically resisted inexplicable events in several ways: by avoiding or denying evidence; by illogical arguments, and by passing the buck between physical and behavioral scientists. Galileo's first telescopic view of Jupiter's satellites and the history of previously unexplained meteorite falls ("stones do not fall from the sky!") were cited as examples of science's attitude toward such reports. In conclusion, Dr. Hall urged scientists not to dismiss hard-core UFO cases, stating "that there is clearly a phenomenon of surpassing importance here. It is going to force some of us to make some fundamental changes in our knowledge."

The late Dr. James E. McDonald, University of Arizona, presented evidence based upon three years of full-time UFO research, which included the personal interviewing of over five hundred UFO witnesses across the country. Included in his presentation was the mention of the *Beverly affair* covered in chapter nine of this book. McDonald contended that UFOs represent one of the greatest scientific problems of our times. He further stated that Colorado UFO Project Chief Edward U. Condon's conclusions did not support the contents of the project's final report, which contained a large number of well-documented unexplained UFO sightings.

Dr. Hynek delivered a paper entitled "21 years of UFO Reports." He concluded that the residue of unexplained UFO reports deserve scientific study because:

1. The same phenomenon is reported from widely separated locations.
2. The reports come from responsible witnesses.
3. The descriptions are not of known processes.
4. The reports resist explanation by known processes.

Philip Morrison of M.I.T., one of the world's most brilliant physicists, was the last speaker. He very eloquently summarized the central thoughts and conclusions of the papers presented at the symposium. The title of his paper was "The Nature of Physical Evidence." He said that he found certain of the reported UFO events "puzzling" but did not personally favor the extraterrestrial or any particular hypothesis. He suggested that only a clear example of a UFO incident will demonstrate whatever hypothesis is being tested. In closing, he cited Biot's investigation of the French meteorite fall as a classic historical example of the proper testing of evidence. Biot's "independent link-by-link test of multiple chains of evidence" is what Morrison stressed must be pursued if scientists are to resolve the UFO problem.

Several years prior to the AAAS UFO symposium there were definite signs that UFOs were finally becoming scientifically respectable. For years, interested scientists felt obligated to study the problem silently among their colleagues because of negative military pronouncements and the lunatic fringe that soon became associated with UFOs. The tide began to turn when the Air Force announced that renowned physicist Edward U. Condon would direct a civilian scientific study of UFOs. Although the study did not prove that UFOs were alien craft from outer space, it nonetheless could not explain a large percentage of the sightings investigated. These included radar-visual and photographic cases by the military, civilians, and our astronauts. As we have already noted, the study proved controversial and was even branded "The Flying Saucer Fiasco" by John Fuller, who wrote an exposé of the project for *Look* magazine.[30] Nonetheless, the study conducted for the Air Force at the University of Colorado became a legitimate springboard for *open* scientific discussion about UFOs at high levels for the first time in UFO history. Even Dr. Condon carefully covered himself and the project by inserting a paradoxical qualifying statement about the matter in his final report. In the Conclusions and Recommendations section of the project's final report, Condon stated:

> Our hope is that . . . this report will help other scientists in seeing what the problems are. . . . If they disagree, it will have been because our report has helped them reach a clear picture of wherein existing studies are faulty or incomplete and thereby will have stimulated ideas for more accurate studies. . . . We have no doubt that support will be forthcoming to carry on . . . studies. We think that such ideas for work should be supported.[31]

Ideas for *more accurate studies* were forthcoming from scientists even before the project report was published. Dr. Felix Zigel of the Moscow Aviation Institute outlined such to American readers of the February 1968 issue of the magazine *Soviet Life* published in this country. He stated that both visual and radar UFO sightings had been occurring in Russia for the last twenty years, adding:

> The hypothesis that UFOs are flying craft from other planets other than earth merits the most serious examination. . . . International cooperation is vital.[32]

Several months later, the House of Representatives Science and Astronautics Committee held a UFO symposium on July 29, 1968. Six prominent scientists presented their findings concerning the physical reality of UFOs. It was proposed, almost as if in response to the Russians, that:

> The United States seek the cooperation of the United Nations in establishing an international clearing house on the subject.[33]

Then after the AAAS UFO symposium was held in 1969, 1970 saw the equally respected American Institute of Astronautics and Aeronautics (AIAA) launch their own UFO investigating subcommittee to check out the negative report issued by the University of Colorado. Their initial findings concluded that:

> We find it difficult to ignore the small residue of well-documented but unexplainable cases that form the hardcore of the UFO controversy.[34]

The following year ushered in Austrialia's first scientific UFO sympoisum during the month of November of 1971. Dr. B. H. Horton, physicist at Adelaide University, told gathered scientists that:

> There is a need for Australian and New Zealand scientists to drop their unscientific attitude toward UFOs. Visual and radar trackings are so numerous that scientists should recognize that there is some phenomenon in our atmosphere that demands an explanation.[35]

Perhaps the result of a poll conducted by *Industrial Research* magazine (April 1971) best illustrates the mounting trend toward respectability for the UFO; 50 percent of the 2700 respondents believed that *UFOs exist;* 80 percent believed that the University of Colorado study was *not definitive;* 70 percent believed that the government was *suppressing UFO information;* and 32 percent believed that UFOs *originated from outer space.* It is significant to note that of the 350,000 subscribers, more than 23 percent have doctor's degrees, 23 percent have master's degrees, and 44 percent have bachelor's degrees.

All of these factors indicate that science is finally beginning to *openly* consider the UFO in a serious manner. Highlighting this fact was the recent publication of a book entitled *The UFO Experience,* by none other than Dr. J. Allen Hynek. Hynek, in addition to his experience as scientific consultant to the Air Force on UFOs, has a very impressive set of credentials. He is currently the director of the Lindheimer Astronomical Research Center at

Northwestern University and chairman of Northwestern's astronomy department. He has also served as associate director of the renowned Smithsonian Astrophysical Observatory in Cambridge, Massachusetts, as well as having headed its NASA-sponsored satellite tracking program. No other scientist is known to have been exposed to as much UFO material in an official capacity. Using the exact methods of science, Dr. Hynek aptly demonstrates that UFOs deserve scientific attention and proposes the means whereby a process of scientific verification can be established.

The aforementioned goal of the *scientific recognition of a new species* appears to be well on its way to being fulfilled. However, difficulties still remain for any *open* scientific study of UFOs. We may indeed have said goodbye to Bluebook and hello to science, but government security orders such as JANAP-146 with their associated restrictive procedures are still in effect. As long as the National Security Council believes that it has a legitimate concern about UFO secrecy, it is doubtful that the federal government will fund open UFO projects or release hard-core UFO evidence to the public at large. The United Nations also shares this concern about UFOs.

United Nations—UFOs Are a Concern

In June of 1967, news commentator Drew Pearson gave our nation the first hint that the United Nations is very concerned about UFOs at its highest levels. In his column, captioned U THANT IS ALSO WORRYING ABOUT UFOs, Pearson made the following revelations:

Washington—In the very middle of the Near East crisis U.N. Secretary General Thant took time to do a very significant thing. He arranged to have one of the top advocates of the theory that flying saucers—UFOs—are from another planet speak before the Outer Space Affairs Committee of the United Nations.

The Middle East war broke on June 5. On June 7 Dr. James E. McDonald of the University of Arizona, a firm believer in UFOs, spoke before the U.N. outer space committee. . . . Interesting fact is that U Thant has confided to friends that *he considers UFOs the most important problem facing the United*

Nations next to the war in Vietnam. [italics mine] U Thant made this statement before the war in the Near East, so it's not known how he rates this last international incident compared with UFOs.[36]

At the referenced address made to the U.N. Outer Space Affairs Group, Dr. McDonald recommended that this group "seek all possible means of securing worldwide attention to this problem." He further stated that "The most probable hypothesis is that these are some type of surveillance probes of extraterrestrial origin."[37]

Perhaps the best way to demonstrate U.N. concern over the UFO problem is to look in on the 821st meeting of the Committee on the Peaceful Use of Outer Space held at Headquarters, New York, on Monday, 8 November 1971, at 3:00 P.M. The following is copied from the Provisional Verbatim Record of this meeting.

Mr. Ibingira, Uganda: The draft convention now before us, and those others to come, are conceived on the basis exclusively that only States from this planet can explore or use outer space. The rights and obligations concern one State in relation to another from our planet. Consequently, we exclude all possibility that we might share outer space with some other space explorers possessed of intelligence and capabilities matching our own, from some undetermined origins.

If there should be any possibility that there might be other co-users of outer space other than from planet earth, it becomes imperative that in a convention such as the one before us or others to come, there must be included a clause ensuring that any State engaged in outer space exploration must conduct itself in such a way as not to prejudice the safety of our planet. If, for instance, a State sent out a spaceship on an exploration voyage into outer space, it should be ensured that such a spaceship must not conduct itself in a hostile manner should it by any chance encounter other spaceships or objects from undetermined origins. It is not enough to leave this to the good sense of the exploring State. The matter is far too important and fundamental. This responsibility to our planet must be appropriately spelled out in a liability convention such as this one before us.

The liability of one space object causing damage on another State on earth is almost nothing compared with the liability a State has to our whole earth in attracting hostile reactions from unknown, undetermined origins, but real all the same.

I know that the problem of whether or not there can be other space travellers has involved great controversy over a long period of time. The official position of all the States involved in exploring outer space seems to be that there is no intelligent life comparable with our own in the universe; that therefore, there are no chances that space explorers from earth would encounter others from other worlds.

These Governments have consistently discredited any suggestion that the unidentified flying objects which have been repeatedly observed at different times in different parts of the world could possibly be interplanetary spaceships. They have concluded that all the alleged sightings of UFOs and flying saucers in our skies are balloons, comets, planets or things of that kind. It is true that a lot of these things could not raise serious thought that they were in fact interplanetary spacecraft. But there is ample evidence to raise a reasonable doubt that some of them just might conceivably be. There are in the United States, in the Soviet Union, and in the United Kingdom, in addition to other countries, serious scientists who believe that some of these unidentified flying objects are interplanetary or intergalactic spacecrafts. Let me quote some of them.

Dr. Herman Oberth, a distinguished space scientist, reputedly one of the people who developed the V-2, one of the founders of modern rocketry, and author of the book *By Rocket to Interplanetary Space,* was quoted by the *Times* newspaper in Alabama, February 1, 1967, to have said as follows:

"According to information available to me there exist more than 70,000 eyewitness reports of UFOs. Eleven per cent of these reports cannot be easily explained. They should not be lies or hoaxes because they involve responsible senior Air Force officers of radar readings or photographs from responsible sources. Their speed can be enormous. Radar measurements have shown up to 11.8 miles per second." And continuing his comments on the UFOs, the distinguished scientist stated:

"(a) They are not built by human beings . . . . today we cannot produce machines that fly as UFOs do.

(b) They are flying by means of artificial gravity. This would explain the sudden changes in direction. . . . This hypothesis also would explain the piling up of these discs into a cylindrical or cigar-shaped ship upon leaving the earth, because in this fashion only one field of gravity would be required for all discs.

(c) They produce high-tension electric charges in order to

push the air out of their path . . . . and strong magnetic fields to influence the ionized air at higher altitudes. . . . This would explain their luminosity."

Another distinguished scientist, the late Dr. James McDonald, Professor of Meteorology and Senior Physicist at the Institute of Atmospheric Physics at the University of Arizona, in October 1966, stated that there was a real likelihood that UFOs are extra-terrestrial probes.

Now, it was stated again in August 1965 by Professor Claudio Anguita of the Cerro Calan Observatory in Chile:

"There is scientific evidence that strange objects visit our planet. . . . It is lamentable that Governments have drawn a veil of secrecy over all this."

I do not want to indulge at length in instances of this nature. These people are not charlatans. These people are not abnormal people. They are responsible people who have got enquiring and serious minds. Not all Governments have been very silent about this matter. I would like to quote the Argentinian Secretary of the Navy, who issued a press release on the sighting of a UFO on 7 July 1965.

"The Naval garrison in the Argentine Antarctica, Deception Island, observed on 3 July at 1940 hours local time, a giant lens-shaped flying object, solid in appearance, mostly red and green in colour, changing occasionally with yellow, blue, white and orange shades. The object was moving on a zig-zag trajectory toward the east but several times it changed course to the west and north with varied speeds and without sound. It passed at an elevation of forty-five degrees over the horizon at a distance estimated to be about ten to fifteen kilometres from the base. During the manoeuvres performed by the object, the witnesses were able to register its tremendous speeds and also the fact that it hovered motionless for about fifteen minutes at an altitude of about three miles. The meteorological conditions for the area of the sighting can be considered as very good. . . . The object was witnessed by the meteorologist together with thirteen members of the garrison and three Chilean non-commissioned officers visiting the base. The observation lasted for twenty minutes and photographs of the object were taken."

I think we cannot completely ignore what these people have had to say. . . .[38]

The United Nations is concerned about UFOs. Why, then, doesn't the U.N. sponsor an international program to study UFOs? Could it be that each major member nation also has its own version of JANAP-146? Is it possible that an international cooperative military scientific study has secretly been conducted over the years? I personally believe this to be the case and that UFOs have been treated as a threat to international security by both Western and Soviet bloc countries.

The Public?—Just as Confused as Ever

Today, the vast majority of the public believe that the Air Force is no longer investigating UFOs since its termination of Project Bluebook. Very few citizens are aware of the fact that this is not true. They have never heard of JANAP-146 or that the Air Defense Command is continuing the UFO investigation for the Air Force.

In response to public requests for information on UFOs, the government replies that UFOs do not exist and that Project Bluebook has closed. However, responsible scientists, including Bluebook's astronomical consultant, Dr. Hynek, state publicly that UFOs do exist. Member nations of the U.N. are concerned. NICAP and other civilian organizations continue to investigate UFO reports initiated by civilians who continue sighting the UFOs that supposedly do not exist! It is no wonder that the public is as confused as ever. Why? Because the military complex in this country and abroad are treating UFOs as a *threat*. In order to maintain efficient national defense postures, they really have no choice but to do so. What are they treating as a threat? That is the question of the century? We have outlined the *situation*. Let us now consider the estimate of the situation.

NOTES

1. Statement on file at NICAP.
2. Personal Files.
3. *Dagens Nyheter*, July 11, 1946.
4. *Aftenposten*, July 20, 1946.

5. *Goteborg Handel* and *Sjofarts Tidning,* July 22, 1946.
6. *Epoque,* August 29, 1946.
7. NICAP, *The UFO Evidence,* p. 129.
8. Ted Bloecher, *Report on the UFO Wave of 1947.*
9. E. U. Condon, *Scientific Study of UFOs,* p. 894.
10. Edward J. Ruppelt, *The Report on Unidentified Flying Objects,* p. 45.
11. Personal Files, Official Air Force Press Release.
12. Ruppelt, *op. cit.,* pp. 154, 162
13. *Ibid.,* p. 197.
14. *Ibid.,* p. 210.
15. *Ibid.*
16. *Ibid.,* p. 218.
17. *Ibid.,* p. 225.
18. John Lear, "The Disputed CIA Document on UFOs," *Saturday Review,* September 3, 1966, p. 45.
19. E. U. Condon *Scientific Study of UFOs,* p. 915.
20. James E. McDonald, Presentation to American Society of Newspaper Editors, Washington, D.C., April 22, 1967.
21. *Ibid.*
22. Lear, *op. cit.*
23. Condon, *op. cit.,* p. 1.
24. Personal files and J. Allen Hynek, *The UFO Experience,* p. 189.
25. JANAP-146, "Communication Instructions for reporting Vital Intelligence Sightings from Airborne and Waterborne Sources," III.
26. *Ibid.,* pp. 3-4.
27. John Lester (staff writer), *Newark Star-Ledger,* December 22, 1958.
28. Ruppelt, *op. cit.,* p. 200.
29. Office of Assistant Secretary of Defense, News Release: "Air Force to terminate Project *Bluebook,*" December 17, 1969.
30. John G. Fuller, "Flying Saucer Fiasco," *Look,* May 14, 1968.
31. Condon, *op. cit.,* p. 2.
32. Felix Zigel, *Soviet Life,* February 1968.
33. *House Document No. 7: Symposium on UFOs,* July 29, 1968.
34. "UFO, an appraisal of the problem," *Astronautics and Aeronautics,* November 1970.
35. *News,* Adelaide, S.A., October 29, 1971.
36. Drew Pearson, *The Boston Globe,* June 27, 1967.
37. James E. McDonald, Statement to Outer Space Affairs Group, June 7, 1967 (Personal Files)
38. Provisional verbatim record of the 821st meeting, United Nations General Assembly, 8 November 1971.

14

THE ESTIMATE— INTERPLANETARY

The most probable hypothesis to account for the UFO phenomena is that these are some kind of surveillance probes of extraterrestrial origin.

DR. J. E. McDONALD
U.N. Address, 1967

Many writers and lecturers at this point of a UFO discussion would ask the obvious leading question—"What are UFOs?"— and proceed to present a reasoned argument to support their particular viewpoint. The most *popular* view is the extraterrestrial hypothesis. However, I prefer to follow the line of reasoning that the late Dr. James E. McDonald[1] and the authors of the previously mentioned Air Force Academy textbook on UFOs have taken.[2] This involves first asking the question "What *aren't* UFOs?" In other words, what are the alternatives to the extraterrestrial hypothesis?

Alternate Hypotheses

The UFO problem, assuming that physical proof really does not exist in the hands of authorities, is readily adaptable to an application of Chamberlain's *method of multiple hypotheses* in the seeking of proposed solutions. That is, one should examine the available UFO data in the light of a number of plausible hypotheses and then propose that hypothesis that best accounts for the observed data. The observed data in most cases consist of anecdotal UFO reports that remain unexplained after careful investigation by competent personnel. In some cases, the anecdotal

256

data is supplemented by inexplicable concurrent radar tracks, photographs, physical traces, and other associated active and passive effects.

The 160 UFO reports used within this book are a small fraction of thousands of similar unexplainable events which originate from all over the globe. If we propose to find an answer other than extraterrestrial origin for cases remaining in the unidentified category, we must first set up a list of counter-hypotheses for consideration. Understandably, there have been few cohesive theories as to the nature of UFOs. Those theories that have been advanced over the course of modern UFO history can be collected under at least seven general group headings: *mysticism, hallucinations, hoaxes, conventional objects, natural phenomena, secret weapons* and *extraterrestrial visitors*. It must be noted that the correct explanation may not be contained in this list. One could speculate upon even more exotic explanations such as visitors from a parallel universe or time-travelers. It would be hard to dispute the fact that such things are very remote possibilities. However, within the reference of our own cultural and technological framework, the foregoing list of hypotheses provides a relatively exhaustive list of the most likely possibilities. Let us now discuss each one in the light of what is known about UFOs.

MYSTICISM

No sooner had the UFO phenomena become widely publicized than *cults* began to spring up everywhere proclaiming that the mission of the "flying saucers" was spiritual in nature. Literally reams of books, pamphlets, records and tapes are being sold on the general premise that the UFOs contain messengers of salvation and occult truth. Some authors of such works even claim direct contact with these heavenly beings and print their messages of peace and love to huge mailing lists of dedicated believers. NICAP investigation into the background of some of the leading personalities of such cults indicates that their statements and beliefs are contradictory and totally lacking in evidence.

One should not overlook the possibility, in spite of such excessive, unsupported claims, that UFOs might represent what could be interpreted as a *spiritual* mission and that all *physical* efforts to explain them must necessarily fail. Researchers in psychic phenomena are convinced of the reality of some inexplicable events and personal abilities, but they have not been able to discover the mechanism responsible for such within the context of *known* physical laws. Solid evidence supporting the mysticism hypothesis is clearly lacking, and one can only speculate on such matters. Further discussion of this hypothesis is beyond the scope of this book. Those interested in pursuing the few scholarly dissertations on this possible aspect of UFOs should refer to the general body of UFO literature.[3] A limited discussion of possible *religious* implications of UFOs will be found in the next chapter.

HALLUCINATIONS

The already quoted Air Force Academy text states the following about hallucinations, mass hysteria and rumor phenomena:

> There is evidence that UFO reports occur in waves and that a rash of sightings in a localized area may be due to increased public sensitivity to an initial report. Some reports received at these times may indeed be inspired by the increased attention to UFOs and not true sightings at all. However, the large number of multi-observer reports from independent observers, and reports from military personnel, airline pilots, policemen, scientists and other qualified witnesses make it unlikely that many UFO reports are the results of hallucinations, mass hysteria, and rumor phenomena. Psychologists and sociologists are unable to estimate what portion of UFO reports may be due to such causes. Analysis of the credentials of witnesses in most cases would indicate that the number would be small.[4]

Civilian UFO researchers would readily agree with the Air Force on this point. Most people who report UFOs have stable personalities and hold down responsible jobs. Are we to suggest that multiple, sometimes independent, stable personalities all hallucinate at precisely the same time? Do animals and birds, which obviously react to the presence of UFOs, hallucinate? I think not! Add to this the list of active and passive effects reportedly manifested in the presence of UFOs and the likelihood of the hallucination hypothesis fades to near insignificance.

HOAXES

In the course of nearly a decade of UFO sighting investigations, I have come across relatively few deliberate hoaxes. Those few which do grace my file involve fake photography and the launching of homemade hot-air balloons. Air Force statistics confirm this little-known truth.

> Confirmed hoaxes are only a small percentage of the total number of UFO reports. Most reports are by reliable witnesses and show no evidence of fabrication or fraud.[5]

People who do plan deliberate hoaxes risk the chance of public exposure and the resultant embarrassment with all its undesirable ramifications. Fortunately, there are relatively few people who would be prepared to take such a gamble.

CONVENTIONAL OBJECTS

The largest percentage of UFO reports can be attributed to common, man-made objects. These include misidentification of aircraft landing, navigational and refueling lights; illuminated aerial advertising banners; weather and research balloons; flares; searchlights; high-flying aircraft reflecting sunlight; and—would you believe it—trucks! I have two *truck* cases on file. In both cases, witnesses had been under the influence of alcoholic beverages. Let us examine one of these cases briefly. (It's a gem!) To avoid embarrassment to the witness, I will not mention his name or the date and place.

The witness decided to park his car in an isolated field to "sleep it off"! He woke up in the middle of the night when he heard a noise. Looking across the field, he saw sparks and strange lights. All of a sudden, a power blackout occurred in the area. House and streetlights bordering the field flickered briefly and went out. Wondering what was going to happen next, he sat up and gazed across the field. Abruptly, red flashing lights appeared and moved over the end of the field. Instantly his mind went back to something that he had read about UFOs' being connected with some power blackouts. He panicked and drove out of the area at top speed!

When his report reached me, I phoned local authorities in the sighting area. Briefly, what happened was this. An automobile struck a utility pole, which woke up our semidrunk witness. Shorted-out wires from the damaged utility pole and the driver's flashlight caused the "sparks and strange lights." The severed power lines caused the blackout, and a repair truck responding to the accident with its red warning lights flashing provided the rest of the stimuli for a UFO report! It is significant to note, however, that the witness did give an accurate description of just what he had observed. It was his *interpretation* that was way out yonder! A few well-placed telephone calls provided an easy solution.

Most *moving lights-in-the-sky* reports that come to my attention are automatically rejected for investigation and evaluated as being probable aircraft. Those few cases of this type that are investigated because of certain peculiarities must still pass a rigid test before being categorized as "unknowns."

Close-encounter, or Type I sightings, on the other hand, leave little room for misidentification. The size, shape, performance and unlikely sighting locale of the Type I sightings do not fit the *conventional object* hypothesis. What conventional object would hover over power lines, power stations, isolated fields, or chase cars and people, or fly within restricted civil air lanes? An example of the latter is a typical airline pilot's report that I personally investigated. The pilot refused to file a CIRVIS report under JANAP-146 and thus was not prohibited from telling his story to me. This report was included in the University of Colorado UFO project's final report.[6] The pilot, Robert W. Fox, stated:

> I will be glad to assist you in your investigation. I looked up the date of my encounter with the saucer in my logbook: Date—23

June 1955; Time—Approximately 12:15 to 12:45 p.m.; Place—
On V-2 (the airway between Utica and Albany, New York).
I was copilot of a Mohawk Airlines DC-3. We were cruising at
3000 feet in the clear about fifteen miles east of Utica, New
York. The ceiling was 4000 feet and there was good visibility
at 3000 feet. We were cruising at 160 knots, eastbound. I saw
the object as it passed approximately 500 feet above us at an
angle of 70 degrees. It was moving along the airway at a great
speed. The body was light gray. It was almost round with a
center line. It was solid above the center line but beneath the
line there were several windows, which emitted a bright blue-
green light. It was not rotating. . . . I could keep good reference
by looking at the lights. Both the captain and I saw it and
watched it for several miles. As the distance between us increased, the lights seemed to change color slightly from greenish
to bluish. A few minutes after it went out of sight, 2 other aircraft . . . reported that they saw it and wondered if anyone
else had seen it. The Albany control tower also reported that
they had seen an object go by on V-2. V-2 also goes between
Albany and Boston. As we approached Albany, we overheard
that Boston radar had also tracked an object along V-2. It
passed over Boston and was still going eastbound. . . . It was
estimated to be moving at 4500 miles per hour.[7]

The University of Colorado analysts made the following remarks about this report:

There are a number of inconsistencies in this report, aside from
the most obvious one: the absence of a devastating sonic boom,
which should have been generated by a 150 ft. ellipsoidal object
travelling at Mach 6 or better in level flight at 3500 ft. . . . The
residue is a most intriguing report. . . . It does appear that
this sighting defies explanation by conventional means [italics
mine].[8]

The absence of a *sonic boom* is just one of several characteristics that would indicate that some reported UFOs are not conventional objects and appear to be immune to the laws of physics
as we presently understand them. In his article, "The Physics and
Metaphysics of Unidentified Flying Objects,"[9] Dr. William Markowitz discusses the UFO problem in light of five basic physical
laws:

1. Every action must have an equal and opposite reaction.
2. Every particle in the universe attracts every other particle with a force proportional to the product of their masses and inversely as the square of the distance between them.
3. Momentum and mass-energy are conserved.
4. No material body can travel at c, the speed of light, in free space.
5. The maximum energy which can be obtained from a body at rest is governed by Einstein's famous equation, $E = mc^2$

Markowitz points out that these basic physical laws have enabled physicists to predict and control many phenomena for practical purposes. They also can be employed in analyzing UFO reports. Although much of the reported UFO data is in harmony with these five laws, some is definitely not. For example, how can one explain how a body moving at supersonic speed can instantaneously stop, resume the same speed at once, perform right-angle turns, create no sonic boom and still remain intact in one piece? It is as if the reported object had no mass and yet retained certain characteristics of a body having mass. It appears solid, it reflects radar waves as if it were solid, and leaves physical traces indicating *weight*. Such data appears to be at variance with one or more of the five listed laws.

Markowitz concludes that our physical laws are firmly established both in theory and in experiment. Thus, the validity of the physical law rather than the reported behavior of a UFO is a more acceptable alternative to the scientist. He cautions, however, that any physical law may be *subject to change* with the discovery of *new evidence*. Do UFOs represent such evidence? If we take the descriptions of thousands of eyewitnesses at face value, the answer must be yes! Especially interesting are the radar-visual cases, in which electronic equipment supplements the eyes of the witnesses. Thus, although a large percentage of reported UFOs do turn out to be conventional objects, there are, nonetheless, thousands of unexplained cases that are highly unconventional in nature.

The authors of the Air Force Academy text on UFOs make the following interesting observations regarding the five basic laws discussed by Markowitz:

Laws number 1 and 3 seem fairly safe, but let us hesitate and take another look. Actually, law number 3 is only valid [now] from a relativistic viewpoint; and for that matter, so are laws 4 and 5. But Relativity completely revised these physical concepts after 1915. Before then, Newtonian mechanics was supreme. We should also note that general relativity has not been fully verified. Thus we have the peculiar situation of five laws which appear to deny the possibility of intelligent alien control of UFOs, yet three of the laws are recent in concept and may not even be valid. Also, law number 2 has not been tested under conditions of large relative speeds or accelerations. *We should not deny the possibility of alien control of UFOs on the basis of preconceived notions not established as related or relevant to the UFOs.*[10]

NATURAL PHENOMENA

Next to conventional objects, misinterpretation of natural phenomena account for many UFO reports. In a real sense, these reports are easiest to evaluate, because in most cases good old mother nature is predictable. In particular, I am referring to bright stars, the planets, the moon, meteor showers and most comets, because their positions during the sighting time is easily determined. Without a doubt, the planet Venus is the queen of the IFOs! Consider a typical case that I investigated not long ago.[11]

A young couple were returning home from a late evening out and were perpendicularly approaching Route 1 in Danvers, Massachusetts. Both sighted a brilliant light source seemingly hovering over this major highway. Turning onto Route 1 they headed north. Much to their surprise, they now found that the bright light was to their right and pacing them. The young man would slow down and then speed up, but the strange light always kept exact pace with them. Terrified, they headed north at high speed with the UFO in hot pursuit! Swinging into a gas station, they ran inside to obtain help. The station attendant came out and, sure enough, there was an intense stationary white light source in the sky. It was brighter than any of the stars. He ran back into the station and phoned the police, who in turn informed the state police, who in turn referred the witnesses to me. I listened quietly as the young couple told me that when they tried to leave the gas station, their car would not start. They actually believed that the UFO was causing some kind of electrical interference that was affecting the ignition system of the car! When they finally managed to get the car started, it was noticed that somehow their gas tank was abnormally low. This too was attributed to the bright UFO in the sky! I then convinced the young lady to repeat their drive over the same route on the following night and explained that she would again sight the UFO in approximately the same position in the sky because *it was the planet Venus!* I pointed out to them that the speed and direction of the automobile caused Venus to appear to chase them. Upon serious reflection about the matter, both witnesses realized that the object was stationary only when they were stationary.

Three points should be made here. First, that many people remain almost totally ignorant of even the most basic astronomical phenomena and misinterpret such as UFOs. Secondly, that a trained investigator recognizes such misinterpretations quite easily. Thirdly, it must be stressed again that most people do give a relatively accurate description of what they observe. If it were not for this fact, evaluation for the field investigator would be extremely difficult.

Unfortunately, some types of natural phenomena are not predictable, such as *ball lightning*. The late James E. McDonald, whose speciality was atmospheric physics, said the following about this rare phenomenon (after dismissing artificially induced plasmas as being significantly responsible for UFOs):

> Now one puzzling and far from understood phenomenon of atmospheric electricity that does lie in the plasma category is *ball lightning,* which, for brevity, will be identified as BL. Only within about the past decade has BL been admitted as a real phenomenon rather than some kind of illusion. In this sense, the history of BL studies is amusingly parallel to that of UFOs. . . . Students of atmospheric electricity have not yet succeeded in developing an adequate theoretical understanding of the baffling phenomena reported under this heading. . . . The range of BL behavior characteristics is so wide that no single mathematical model has fit very satisfactorily the reported effects.[12]

Thus, ball lightning is a rare and still not completely understood phenomenon. This knowledge, coupled with the fact that we are dealing with reports not of small, luminous, short-lived balls but with structured, machine-like objects would eliminate ball lightning as a stimulus for most UFO reports.

What natural phenomenon would appear to resemble an artificial, metallic-appearing, domed oval object? The answer obviously is that there are no known natural phenomena that can successfully account for the hard-core residue of UFO reports that continue to remain "unknown" after careful investigation.

SECRET WEAPONS

Some UFO reports stem from the observation of secret or experimental aircraft and missiles. Most of these consist of rocket firings, which can be seen at great distances from the launching sites. Some involve satellite reentries. Very few actually involve experimental aircraft, as normally their flight is restricted to the boundaries of secret test ranges. However, early in UFO history, the United States Air Force did fear that the mysterious objects were Russian secret weapons. Dr. G. E. Valley, member of the Scientific Advisory Board for the Air Force Chief of Staff, wrote the following in a formerly secret document issued in February of 1949:

> The objects may be Russian aircraft. If this were so, then . . . we would have plenty to worry about. It is the author's opinion that only an accidental discovery of a degree of novelty never before achieved could suffice to explain such devices. It is doubtful whether a potential enemy would arouse our curiosity in so idle a fashion.[13]

A more recent statement regarding the *secret weapon* hypothesis is from the 1970 edition of the Air Force Academy text on UFOs.

> Thus, while some current UFO reports may be attributable to space vehicle re-entries or satellite launches, the reports in the late forties and early fifties cannot be attributed to these causes. Similarly, advanced weapon systems in the development and test stages [secret weapons] now would give rise to a different

type of UFO report from those of earlier eras. The variety and world-wide distribution of UFO reports make it unlikely that the reports are due to sightings of products of an advanced terrestrial technology.[14]

Again, it is quite apparent that secret weapons do not account for the hard-core UFO sightings reported on a global scale. Secret weapons do not fly in commercial airlanes. They do not hover over cars, houses, fields, ponds and power lines at low level! The configuration, maneuvers and effects of UFOs reported are totally inexplicable in terms of any terrestrial power's capability either in the past or the near future. It is no wonder that the writers of the Air Force Academy text conclude: "Very few people accept this as a credible suggestion." This leaves us with the last and the most controversial explanation on our list.

EXTRATERRESTRIAL VISITORS

According to former Air Force UFO Project Chief Edward J. Ruppelt, the Air Technical Intelligence Center (ATIC) had concluded as early as August 1948 that UFOs must be interplanetary.

> The people at Air Technical Intelligence Center decided that the time had come to make an Estimate of the Situation. The situation was the UFOs; the estimate was that they were interplanetary. It was a rather thick document with a black cover and it was printed on legal-sized paper. Stamped across the front were the words TOP SECRET. It contained the Air Force's analysis of many . . . incidents. All of them had come from scientists, pilots, and other equally credible observers, and each one was an unknown.[15]

Ruppelt goes on to say that this report worked its way up into the higher echelons of the Air Force.

> It got to the late General Hoyt S. Vandenberg, then Chief of Staff, before it was batted back down. The General wouldn't buy interplanetary vehicles. The report lacked proof. A group went to the Pentagon to bolster their position but had no luck.[16]

Now, what can we conclude about this? It is very possible that the ATIC *estimate,* unbeknown to ATIC, was taken more seriously by the Air Force Chief of Staff. Perhaps the good general's attitude was just a cover for a higher-level UFO enquiry that depended upon ATIC for data but that discouraged ATIC from drawing conclusions. Such conclusions would be for the level of Chief of Staff and higher levels. This, of course, is pure speculation on my part. Most probably, at least at this early date, General Vandenberg did exactly what Ruppelt attributes to him. In either case, one significant fact stands out very clearly. Regardless of what the general or the Pentagon thought, those who actually researched the UFO problem *firsthand* at ATIC were convinced beyond the shadow of a doubt that the unidentified flying objects were *interplanetary!*

The theory that UFOs were extraterrestrial visitors did not die. In December of 1948, about four months after the ATIC estimate of the situation, Dr. J. E. Lipp, scientific consultant to the Air Force, wrote the following, now declassified memo to the Air Force Director of Research and Development—Brigadier General Putt. After a lengthy discussion about possible intelligent life existing elsewhere in our solar system, Dr. Lipp concluded that *Mars* presents a possibility.

One other hypothesis needs to be discussed. It is that the Martians have kept a long-term routine watch on Earth and have been alarmed by the sight of our A-bomb shots as evidence that we are warlike and on the threshold of space travel. . . . The chance that Martians . . . . would have a civilization resembling our own is extremely remote. It is particularly unlikely that their civilization would be within a half century of our own state of advancement. Yet in the last 50 years we have just started to use aircraft . . . and in the next 50 years we will most certainly start exploring space.[17]

Moving into the 1951-1953 time frame, we now find that behind the scenes, scientists working with the Air Force had concluded that UFOs were interplanetary. Ruppelt briefed groups of these scientists on UFOs as part of his function as chief of

Project Grudge and, later, Bluebook. He says of one such group that:

> These people were not pulp writers or wide-eyed fanatics, they were scientists—rocket experts, nuclear physicists, and intelligence experts. They had banded together to study our UFO reports because they were convinced that some of the UFOs that were being reported were interplanetary spaceships.[18]

If this were the case, why weren't these scientists announcing their personal convictions to the public at large? The answer is quite simple. *Facts* about UFOs were classified. Absolute *proof* was lacking. As Ruppelt so aptly put it:

> Normally scientists are a cautious lot and stick close to proven facts . . . but when they know that there is a sign on a door that says "Classified Briefing in Progress," inhibitions collapse like theories that explain all UFOs away. People say just what they think.[19]

It was about this point in time that the CIA-sponsored Robertson Panel sessions were held in secret. Since Ruppelt and later Air Force releases about the panel's conclusions are at variance with each other, we will probably never know what the panel actually accomplished and concluded. One thing is certain, however: the UFO was systematically debunked by the Air Force from that point of time onward. Year by year the UFO sightings continued and year by year the Air Force issued typical releases to the national press:

> To date, no unidentified aerial phenomenon has given any indication of threat to national security; there has been no evidence submitted to or discovered by the Air Force that unidentified sightings represented technological developments or principles beyond the range of our present day scientific knowledge; and finally, there has been nothing in way of evidence or other data to indicate that these unidentified sightings were extraterrestrial vehicles under intelligent control.[20]

This particular release is dated February 15, 1964.

Then, in 1968, an enterprising UFO buff discovered that a

space science textbook used at the Air Force Academy plainly
stated that *there was evidence* for the extraterrestrial origin of
UFOs. I have already quoted from this text several times. In any
event, the UFO buff secured a copy of the text and sold a story
about his discovery to a national newspaper.[21] When the news
article was called to my attention, I immediately sought to obtain
the textbook through a contact I knew who was an Air Force
officer. Because of his position, he was able to secure a copy of
the complete textbook from the academy. However, when he
turned to the section on UFOs, he found that it had literally been
ripped out and replaced with photostats of typewritten sheets with
unmatching page numbers! A letter accompanied the textbook
explaining that the *removed* section was outdated! My friend
rightly observed, in his letter to me, "How does such material,
especially if they are citing historical items, become outdated?"[22]

Nonplussed by this turn of events, I turned to still another
contact for help. I was determined to see what the Air Force was
apparently attempting to hide. Several weeks later, I managed to
obtain photostats of the pertinent pages from the textbook. It was
very interesting indeed and contained statements that were completely contradictory to the Air Force press release just quoted.
For example:

> The most stimulating theory for us is that UFOs are material
> objects which are either "manned" or remote-controlled by
> beings who are alien to this planet. *There is some evidence
> supporting this* viewpoint [italics mine].[23]

Among the evidence presented were several classical cases.
One of these, briefly mentioned in chapter two, had taken place
at Socorro, New Mexico, on April 24, 1964. It involved a highly
trustworthy police officer who had seen a UFO land and walked
within one hundred feet of it before it took off. The Air Force
text states that Officer Lonnie Zamora had driven as close as he
could to the object before leaving the police cruiser and approaching it on foot. The following account revealed details about this
sighting that had never been printed before in regard to the
occupants he had observed near the strange craft:

He radioed that he was investigating a possible wreck and then worked his car up onto the mesa and over the edge of the gully. He parked short, and when he walked the final few feet to the edge, he was amazed to see that it was not a car but instead was a weird egg-shaped object about fifteen feet long, white in color and resting on short metal legs. Beside it, unaware of his presence were two humanoids dressed in silvery coveralls. They seemed to be working on a portion of the underside of the object. Zamora was still standing there, surprised, when they suddenly noticed him and dove out of sight around the object. Zamora also headed the other way, back toward his car. He glanced back at the object just as a bright blue flame shot down from the underside. Within seconds the egg-shaped thing rose out of the gully with "an ear-splitting roar." The object was out of sight over the nearby mountains almost immediately, and Sergeant Zamora was moving in the opposite direction almost as fast when he met Sergeant Sam Chavez who was responding to Zamora's earlier radio calls. Together they investigated the gully and found the bushes charred and still smoking where the blue flame had jetted down on them. About the charred area were four deep marks where the metal legs had been. . . . An official investigation was launched that same day, and all data obtained supported the stories of Zamora and Chavez. It is rather difficult to label this episode a hoax, and it is also doubtful that both Zamora and Chavez shared portions of the same hallucination.[24]

Other samples of evidence employed by the Air Force Academy textbook to support the *extraterrestrial visitors* hypothesis was the famous Betty and Barney Hill case investigated by Walter Webb of NICAP. Concerning the description of UFO occupants by Zamora, the Hills and many others who have observed occupants near landed UFOs, the Air Force text continues:

The most commonly described alien is about three and one-half feet tall, has a round head (helmet?), arms reaching to or below his knees, and is wearing a silvery space suit or coveralls. Other aliens appear to be essentially the same as earthmen, while still others have particularly wide (wrap-around) eyes and mouths with very thin lips. And, there is a rare group reported as about four feet tall, weight of around 35 pounds, and covered with thick hair or fur (clothing?). Members of this last group are described as being extremely strong.[25]

Reports of such UFO landings with occupants by trustworthy people are more widespread than most people think. Dr. William T. Powers, assistant to Dr. J. Allen Hynek, gives us some interesting statistics along these lines in the pages of the prestigious journal of the American Association for the Advancement of Science, *Science.*

> Over 200 world-wide landings were reported for the year 1954 . . . many with occupants. . . . Over 100 witnessed by more than one person. . . . In all these sightings at least 624 persons were involved, and only 98 of these people were alone. [18 cases involved independent groups] In 13 sightings, there were more than 10 witnesses for each.[26]

This book contains just a small fraction of the known UFO record. Because of my circumstances, the majority of cases reported in this book are highly localized. The significant fact is, however, that this local sample is in harmony with the global record. People are seeing and reporting the same types of flying objects whether they are in rural New Hampshire or a plantation in South Africa. What are they observing? They describe metallic, machine-like objects in the air and on the ground. A small percentage include the sighting of occupants associated with the objects. *What* and *who* are they? Well-witnessed and documented global reports of this nature cannot rationally be explained in terms of *mysticism, hallucinations, hoaxes, conventional objects, natural phenomena,* or *secret weapons.* Only the *extraterrestrial visitors* hypothesis fits *all* the reported facts about UFOs. Indeed, the Air Academy text concludes that:

> This leaves us with the unpleasant possibility of alien visitors to our planet. . . . However, the data are not well correlated and what questionable data there are suggest the existence of at least three and maybe four different groups of aliens (possibly at different stages of development). This too is difficult to accept. It implies the existence of intelligent life on a majority of the planets in our solar system, or a surprisingly strong interest in Earth by members of other solar systems.[27]

If UFOs do represent visitation of aliens from other worlds, the question immediately arises—*Why no contact?*

Why No Contact?

The Air Force text that I have been quoting from answers this question in several ways:

> 1. We may be the object of intensive sociological and psychological study. In such studies, you usually avoid disturbing the test subject's environment.
> 2. You do not *contact* a colony of ants, and humans may seem that way to any aliens (variation: a zoo is fun to visit, but you don't *contact* the lizards).
> 3. Such contact may have already taken place secretly.
> 4. Such contact may have taken place on a different plane of awareness and we are not yet sensitive to communications on such a plane. These are just a few reasons. You may add to the list as you desire.[28]

We could indeed add to this provocative list. If UFOs are hostile and are planning a classical *invasion,* it would be to the advantage of an advanced reconaissance party to maintain complete aloofness from us until a larger force arrived. Hopefully, such is not the case. However, the reverse might be true. They may, in spite of their technological advantage, consider us too dangerous to contact! Under the heading Human Fear and Hostility, the Air Force Academy text makes the following observations.

> Contacting humans is downright dangerous. Think about that for a moment! On the microscopic level our bodies reject and fight (through production antibodies) any alien material; this process helps us fight off disease but it also sometimes results in allergenic reactions to innocuous materials. On the macroscopic (psychological and sociological) level we are antagonistic to beings that are "different." For proof of that, just watch how an odd child is treated by other children, or how a minority group is socially deprived, or how the Arabs feel about the Israelis (Chinese vs Japanese, Turks vs Greeks, etc.) In case you are hesitant to extend that concept to the treatment of aliens, let me point out that in very ancient times, possible extraterrestrials may have been treated as Gods, but in the last two thousand

years, the evidence is that any possible aliens have been ripped
apart by mobs, shot and shot at, physically assaulted . . . and
in general treated with fear and aggression. In Ireland about
1,000 A.D., supposed airships were treated as "demon-ships."
In Lyons, France, "admitted" space travellers were killed [840
A.D.].[29]

The text then goes on to document a few more recent events.

More recently, on 24 July 1957, Russian anti-aircraft batteries
on the Kouril Islands opened fire on UFOs. Although all Soviet
anti-aircraft batteries on the Islands were in action, no hits were
made. The UFOs were luminous and moved very fast. We too
have fired on UFOs. About ten o'clock one morning, a radar
site near a fighter base picked up a UFO doing 700 mph. The
UFO then slowed to 100 mph, and two F-86's were scrambled
to intercept. Eventually, one F-86 closed on the UFO at about
3,000 feet altitude. The UFO began to accelerate away but the
pilot still managed to get within 500 yards of the target for a
short period of time. It was definitely saucer-shaped. As the
pilot pushed the F-86 at top speed, the UFO began to pull
away. When the range reached 1,000 yards, the pilot armed his
guns and fired in an attempt to down the saucer. He failed, and
the UFO pulled away rapidly, vanishing in the distance.[30]

A similar incident occurred on June 26, 1972, at Fort Beau-
fort, South Africa. Investigating police fired at a glowing metallic
object on the ground from a distance of only eight yards. It took
off with a humming sound into the brush.

Even UFO occupants have been shot at! The Air Force text
describes such a case very vividly.

On Sunday evening, 21 August 1955, eight adults and three
children were on the Sutton Farm (one-half mile from Kelly,
Kentucky) when, according to them, one of the children saw
a brightly glowing UFO settle behind the barn, out of sight
from where he stood. Other witnesses on nearby farms also
saw the object. However, the Suttons dismissed it as a "shooting
star," and did not investigate. Approximately thirty minutes later
(at 8 P.M.), the family dogs began barking so two of the men
went to the back door and looked out. Approximately 50 feet
away and coming toward them was a creature wearing a glowing

silvery suit. It was about three and one-half feet tall with a
large round head and very long arms. It had large webbed hands
which were equipped with claws. The two Suttons grabbed a
twelve-gauge shotgun and a 22-caliber pistol, and fired at close
range. They could hear the pellets and bullets ricochet as if off
of metal. The creature was knocked down, but jumped up and
scrambled away. The Suttons retreated into the house, turned
off all inside lights, and turned on the porch light. At that
moment, one of the women who was peeking out of the dining
room window discovered that a creature with some sort of helmet
and wide slit eyes was peeking back at her. She screamed, the
men rushed in and started shooting. The creature was knocked
backwards but again scrambled away without apparent harm.
More shooting occurred (a total of about 50 rounds) over the
next 20 minutes and the creatures finally left (perhaps feeling
unwelcome?). After a two-hour wait (for safety), the Suttons
left too. By the time the police got there, the aliens were gone
but the Suttons would not move back to the farm. They sold it
and departed. This reported incident does bear out the contention though that *humans are dangerous* [italics mine]. At no
time in the story did the supposed aliens shoot back, although
one is left with the impression that the described creatures were
having fun scaring humans.[31]

The whole concept of communication with superintelligent
aliens is so novel and so outside of man's past and contemporary
experience that he finds it hard to visualize or even take the possibility seriously. It would do us well to consider the fact that
although man has evolved along with a myriad of other creatures
on this planet, he has yet to truly communicate with any of them
except in the family pet sense. Why? We do not know *how* to and
we do not *want* to. Perhaps this is because we believe that other
so-called *lower* life-forms are not capable of overt communication
in the human sense of the word. This is not to say that we are
not intellectually interested in these animals. We go to great
lengths to study their habits, environment and idiosyncracies. Consider the following analogy.

A black bear is out rummaging for food in a heavily wooded
area that he shares with a goodly number of other creatures.
Sniffing the air cautiously, he cuts across a large field on the way
to a river to fish for salmon. Suddenly a foreign noise coming from

above causes him to look up. Terrified, he sees a strange, noisy, whirring, birdlike thing hovering directly above him. He starts to run back to the woods with the "huge bird" in hot pursuit. Suddenly a sharp but short-lived pain stabs into his side. He continues to run but an inexplicable feeling of drowsiness overwhelms him. The bear slumps to the ground in a sound sleep.

The "bird" lands. It is a helicopter and out of it step several scientists. One still holds the rifle that has just fired a tranquilizer-filled dart into the fleeing bear. Carefully, a wildlife biologist tags the bear and places a radio transmitter collar and temperature probe about the sleeping bear's neck. The scientists then board the helicopter and depart.

Later, the bear stirs. Perhaps vague images of the frightening chase still linger in his mind but most likely are dismissed as having been a bad dream brought on by his eating some decayed rabbit meat earlier that morning! So, off to the river he lumbers. There are fat migrating salmon just waiting to be caught and he is hungry.

Seven hundred miles above him, a highly sophisticated satellite dubbed Nimbus wheels around the planet in a predetermined course. It signals the radio transmitter attached to the bear, which in turn begins to transmit data gathered by special sensors. Nimbus, in return, retransmits the signals to a ground radio station at Fairbanks, Alaska.[32] The data is then sent to Goddard Space Flight Center at Maryland, where it emerges as a computer readout. Meanwhile, the bear continues to fish, hunt, sleep and hibernate. He remains completely oblivious to the fact that his bodily functions and exact whereabouts are being monitored by a super-intelligent species—man!

How could a bear even begin to comprehend such a thing? Who would seriously consider attempting to communicate this knowledge to the bear. The answer is obvious—no one!

Have you ever considered that we might be thought about in the same way by highly advanced beings from another planet?

"But," you say, "we are different. We are rational beings and are part of a technological society."

Such a reaction could be analogous to the following situation.

For several months, a new air route caused modern airliners to overfly some remote New Guinea Islands. These huge shiny "birds" caused awe and consternation on the part of a primitive people who dwelt on these islands. One day, several islanders were collecting shellfish washed up on the beach when, suddenly, one of the huge shiny "birds" buzzed the handy shoreline. The captain of the airliner was giving his passengers a special sightseeing treat!

The natives ran back and reported to the chief and the witch doctor that these "birds" carried people inside of them. They excitedly told how they actually saw such people waving at them through holes in the bird's body! After much consultation with the witch doctor and elders, the chief told the tribe that it had been decided such a story could not possibly be true. If people were flying inside the birds, surely they would land and trade bones and colored feathers with them! After all, their tribe was known throughout the island chain for their carved bones and beautiful feathers.

We smile at this story and find it quite hard to accept if it is applied to us. However, we should not overlook the fact that this story would not be completely analogous to the situation we are presently discussing. The aborigine is *man*. The passengers in the low-flying aircraft are also *man*. What would extraterrestrial aliens be? How would one communicate with a superintelligent being from a planet and environment perhaps totally alien to that of the planet Earth? Let us see what some experts think about such a situation.

Communication with Aliens

In September 1965, a military electronics conference was held to discuss communication with extraterrestrial intelligence. The sessions were chaired by Dr. Harold Wooster, Air Force Office of Scientific Research. It would do well for us at this point to relive some of the minutes of these thought-provoking sessions as we consider the subject *communication with aliens*.[33]

Dr. Wooster opened the meeting by introducing the subject and members of a carefully selected panel of experts.

In a discussion of this nature, we quite obviously need a linguist—a very special kind of linguist who specializes in monolingual field work . . . I believe that Paul L. Garvin fills the bill perfectly.

Obviously, too, a cryptologist was needed. I chose Lambros D. Callimahos, a highly qualified expert from the Department of Defense.

Let us examine the word "extraterrestrial." *Terrestrial* means "earth or land" and *extra* means "outside of." An ideal choice would be someone who has actually lived with, worked with, and talked with an extraterrestrial species. Therefore we have with us Dr. John Lilley, who works with dolphins.

William O. Davis is a physicist, a rather free-thinking one, who was invited on the grounds that we should have somebody on the panel whose comments are seldom predictable.

"Extraterrestrial" has other connotations. Since there is an astronomical aspect to this whole question, a learned astronomer would be an excellent person to have on the panel. And so we have Father Heyden.

Panel members will each have an opportunity to state their positions. They will then be allowed to—using a nice sociological word—interact.

Now that Dr. Wooster has kindly introduced the panel, let us summarize what each had to say about this fascinating subject. We shall first hear from Dr. Paul Garvin.

THE LINGUIST

I should first like to say that I am professionally concerned with "terrestrial" communication—that is, with natural language. The field of linguistics that I represent on the panel is limited mainly to this aspect, although obviously we are forced to recognize that there are other forms of communication. We deal primarily with natural languages, so that in a certain sense I should be the last person to ask to discuss the question of extraterrestrial communication. . . . The most common "substance" for transmitting natural language is sound, and sound of a particular kind. There is a certain frequency range, a certain pace, at which the sounds are produced. The sounds have well-known characteristics—such as vowel properties, consonant properties, etc.—and certain other much less well-known characteristics.

In addition, in a situation of monolingual field work we take advantage of a particular kind of behavior, which I like to call naming behavior—that is, the observation that in all human societies people have the habit of pointing at things and having consistent names for them. Naming behavior is one essential prerequisite for this type of monolingual communication.

Another question that arises is: What kinds of extraterrestrial beings could we communicate with in this form—that is, in a form analogous to the one used when we talk to other humans? One problem is that we presuppose a structurally complex system; this assumption, in turn, requires that the entity using a language similar to ours be of a high order of complexity as far as intelligence and, therefore, brain and nervous system are concerned. So when we talk about communication, these beings would need to have a high order of intelligence if we hope to succeed in the use of linguistic methods in establishing communication. Furthermore, they would presumably have to have a type of intelligence somewhat similar to the human intelligence, at least in the sense that the complexities which we use in signaling by natural languages might be shared by these beings.

Can we conceive of an equally flexible communication system that would not have some of the properties of natural language? Is it conceivable for instance, to have a very flexible communication system that does not differentiate between things that are like letters and things that are like words?

The next question involves the substantive characteristics of human language. Again, in establishing monolingual communication we take a great many things for granted. Just try to imagine how you could establish communication by pointing without being able to use your voice to name the things you point at. This is very hard for us to visualize, so the first prerequisite is that *there should be vocal signals.*

The second prerequisite is that not only should there be vocal signals but that *these be within a certain frequency range,* because obviously if the other beings use frequencies that we are unable to hear or to manipulate, we will find it very difficult to learn their system of communication.

Another characteristic of the substantive aspect of natural languages is that there is a phonological system—and by that I mean the details of the functioning of vowels and consonants—which is correlated to a certain structure of the human vocal tract. We have a tongue, we have vocal cords, we have teeth, we have different cavities in our respiratory tract from vocal cords up.

All of these things are taken for granted when you approach another human being for the purposes of establishing communication, and by taking them for granted you unconsciously are able to manipulate them. With another human being you anticipate being able at least in part to imitate what he says. If you successfully establish communication and you can correlate your gestures with some noises that you hear, there is a chance that you will be able to repeat the "conversation." However, the prerequisite for this procedure is a human vocal tract, which implies the presence of vocal cords and a mobile tongue, as well as musculature that allow the sizes of cavities and the entrances and exits of the cavities to be manipulated.

This means, at least in terms of evolution on earth, that you have to have erect gait, which allows you to develop the kind of skull and jaw structure that in turn permits the development of a vocal tract. There have been experiments, for instance, in trying to teach certain of the higher primates to speak, and one of the difficulties was that they haven't the necessary physiological and anatomical attributes. Whether such attributes are present is, in fact, the basic question that a linguist would ask.

In order for extraterrestrial communication to work, what kind of extraterrestrials can we deal with? The answer is that they should be, preferably, beings with erect gait, vocal organs, a frequency range not too far different from our own, some pointing organs, and a pace of their physiologic processes that is in some way commensurate with our own.

If these beings are substantially different from this, then linguistics does not readily have anything to contribute. I will not say that we couldn't possibly advance the field and contribute even in very strange cases, but it would be considerably more difficult.

The next person to speak was Dr. Callimahos of the National Security Agency.

THE CRYPTOLOGIST

We are not alone in the universe. A few years ago, this notion seemed farfetched; today, the existence of extraterrestrial intelligence is taken for granted by most scientists. Sir Bernard Lovell, one of the world's leading radio astronomers, has calculated that, even allowing for a margin of error of 5000 percent, there must be in our own galaxy about 100 million stars that have planets of the right chemistry, dimensions, and temperature to support organic evolution. If we consider that our own galaxy, the Milky Way, represents only one of more than a billion galaxies similar to ours in the observable universe, the number of stars that could support some form of life is, to reach for a word, astronomical.

If another civilization were trying to establish communication with us, it would first embark on attention-getting signals of such a nature that we could distinguish them from random cosmic noise; once we receive a recognizable signal, we have a good chance of understanding the message. For example, they could start with trains of signals corresponding to the natural numbers 1, 2, 3 . . . , followed perhaps by prime numbers. They might continue with equal-length extended signals consisting of start and stop impulses, with occasional pulses in between; when these signals are aligned flush over one another, they would show a circle, the Pythagorean theorem, or similar geometric design. These attention-getting signals would be followed by early "language lessons," interspersed with items of technical information to help bring us up to "their" level.

It may be assumed that the sense of sight, or an equivalent, is possessed by all higher forms of life; the problems of communication could thus be greatly simplified through the medium of a "raster" representation, such as that of a television screen.

After we resolve our pressing scientific questions, it might be appropriate to make discreet inquiries as to how we could live in harmony and peace with our fellow man—that is, if we aren't eaten or otherwise ingested by the superior civilization that had the good fortune to contact us. But as far as the cryptologist is concerned, he (and generations of his descendants who might experience the thrill of their lives when we hear from "them") must keep a level head and be prepared to cope with problems that are out of this world, so to speak.

THE SPECIALIST

Dr. John C. Lilley, director of the Communication Research Institute, was introduced to the panel. He founded this independent organization in 1959 for studies on methods of communication between man and other species. He is the author of *Man and the Dolphin* and coauthor, with Dr. Ashley Montagu, of *The Dolphin in History*. He has also written some ninety published papers on his scientific research in this area. His concluding thoughts about the subject at hand are somewhat humbling. If true, they would strike a hard blow to man's already faltering ego.

In essence, then, this is the problem of communicating with any nonhuman species or being or mind or computer. We do not have, however, the full support in basic beliefs in the scientific community for these postulates. Obviously, we as a species do not believe, for example, that a whale, with a brain six times the size of ours, has a computer worth dealing with. Instead, we kill whales and use them as fertilizer. We also eat them. To be fair to the killer whale, I know of no instance in which a killer whale has eaten a human, but I know of many instances in which humans have eaten killer whales.

Therefore, on an historical basis, I do not feel that at present there is much chance that any species of greater attainments than ours will want to communicate with us. The dolphins want to communicate only with those people who are willing to live with them on the terms the dolphins set up and that certain kinds of human beings set up. Other types the dolphins drive away. Every year we lose people from the dolphin research program. Usually it is because of fear of the power of these animals and fear of damage, even though in the history of the laboratory no one has yet been injured by the dolphins. Sometimes we think that these people who are lost are projecting their own hostilities outward onto the animals in a very unrealistic fashion. The people who survive either realize that this mechanism is operating and conquer it, or else their nature is such that they do not have hostilities to project.

THE PHYSICIST

As Dr. Wooster had predicted, Dr. William O. Davis's comments were certainly "free-thinking," to say the least. They prove to have been the most speculative and appropriate contribution of the whole conference!

Now, let's assume we discover that there is life. This life need not have the same chemical form as our life. All that is required for it to be life is that there be a local reversal of the second law of thermodynamics; and if we see that there is, we suspect there is something living present. If we find that nuclear reactions that we know take place in a certain way are going

the other way on a certain planet, then I would look for life
at the nuclear level.
How do we communicate? Well, we have talked about the
linguistic approach. We have talked about Dr. Lilley's approach
with non-human forms. I think I would like to break the
problem down a little more.
There are really three different cases we should worry about.
First of all is an encounter with a lower order of intelligence
than our own. This would be the case if we should land on a
planet and find it occupied with life at the level of bees or cows
and presumably nonintelligent, or at least not yet at our level.
In this particular case, I think that the best we could hope for
would be the type of communication we establish with dogs
and horses, a symbiosis or—and this is disputable—a telepathic
rapport with them. It would be unlikely that we could establish
communication at the verbal level or at the level of symbology.
The *second* case is where we find people of precisely equal
evolution. Now, this is very improbable, as was pointed out
earlier. Even 15 years in our history would make a tremendous
difference, either backwards or forwards. If you look at the
technological trend curves, for example, you find that by the year
2000 everything is asymptotic, and it is extremely likely that
technological revolution per se will have played itself out by that
time. Other trends indicate that from here on increasing emphasis
is going to be on understanding the mind and how it operates.
Some of the work that Dr. Puharich has done is a little controversial, too, such as studying extrasensory perception with
people having extreme talents, which indicates that there are
relationships between these ESP talents and other natural phenomena, and indicates that as we go on we may be able to
learn how to improve our ability to communicate, at least at
the symbolic level, by ESP means. Certainly even today we do
a great deal, I suspect, of our communication at the emotional
level by extrasensory means.
If we were to encounter somebody of equal intelligence, I
think we would have a problem. We would undoubtedly fight
them. This, to my way of thinking, is the least probable and
the most dangerous of the three cases.
In many respects the most probable encounter is with a
higher form of life, or at least a more advanced form, because
these beings would be more likely to reach us first than vice-
versa. If we assume that they understand more about the mind
than we do—and let's say they understand more about ESP or
it turns out to be a human-type phenomenon—they should be

able to detect us. After all, we know all kinds of fields associated with the physical world, the world of entropy. It is not illogical to assume that life may have as yet detected fields and radiation associated with it. They wouldn't have to scour the whole universe for us. They would simply focus their life-detecting device.

The nice thing about this hypothetical contact is that communication would be their problem. We wouldn't have to worry too much about it. They would come to us. As a matter of fact, I strongly suspect that the first communication is very likely to be telepathic; perhaps it will just involve a sense of being friendly. As Dr. Lilley pointed out earlier, some dolphins want to communicate and others don't, and they apparently can detect which people wish to communicate with them and which don't. I think that if this first form of communication were achieved, more detailed forms would probably follow.

The problem of language is that you require some kind of a cultural reference. In just learning to speak a European language, for example, you may know all the words and be able to translate them into English, but if you know nothing of the culture of the country, you will not really understand the subtleties of what you are saying. This sort of problem will be incredibly more complicated in communication with an alien race. In fact, I suspect that language communication will be almost the last thing to take place.

In summary, I would say that the most probable case of communication with extraterrestrial beings is an encounter with a race more advanced than we; therefore, the problem would be primarily psychological on our part. We would undoubtedly be deeply upset by this state of affairs. Thus these beings, if they are really advanced and subtle, would know this and would approach us in such a way as not to frighten us. If I were on their staff, I think I would use my advanced knowledge to learn the languages of the human race through one means or another, imitate human structure and appearance, and send representatives down to mingle with the earth's people. Gradually I would begin to understand the earth's culture and develop means of communication to a point at which at a later time communication could be established in the proper verbal manner. Thus, it is entirely possible and maybe even probable that *extraterrestrial races are already amongst us!* [italics mine]

Father Francis J. Heyden was the closing speaker and tempered the preceding presentations by discussing the astronomical aspects to this intriguing subject.

THE ASTRONOMER

Let's assume that we do pick up a communication. Suppose this "Rosetta Stone of space" does sometimes occur. If the signal were coming from a planet, probably some thousands of light-years away, the energy needed for that transmission would be roughly equivalent to all the energy that we can now generate on this earth at one time. Of course, it would take more than an International Geophysical Year to get wired up for it on earth.

If the same signal were coming from about 100,000 light-years away the dilution would become much greater. . . . I can't say as an astronomer that we have ever heard any such signal. However, if we did find something that could be interpreted, let's suppose that the thing said, "Hello there." We would answer by asking "Where are you?" It might take about 400 years for a signal to come back, saying, "Out here." . . . I can't predict whether we will ever have telepathic tennis players racketing news back and forth from distant parts of space. I hope that when we do unravel the mysteries of telepathy it will not be tied down by the speed of light, which brings down a light curtain upon all of us when we try to talk about interplanetary or interstellar communication. Telepathy may, as Aristotle said, need *no time to travel through space* [italics mine].

One can sense already the tremendous difficulties associated with any attempt on our part to communicate with alien beings from another planet. We can only speculate about the tremendous cultural impact that would result if discovery of and eventual *contact* with superior alien beings were actually to take place. The advent of UFO sightings in this country and abroad probably signifies that we are already on the threshold of this mind-shattering event! If accounts of telepathic communication with aliens (such as the case of Mr. and Mrs. Barney Hill) are true, communication has already begun!

NOTES

1. James E. McDonald "UFOs—An International Scientific Problem," p. 15.
2. Major Donald G. Carpenter, *Introductory Space Science, II.*
3. Lynn Catoe, UFO Bibliography, Library of Congress.
4. Carpenter, *op. cit.,* p. 3 (1970 edition).
5. *Idem.*
6. Edward U. Condon, *Scientific Study of Unidentified Flying Objects,* p. 143.
7. Personal Files, UFO Report No. 55-1.
8. Carpenter, *op. cit.,* p. 143.
9. William Markowitz, "The Physics and Metaphysics of Unidentified Flying Objects," *Science,* CLVII, 1274-1279.
10. Carpenter, *op. cit.,* p. 466 (1968 edition).
11. Personal Files, UFO Report No. 72-10.
12. McDonald, *op. cit.,* p. 19.
13. Project Sign, Technical Report No. F-TR-2274-IA: "Unidentified Aerial Objects," p. 25.
14. Carpenter, *op. cit.,* p. 3 (1970 edition).
15. Edward J. Ruppelt, *The Report on Unidentified Flying Objects,* p. 41.
16. *Ibid.,* p. 45.
17. Ruppelt, *op. cit.,* pp. 29, 30.
18. Ruppelt, *op. cit.,* p. 109.
19. *Ibid.,* pp. 191, 192.
20. Project Bluebook, Public Information Sheet, February 15, 1964, p. 2.
21. Lloyd Mallan, *The National Enquirer,* October 11, 1970.
22. Personal Files, correspondence dated November 13, 1970.
23. Carpenter, *op. cit.,* p. 461 (1968 edition).
24. Ibid., p. 460.
25. Ibid., pp. 461, 462.
26. William T. Powers, Letters, *Science,* April 7, 1967.
27. Carpenter, *op. cit.,* pp. 466, 467 (1968 edition).
28. *Ibid.,* p. 462.
29. *Idem.*
30. *Ibid.,* pp. 462, 463.
31. *Ibid.,* p. 463.
32. *The National Geographic,* "Studying Wildlife by Satellite," January 1973, pp. 120-123.
33. *IEE Spectrum,* "Communication with extraterrestrial intelligence," March 1966, pp. 153-163.

15

THE IMPACT—
DISINTEGRATION
OR SURVIVAL?

If superintelligence is discovered, the results become quite unpredictable. . . . It has been speculated that, of all groups, scientists and engineers might be the most devastated by the discovery of relatively superior creatures.

Brookings Institution
House Report 242/1961

Edward J. Ruppelt, former chief of the United States Air Force Project Bluebook, wrote:

No one . . . in the Air Force . . . was qualified to give a final yes or no answer to the UFO problem. Giving a final answer would require a serious decision—probably one of the most serious since the beginning of man.[1]

These are strong words. They give us some insight into the philosophy behind the Pentagon's public information statements about UFOs. In this chapter, we are going to *assume* that a final answer has been secretly determined and acted upon at the very highest military and governmental levels. The final answer is that UFOs are alien machines from an unknown source not of this earth. If such were the case, what implications would such a dramatic discovery hold for mankind?

Military Implications

The United States Air Force is heavily committed to defending the air space of this country and to retaliate in the event of

286

an enemy attack. In order to carry out this mission, it employs some of the finest aircraft, missiles and support systems in the world. However, time and time again its weapons systems have proved no match for the UFO. We have already noted in the previous chapter that one admitted attempt by an Air Force fighter to shoot down a saucer-shaped UFO ended in total failure.[2] This pilot was fortunate. Others have not been so fortunate.

During the latter part of 1955, UFO reports were so abundant in the state of Ohio that Leonard H. Stringfield, a respected civilian UFO researcher, was asked to cooperate with local Air Force authorities. On September 9, 1955, the Air Defense Command cleared his home telephone to report UFOs directly to the Air Force Filter Center in Columbus, Ohio. Civilians reporting UFOs to his home phone had their observational data relayed to the Air Defense Command for immediate action if so required. Stringfield's research activities exposed him to a variety of UFO information from Ground Observer Corps observers, active and reserve Air Force officers. In a privately published book, he relates some of this data. Some of it concerned information relating to Air Force fighter aircraft that were lost when attempting to intercept UFOs. He quotes a source that quoted General Benjamin Chidlaw (who had been in charge of our continental air defenses) as saying that "we have many men and planes trying to intercept them."[3] During the UFO wave in the Cincinnati area in 1955, a Ground Observer Corps supervisor told Stringfield that an Air Force officer had admitted to him that the Air Force was losing many aircraft during UFO intercept missions.[4] Another reliable military source informed him about a case involving a jet fighter falling out of the sky as base operations vectored it into the vicinity of two UFOs recorded on radar. The plane crashed into the sea, and the adjutant of the overseas American air base wrote the surviving relatives that the pilot and radar operator had met death during a routine mission. Such stories admittedly fall into the *hearsay* class, but the source of the data in each case would appear to be trustworthy.

One of the most fantastic accounts of this nature was recently brought to my attention by the *Mutual UFO Network*.[5] It in-

volved the disappearance of a jet fighter and its radar officer
during a UFO intercept mission originating from Otis Air Force
Base in June of 1953. Here is a written report from one of the
airmen who investigated this bizarre event—Master Sergeant (retired) Clarence O. Dargie:

> This is an account of the disappearance of an F-94C jet
> fighter-interceptor which has puzzled me for many years. I have
> personal knowledge of the circumstances because I was directly
> involved in the resultant investigation. . . . This happened at Otis
> Air Force Base . . . on Cape Cod about 12 miles east of Buzzards
> Bay at the edge of old Camp Edwards. Just after dark an F-94C
> with classified electronic gear aboard took off in a westerly
> direction. The crew consisted of the pilot, Captain Suggs, and
> the radar officer [R/O], Lt. Barkoff. According to the pilot's
> sworn testimony, shortly after breaking ground—at an altitude
> of 1500 feet over the Base Rifle Range—the engine quit func-
> tioning and the entire electrical system failed. As the aircraft's
> nose dropped towards the ground at an ever-increasing angle,
> the pilot stopcocked the throttle and yelled to the R/O to bail
> out.
>
> The normal bail-out sequence in this particular type of air-
> craft calls for the R/O to jettison the canopy by pulling a lever
> which activates explosive bolts, then pulling a second handle
> which ejects him from the aircraft by means of an explosive
> device under the seat. The pilot, upon hearing the second ex-
> plosion, which tells him that the R/O is clear of the aircraft, is
> then free to eject. In this case, however, the pilot ejected im-
> mediately after the R/O jettisoned the canopy because the air-
> craft had now descended to about 600 feet at a steep angle and
> was about 3 seconds from impact.
>
> The parachute opened and acted as an airbrake to slow the
> pilot down and stopped his forward motion just as his feet hit
> the ground. He landed in the backyard of a house near the base,
> and the first indication that the owner had that there was some-
> thing amiss was when he heard Captain Suggs calling out to his
> R/O, "Bob, where are you?"
>
> The R/O could not be found and the pilot had a difficult
> time convincing the owner that his aircraft had crashed because
> the man had been sitting near an open screened window and had
> heard nothing. The crippled plane should have crashed near
> where Suggs landed but it wasn't there.

This caused one of the most extensive and intensive searches I have ever seen. . . . The Cape was literally combed, both on foot and from the air for three months without turning up a thing. The aircraft and the R/O were never found.

There are all sorts of points to ponder in this case. For example, if the aircraft did not impact on land, then it must have somehow reached Buzzards Bay some 12 miles away and crashed in the water. If this happened then someone would most certainly have seen or heard it because the bay is crowded with pleasure and commercial watercraft at this time of year. No one saw or heard it. In addition, the aircraft had a full fuel supply aboard and if it did not explode in flames on impact, it would have left a large fuel slick on the surface. There was no fuel slick. The Navy dragged the bay from end to end but no wreckage was found.

In view of the fact that the pilot stopcocked the throttle and the aircraft was descending at a steep angle only 600 feet from the ground when the pilot ejected, we can discount the possibility that the crash occurred in the water. This leaves us with the only other alternative and that is the fact that the aircraft, in all logic, impacted on the ground. This whole event took place in a well-populated area at the height of the tourist season. If it did crash in that area, it would have created a detonation heard for miles; yet, no explosion was heard, no flames were seen and no wreckage was found.

What caused the complete and simultaneous failure of all engine and electrical systems? Aircraft systems have their own separate power sources so if one power source fails, the others are not affected; yet the pilot swears that, without warning, the cockpit lights, navigation lights, instruments, radio and engine simply went dead.

In the final analysis, it would seem that the aircraft and the R/O literally vanished into some form of oblivion in the 3 seconds between the time that Captain Suggs left the aircraft at 600 feet and the time it should have crashed to earth. As far as I know, the aircraft and the R/O were never found. At least it hadn't been located as of December 1954, when I was reassigned to an overseas station. Where are they? . . . Some of the circumstances involved in this case were classified and I have had to frame my story around them. Jets of this nature were dispatched to intercept aerial objects that failed to respond to radar identification. *It was on just this type of mission that this aircraft vanished* [italics mine].[6]

I attempted to find others who were stationed at Otis Air Force Base during the sighting time frame in order to supplement Mr. Dargie's account. I managed to talk to quite a few Air Force pilots who had been stationed at Otis and Westover Air Force Bases in Massachusetts but none during June of 1953. Interestingly enough, every pilot I talked to had had at least one experience with UFOs! The closest I came to independently verifying the event was a personal chat with a former R/O who had been discharged from Otis Air Force Base in May of 1953. He had continued flying with the Air National Guard stationed at nearby Logan Airport in Boston. He told me that he definitely remembers hearing the story passed around by Air National Guard pilots. Another person stationed at Logan in the Air Guard told me that F-94s were continually being dispatched to identify unknown targets picked up on radar. He said that returning pilots were not allowed to talk about the incidents but would often remark that if they hadn't seen it they never would have believed it! I checked on the background of Mr. Dargie through an acquaintance of mine on the staff of the *Mutual UFO Network* (MUFON). He knew the former master sergeant very well and vouched for his honesty and integrity. I requested further information from Mr. Dargie and he wrote me the following letter:

18 March 1973

Dear Ray,

Walt Andrus asked me to write to you about the Otis AFB case of the lost F-94C. I started this letter last week and am just getting around to finishing it now. I have been busy with quarter finals at school. I am going to school full-time at Southern Illinois University and, believe me, I really have to hump in order to keep up with these kids today.

I really don't have much more to add to what was written in the *Skylook* account. To the best of my knowledge, the aircraft was never found. As I recall, the canopy was found on the rifle range, which would indicate that whatever happened took place in close proximity to the airfield proper. I have since lost track of the people who worked on this case. The NCO in charge at that time was a Master Sergeant George Kimmel. I have no idea where he is now. I believe that the Operations Officer was a Major Ralph Nelson. The missing R/O was a Lieutenant Robert Barkoff. I believe he was from Detroit. His mother was either a widow or divorced. At least, there was no mention of his having a father. She arrived on the Cape shortly after the incident and stayed there until the search was called off in September.

I would appreciate it if you would pass on to me any further information you may discover. This has been puzzling me for over twenty years.

Sincerely,
CLARENCE O. DARGIE

I would add to Mr. Dargie's closing remarks that incidents like this have given our government and other governments plenty to worry about over the past two or more decades! In fact, just five months after the Otis AFB incident, a similar event occurred concerning an Air Force interceptor flying out of Kinross AFB in Northern Michigan. NICAP has thoroughly documented this case and the following summary is quoted from its impressive documentary—*The UFO Evidence.*

THE KINROSS CASE

On the night of November 23, 1953, an unidentified flying object was detected over Lake Superior by Air Defense Command radar. An F-89C all-weather interceptor was scrambled from Kinross AFB, near the Soo Locks in northern Michigan. Guided by radar, the jet sped northwest across the lake on an intercept course. On the radar screen, ground controllers saw the F-89 close in on the UFO blip, and then the two blips merged and faded from the screen. From all appearances, the aircraft and the UFO had collided. No trace of the jet has ever been found.

The last radar contact with the F-89 showed it to be at 8000 feet, 70 miles off Keeweenaw Point, and about 160 miles northwest of Soo Locks. Later, the Air Force reported that the "UFO" was identified by the F-89 as a Royal Canadian Air Force C-47. After identifying the friendly plane, the Air Force states, the F-89 turned back to base. From that time, "nothing of what happened is definitely known." (Air Force information sheet; copy on file at NICAP). The C-47 was "on a flight plan from

Winnipeg, Manitoba, to Sudbury, Ontario, Canada." (Air Force
letter to NICAP . . .)

The original report released by the Air Force PIO at Truax
AFB, Wisconsin, stated that contact was lost with the F-89 when
it appeared to merge with the UFO. There is no mention of
tracking the jet after that.[7]

NICAP investigation indicated that the Royal Canadian Air
Force had no record of one of its aircraft being in the Lake
Superior area on the date of the incident. On letter from Flight
Lt. C. F. Page, for the Chief of Staff, Royal Canadian Air Force
stated:

> A check of Royal Canadian Air Force records has revealed no
> report of an RCAF aircraft in the Lake Superior area on the
> above date.[8]

A double check with Canadian authorities by NICAP pro-
duced the same information. A letter from the Department of
National Defense, Royal Canadian Air Force from W. B. Totman,
Squadron Leader, Acting Director of Public Relations, stated:

> We have been unable to come up with any information re-
> garding an intercept of a RCAF C-47 by a USAF F-89 on No-
> vember 23, 1953.[9]

How does the Air Force account for the disappearance of the
F-89 interceptor along with its pilot, Lt. Felix Moncla, Jr. and
radar operator, Lt. R. R. Wilson? At least two fine aircraft and
three personnel vanished from the face of the earth within a
period of five months. How many other military aircraft have met
the same fate chasing UFOs? NICAP would have never known
about the Kinross event if the Public Information Officer at Truax
Air Force Base had not let the proverbial cat out of the bag. The
Pentagon completely denied the incident until it learned of the
PIO's statement to the Associated Press! The AP wire at Sault
Sainte Marie, Michigan read: "The plane was followed by radar
until it merged with an object 70 miles off Keeweenaw Point in
upper Michigan." The release, however, was short-lived. Other

than a short story in the early edition of the *Chicago Tribune* headlined, "Jet, Two Aboard, Vanishes Over Lake Superior," it was deleted from all other editions.[10] The Air Force information sheet on this case explains the bizarre incident away as follows:

> It is presumed by the officials at Norton AFB (Flying Safety Division) that the pilot probably suffered from vertigo and crashed into the lake.[11]

This is not a satisfactory answer. The weather reports for that day and time indicate that the pilot would have been flying on instruments. Vertigo (dizziness resulting from visual observation) would be very unlikely. There is also no explanation as to why radar tracked the aircraft perfectly for 160 miles and only lost contact when the blips of the aircraft and UFO merged. An intensive search failed to find any trace of the aircraft or its crew.

Other Air Force crewmen have been more fortunate. They have escaped with their lives although losing their aircraft during UFO intercepts. A tragic example, which involved loss of civilian lives and property, took place high in the skies above the village of Walesville, New York. On July 2, 1954, at 11:05 A.M., reports of an unidentified balloonlike object came into the Air Force Depot at Rome, New York. At the same time, F-94C aircraft number 51-13559 was diverted from a routine training flight to check on two unidentified radar tracks. The first was identified as a C-47 transport. The second was never identified. The official Air Force account states:

> As the pilot started a descent, he noted that the cockpit temperature increased abruptly. The increase in temperature caused the pilot to scan the instruments. The fire warning light was on . . . the engine was shut down and both crew members ejected successfully.[12]

The F-94C crashed into the village of Walesville and hit two buildings and an automobile. Four people were killed including two children. The pilots were forbidden to talk further about the incident. The official Air Force accident report stated that the

UFO was probably a balloon. During the Air Force-sponsored University of Colorado UFO Study, I received a letter from the administrative assistant to the project's director, Dr. Edward U. Condon. It read, in part:

> I am trying to obtain some information on a UFO sighting that occurred in July of 1954 in the Utica, New York, area, in which . . . jets were sent, on an "interceptor" mission, after a UFO. . . . There's a good deal of indication of an Air Force "conspiracy" or foul-up in communications. Frankly, on this case, I suspect the former.[13]

I was able to supply the names of the pilot and R/O for further follow-up, but all that appears in the University of Colorado UFO Study's final report is a few excerpts from the accident report. Major Donald E. Keyhoe, U.S.M.C. (retired), who was the director of NICAP at that period of time, also was unable to obtain further information on the hushed-up incident. The Air Force press desk merely told him that it was "a classified Air Defense report."[14]

Thanks to NICAP's obtaining formerly classified Project Bluebook Reports 1-12, former Bluebook chief Edward Ruppelt's admissions, and the fact that many former military personnel are now recounting their UFO experiences—civilian researchers are now documenting evidence that UFOs have consistently outclassed any aircraft we or any other country have in the skies! This also applies to ground-based weaponry.

During the UFO waves of especially 1966 and 1967, UFOs were making frequent appearances over this country's Minuteman Intercontinental Ballistic Missile sites. I understand that Titan ICBM sites were also visited by UFOs. During my course of work in the Minuteman Program Office within the defense industry, I talked with civilian and military personnel who were located on these ICBM bases. They informed me of the UFO sightings. What disturbed me was the reported electromagnetic effects from the UFOs that were affecting strategic electrical equipment essential to the operation of emplaced Minuteman missiles that our country counted upon for defense! Attempted intercepts by Air Force fighters proved futile. In one case, communications between land strike-teams and intercepting aircraft were completely blocked out by strong radio interference. Dr. J. Allen Hynek managed to obtain a nonclassified summary of this particular case and brought it to the public's attention in December of 1966. Excerpts from his report are as follows:

> On August 25, 1966, an Air Force officer in charge of a missile crew in North Dakota . . . found that his radio . . . was being interrupted. . . . He was in a concrete capsule 60 feet below the ground. . . . Other Air Force personnel on the surface reported seeing a UFO. . . . It appeared to be alternately climbing and descending. Simultaneously . . . radar . . . picked up the UFO at 100,000 feet. . . . When the UFO climbed, the static stopped. . . . It then appeared to land. . . . Missile-site control sent a strike-team . . . to check. When the team was about ten miles from the landing site, static disrupted radio contact with them. . . . The UFO took off. Another UFO was visually sighted and confirmed by radar. . . . The one . . . first sighted passed beneath the second. Radar . . . confirmed this. The first made for altitude toward the north and the second seemed to disappear with the glow of red.[15]

Later, in one of those strange coincidences that have occurred in the course of my UFO investigations, I met an Air Force officer who was directly involved in this particular event. I was working at my desk one day when a contract administrator walked by with an Air Force officer. He stopped by my desk and pointed me out to the officer with a big broad grin and said, "Let me introduce you to Ray Fowler. He believes in UFOs. Ha-ha!"

The officer did not grin but shook my hand and said, "I used to laugh like that about UFOs but I don't anymore after what I experienced."

My friend, the contract administrator, somewhat taken aback by his statement suggested that he introduce the officer to some other people and they walked away. I soon looked up the officer and talked to him alone. Amazing as it might seem, he had been in the Minuteman Launch Control Facility, sixty feet underground, when the incident that Dr. Hynek made public had taken place! He confirmed what Hynek had written and told me that nothing on earth could have caused such equipment malfunctions from an altitude of 100,000 feet.

"From that day on, I believed in UFOs!" he said.

He told me that those who were interrogated by Air Force intelligence teams were told not to talk about the incident. He had been in training and was not interrogated. Time after time I had been told this by military personnel who related their sightings to me. The government did not want such things made public. It is to Dr. Hynek's credit that he took advantage of an unclassified memorandum on the case just cited. Even field representatives from the same company that I am employed by were silenced. For several weeks, these fellow employees had relayed UFO information to me directly from a missile site. One day I was informed that they had been asked by the Air Force not to say any more to me about the UFO incidents. When I checked on one of the missile malfunctions through the representative of another company involved with Minuteman, I was told that the assistant base manager for his company had informed him that the incident was "a hot potato and highly-classified!" This particular malfunction had also taken place concurrently with a UFO sighting.

The military implications that can be drawn from just these several examples are obvious. Again, if we take these accounts at full face value, it would appear that UFOs can willingly violate any country's airspace at any time for any purpose! If UFOs are interplanetary vehicles, this would be just what we might expect. The technology and weapons of a race capable of interplanetary, especially interstellar, flight would appear magical to us. This being the case, no major military power could afford to admit to the general populace that alien machines are flagrantly violating our planet's air space. Questions relating to where they come from and why they are here, coupled with the obvious fact that there is no adequate defense in the event of hostility, would leave many questions without answers. No government would want to intentionally expose its people to such a cultural shock. A top priority effort would be initiated both to try to understand all aspects of the UFOs and to achieve space travel capability ourselves. All information relating to scientific and technical data gained from the study of UFO reports would be classified and jealously guarded from foreign countries. Attempts would be be made to understand and use such data in our own research and development programs.

I am personally convinced that the major governments are working at a feverish pace on the UFO problem but at a very high level of secrecy. It behooves us to practice patience and tolerance toward the often absurd *cover stories* that are generated from the Pentagon to explain UFOs away. Apparently, someone has decided, on the basis of what is now known (or unknown), that such secrecy, in the long run, is for our own good. I think that I might find some support for this view by some of my readers as we continue to discuss other implications of the UFO problem.

Political Implications

HOSTILE ALIEN VISITORS

Have there been well-documented UFO reports that indicate *unprovoked* overt acts of hostility? I shall say at the very outset that the vast majority of cases do not indicate any hostility. In those cases where human beings or equipment have been physically affected or damaged, the UFOs' action could be interpreted as either accidental or defensive in nature. However, there are a few real exceptions that, on the surface, appear to be unprovoked hostile acts. One such event took place at Beallsville, Ohio, just after 8:30 P.M. on March 19, 1968. The following account is quoted from a NICAP special report entitled *Strange Effects from UFOs,* which isolates cases like these from the general body of UFO reports.

> Young Gregory L. Wells, of Beallsville, Ohio, was returning from his grandmother's house to his own home next door when he saw an oval-shaped UFO hovering just over some trees. It was shortly after 8:30 P.M., March 19, 1968.
> The large red object was so bright that it illuminated the road, according to Mrs. James E. Wells, the boy's mother. It had a band of dimmer red lights flashing around its center.

"I stopped," Gregory recalled. "I wanted to run or scream but suddenly a big tube came out of the bottom which moved from side to side until it came to me and a beam of light shot out."

Gregory turned away as the light beam hit the upper part of his arm, knocking him to the ground. His jacket caught fire and the boy rolled around on the ground screaming with fright. Both his mother and grandmother responded. . . . Mrs. James Wells also reported seeing the UFO, which just "faded away."

During the sighting, a large night light on a nearby pole went out. This was confirmed later by Gregory Wells's father. There was also electromagnetic interference to a television set, and the grandmother's dog reacted violently.

The witness was taken to Beallsville Hospital after the encounter and was treated for second-degree burns. Bruce Francis, who reported the incident to NICAP, confirmed the burns and said the scar was still visible three months later.

Sheriff F. L. Sulsberger, of Monroe County, investigated. He said he could find no explanation. The sheriff sent the burned jacket to the Ohio Bureau of Criminal Investigation (OBCI) in London for analysis. OBCI officials said they found no evidence of radioactivity.

Civil Defense Director Ward Strikling, who combed the area with a Geiger counter, also found no radiation. He stated, however, that there are types of radioactive beams that leave no detectable traces.

"In the course of checking this case," wrote Dr. James E. McDonald, "I interviewed a number of persons in the Beallsville area, some of whom had seen a long cylindrical object moving at very low altitude in the vicinity of the Wells property that night. . . . My conversations with persons who know the boy, including his teacher, suggest no reason to discount the story, despite its unusual content.[16]

What are we to make of this and similar incidents? My own opinion is that events such as this may possibly be analogous to human behavior. In this case, perhaps this really was an intentional act of unwarranted aggression. Our country's recent involvement in Vietnam has brought news of atrocities committed against innocent civilians by U.S. servicemen. Someone told me that he knew of cases where U.S. soldiers had shot at Vietnam civilians for the fun of it. We shudder at such stories and rightly so. Men have been brought to trial and justice because of such atrocities. However, we do not condemn the majority of U.S. servicemen for the wrong actions of a few. This incident which occurred at Beallsville, Ohio, may be a similar type of event.

It may, on the other hand, be considered as a purely amoral act by a higher life-form to a lower life-form. Take, for example, our attitudes and paradoxical behavior towards animals and insects. Cattle, which we go to great lengths to provide food and shelter for, may, in their own way, worship us as great benefactors until we slaughter and devour them with no conscience at all! I have often rescued an insect from certain death in a spider's web down in my cellar. Sometimes, it has taken much care and effort on my part to do this without being stung, if the insect happens to be a hornet! Nonetheless, feeling very much like the young boy scout doing his good deed for the day, I capture the insect in a jar and let it loose outside. An hour later, I might see the same insect in the kitchen. Without even a second thought, I would promptly squash it and dump it in the wastebasket to be incinerated! The poor insect had no way of knowing why the cellar was a safer place for him to be than the kitchen. In the same way, the young boy from Beallsville, Ohio, may ignorantly have been in the wrong place at the wrong time as far as the UFO was concerned. Now, I personally have not declared war on *all* insects because one happened to trespass in my kitchen. Neither should we assume that the controlling force behind the UFO phenomena is hostile to the human race because of a few isolated cases suggestive of unprovoked hostility.

Nonetheless, if UFOs proved to be hostile and began committing well-publicized acts of open and obvious aggression, a number of implications would arise. In the United States the civilian populace would demand immediate protection from its government through its representatives and through the now familiar demonstration marches and riots. The political party in office would find itself in the unenviable position of assuring the citizenry that it was able to cope with the situation when, in reality, it found itself completely helpless against the UFOs. The public would certainly demand that its government put aside international differences to present a united front against the UFOs. In addition, there would be a constant public clamor for information and assurance about the UFOs.

The government, in the meantime, would be in an unprecedented quandary. Top level cooperation and coordination with other governments would be essential. This would mean a complete self-imposed breach of *national* security on the part of all cooperating nations in an attempt to establish *international* security against an interplanetary foe!

The following statement made by General Douglas MacArthur would prove to have been prophetic in nature:

> The nations of the world will have to unite, for the next war will be an interplanetary war. The nations of the earth must someday make a common front against attack by people from other planets.[17]

But what if some nations refused to cooperate? What if some segments of the civilian and military populace refused to fight an unimaginably superior extraterrestrial enemy? It is hard to imagine all of the political implications and ramifications that would arise in such an event. Government, as we know it, would probably collapse, because it ultimately depends upon the ability to control and protect its country by superior force. Such a force would be physically and psychologically neutralized by weaponry beyond our understanding!

FRIENDLY ALIEN VISITORS

Friendly alien visitors might do little more than study us and depart without overt communication. However, suppose somehow the tremendous barriers to rational overt communication were overcome. Let us suppose that the aliens, in their own way, communicated with us. What, then, could happen to the political structure of our government? One could speculate that some elements of the civilian populace would *transfer allegiance* to the alien powers because of its advanced wisdom and power. Perhaps the aliens would even intervene in national and international affairs to accomplish what they (but not necessarily we) consider best for us. This in turn could cause a *loss of confidence* in earthly government by some and antagonism towards the aliens by others. Realization of our primitive backwardness as compared with the advanced technology of the aliens might also result in a *loss of national pride*. Alien advice and coercion might cause a complete reorganization of the political system of any given government. Governments might be forced to work together under circumstances that would destroy all vestiges of nationalism.

Many of the situations I have just described have already had earthly counterparts during the colonization of primitive tribes by nations with an advanced technology. Others might be considered analogous to anthropological studies of primitive cultures by more advanced societies. However, all of these situations in the final analysis may be proved to have been self-centered anthropomorphisms. They presuppose that such beings would consider us worthy of contact. This would probably be the case only if the aliens were only slightly more advanced than we and were similar to us in biological structure and form. Highly advanced beings would probably have no more to do with us than we do the animals of the forest. In any event, alien hostility, friendliness or neutrality could change our present political systems beyond recognition!

Sociological Implications

The military and political implications that we have just discussed are specialized aspects of a more overall sociological impact. I shall discuss such an impact in terms of the society that I am most familiar with—Western culture.

It is interesting to note that cultures on this planet vary from the highly technological societies in developed countries to the primitive aborigines located in underdeveloped countries. A tremendous knowledge gap exists between the extremities of such cultures. Anthropological studies have indicated that significant cultural impact occurs when, for example, a stone-age culture is confronted with an advanced technological civilization. In a special report prepared by the Brookings Institution for NASA, it is written that:

> Anthropological files contain many examples of societies, sure of their place in the universe, which have disintegrated when they had to associate with previously unfamiliar societies espousing different ideas and different life ways; others that survived such an experience usually did so by paying the price of changes in values and attitudes and behavior.[18]

If this is true of societies within the same species who have developed and coexisted under identical environmental circumstances on the same planet, a question immediately arises in one's mind. How can we even begin to predict the overall impact that overt contact (hostile or benevolent) with totally alien beings from another planet would have upon earthly societies? The Brookings Institution report concludes that:

> The consequences of such a discovery are presently unpredictable because of our limited knowledge of behavior under even an approximation of such dramatic circumstances.[19]

The report goes on to recommend research in two areas. First:

> Continuing studies to determine emotional and intellectual understanding and attitudes—and successive alterations of them if any —regarding the possibility and consequences of discovering intelligent extraterrestrial life. . . . A possible but not completely satisfactory means for making the possibility "real" for many people would be to confront them with present speculations about the I.Q. of the porpoise and to encourage them to expand on the implications of this situation. Unfortunately, the semantics of "animal" at least for Americans, is such that even a human level I.Q. would not be as threatening as a "being" which wasn't an earth animal.[20]

It is humbling to realize that a similar situation would most probably exist between a superintelligent alien and even the most sophisticated earthman. *We* probably would be regarded as the *animal!*

Secondly, the report suggests:

> . . . . historical and empirical studies of the behavior of peoples
> and their leaders when confronted with dramatic and unfamiliar
> events or social pressures. Such studies might help to provide
> programs for meeting and adjusting to the implications of such
> a discovery. Questions one might wish to answer by such studies
> would include: How might such information, under what cir-
> cumstances, be presented to or *withheld from the public* [italics
> mine] for what ends? What might be the role of the discovering
> scientists and other decisionmakers regarding release of the fact
> of discovery?[21]

It is further suggested that

> Such studies would include historical reactions to hoaxes, psychic
> manifestations, unidentified flying objects, etc. Hadly Cantrel's
> study, *Invasion from Mars* (Princeton University Press, 1940),
> would provide a useful if limited guide in this area.[22]

Nonetheless, study as we may, one can only theorize in this
area of *sociological implications.* Confrontation between earthman
and superintelligent alien life may indeed have some similar par-
allels to draw upon within the context of interaction between societies of the same species originating on this planet—but actual
realization of such an event would be unprecedented, hence unpredictable!

Scientific Implications

One would like to think that out of all the disciplines within
the society of mankind, scientists and engineers would be the least
affected by an encounter with superintelligent life-forms. According to the Brookings Institution report, this might not be the
case!

> It has been speculated that, of all groups, scientists and engineers
> might be the most devastated by the discovery of relatively
> superior creatures, since these professions are most clearly as-
> sociated with the mastery of nature, rather than with the under-

standing and expression of man. Advanced understanding of nature might vitiate all our theories at the very least, if not also require a culture and perhaps a brain inaccessible to earth scientists.[23]

One might use an analogy to gain some insight into the impact such a confrontation would have upon science and engineering. Scientists and engineers have became elite members of technological societies wherever they are found. Their counterparts in a primitive society would be most certainly the witch doctors. Think for a moment upon the impact that would occur to witch doctors if suddenly confronted with the intrusion of modern hospitals into their area of operation. They could not begin to grasp modern medicine with all of its specialized equipment and scientific ramifications. Their inability to comprehend, duplicate and practice the feats of modern medicine would cause a severe loss of ego and prestige among the peoples they served. An initial reaction on their part would probably be an attempt to debunk the medical doctors, medicine and equipment in order to retain their hold on the native people and their world view. Again, we are using an analogy between the same species on the same planet. One can only wonder what advanced alien technology might be like.

UFOs and psychic phenomena are *anathema* to all but a few open-minded scientists today. Why? Are we seeing a parallel to our witch doctor analogy in real-life operation today? The modern scientist has carefully built a rational model of the world and the general scheme of things. Historically, things that "do not fit" scientific models have been rejected from serious discussion. Indeed, Dr. Robert J. Low, project coordinator for the Air Force-sponsored University of Colorado UFO Study reveals just such an attitude in a memorandum written to university officials *before* the university accepted the Air Force contract. Take the following excerpts from this memo, for example:

> In order to undertake such a project one has to admit the possibility that such things as UFOs exist. It is not respectable to give serious consideration to such a possibility. . . . Branscomb suggested that one would have to go so far as to consider the

possibility that saucers, if some of the observations are verified, behave according to a set of physical laws unknown to us. The simple act of admitting these possibilities just as possibilities puts us beyond the pale, and we would lose more prestige in the scientific community than we could possibly gain by undertaking the investigation. . . .[24]

Need I say more?

Religious Implications

Man is a religious being. This fact is much in evidence whereever we might go. Whether it be the steeples, temples and shrines of advanced civilizations or the crude stone altars, idols and fetishes of primitive societies, the phenomenon of religion is universally present.

When faced with a possible threat against which there was no practical defense, multitudes would probably turn to their religious beliefs for help and comfort. It is probably very fitting that in the final scenes of the movie version of H. G. Wells's *War of the Worlds*, we find helpless people huddled in churches seeking divine help against the invading Martians. Help does come in a most dramatic way. The Martians succumb to the very disease-carrying microbes that man had built up immunity against during the course of his evolution.

We might also consider that some would turn from one religion to another in feverish desperation if no divine help appeared in answer to their petitions. Some awestruck cultures might turn from their traditional religions to worship the aliens themselves! Not long ago, I read an account from Vietnam that told of a helicopter making an emergency landing in a remote village. The natives greeted the crewmen as gods and offered sacrifices to them! You will recall that the Spaniard, Cortez, was better able to conquer the Aztec nation because he was mistaken for a god. Cortez forced the subdued Aztecs to accept Roman Catholic Christianity.

Indeed, much of the initial exploration of our own planet was motivated by Christian missionary zeal. One might wonder if this motivation exists on an interstellar scale! Would the aliens attempt to evangelize our planet with totally new religious concepts? Such a thought in turn creates further speculation into this area. Some religions, including Judaism and Christianity, are based upon written records concerning superhuman manlike beings who brought religious teachings from the sky. Could, for example, the *angels* (messengers) mentioned in the Bible actually have been alien evangelical missionaries? I, among others, have pondered much about such a possibility and shall discuss this possibility in some detail towards the end of this chapter. In the meantime, what does the report from the Brookings Institution say concerning the impact that the discovery of advanced extraterrestrial life would have upon religion?

Unfortunately, very little is said on this matter except that

> the positions of the major American religious denominations, the Christian sects, and the eastern religions on the matter of extraterrestrial life need elucidations.[25]

It goes without saying that both Catholic and Protestant theologians have realized the implications of the vastness of the universe. Angelo Secchi, the great Jesuit astronomer, asked the following thought-provoking question as early as the middle of the nineteenth century:

> Could it be that God populated only one tiny speck in the cosmos with spiritual beings? . . . It would be absurd to find nothing but uninhabited deserts in these limitless regions. No! These worlds are bound to be populated by creatures capable of recognizing, honoring and loving their Creator.[26]

Dr. Earl L. Douglass, well-known Protestant Bible scholar and editor, wrote the following in 1952:

> May it not be that there are *unfallen* beings in the universe? . . . Would they not—if for no other reason save that they are morally our superiors—have advanced far beyond us?[27]

In January 1966, *The New Hampshire Churchman*, published

by the Episcopal Church, carried an article entitled "UFO I Cannot Doubt, I Believe." The author was the Reverend John D. Swanson, the busy rector of Christ Church, Portsmouth, New Hampshire.

The story of the Hills' experience of being taken aboard a strange ship, being examined and questioned and finally released is by now well known to the New Hampshire public. And, although some of us who are friends of the Hills had known about it for some time, the publication of the story, in conjunction with the recent rash of U.F.O. sightings in the Seacoast area, made U.F.O. the subject of the day in Portsmouth . . . and sent many of us into a new consideration of the implications of the kind of experience the Hills had. For those of us in the Church, one of our first thoughts was the religious implications of these matters. . . .

First let it be said that I do not and cannot doubt the veracity of the Hills' account and I believe in the factual reality of their experience. Anyone who has spoken with them, has heard the recordings made when they were under hypnotic recall, and has examined all the evidence, cannot doubt that what they describe did in actuality happen. It also seems quite clear that the race of beings they encountered were indeed rational and technically skilled to a degree well beyond our own present tchnology . . . which brings us to the classic second consideration: what is the spiritual state of these beings? Have they Fallen? . . . If they know sin, do they also have a Redeemer? Do they have an equivalent to our Christ? Or is Christ the same there as here? . . . If they are unfallen, would they be susceptible to the evil of this world? . . . . Might they have watched our planet for generations, and only now that we begin to move out of our world do they believe they must do something about this "bent" planet? To keep its evil contained? . . . As Christians we ought to make it our concern now to pray that whatever commerce we might have with these beings from outer space will prove mutually beneficial and not mutually destructive.

Not all those who profess Christianity would be as open-minded as the Reverend Swanson. According to the Brookings Institution report,

the fundamentalists (and antiscience) sects are growing apace around the world, and, as missionary enterprises, may have schools and a good deal of literature attached to them. One of the important things is that, where they are active, they appeal to the illiterate and semiliterate (including, as missions, the preachers as well as the congregation) and can pile up a very influential following in terms of numbers. For them, the discovery of other life—rather than any other space product—would be electrifying. . . . Scattered studies need to be made both in their home centers and churches and their missions, in relation to attitudes about space activities and extraterrestrial life.[28]

Whether such studies have ever been conducted since the report was written, it is hard to say. I have seen very little published in this area. However, I can vouch for the general accuracy of this statement. Much of my church life has been centered within Fundamentalist and Evangelical circles. The majority of people within these groups with whom I have discussed the UFO subject tend to either deny or ignore any implications that would affect their personal beliefs. I have heard some within these circles attribute the UFO phenomena to Satan himself, who, they say, is "the prince of the power of the air." (Ephesians 2:2) These same people, if they had lived in another age, might have cast the same suspicions at Galileo and the Wright brothers!

In any event, it is interesting to note that Christianity still thrives regardless of the fact that the earth is not the center of the universe and that man is able to fly. For the Church, such discoveries and events have meant the painful process of reinterpreting the Scriptures and expanding its theology to be in harmony with current scientific thought. Unfortunately, because of the very dogmatic nature of both theology and science, it takes many years to introduce new concepts into either discipline.

I shall now bring this discussion on religious implications to a close with some personal speculations. They are, because of my background, centered around Christianity. If I were of a different persuasion, I am sure that I would discuss UFOs in another context. The closing paragraphs are taken almost verbatim from previous articles that I have authored on this matter. They reflect my thoughts as a Christian layman on some *possible* implications that UFOs might have upon the Christian Faith. Permission to use this material has been kindly granted by the editors of *Christian Life.*[29]

As mentioned earlier in this book, I have been following the UFO problem since 1947. I was converted to Christianity in 1950 and began reading the Bible seriously for the first time in my life. By 1953, it became quite apparent to me that some of the aerial objects described in Biblical accounts were very similar in description to the modern UFOs.

Dr. Carl Sagan, prominent space biologist and a member of the Space Science Board, in regard to the possibility of extraterrestrial visits in the past, states, "It is possible that they have visited us since the dawn of civilization?"[30] Dr. Frank Drake, renowned American radio-astronomer involved in a program listening for intelligent radio signals from outer space, mentions the account in the "first three chapters of Ezekiel" as a possible such record.[31]

We read in chapter one of Ezekiel, in the Bible, that the prophet Ezekiel was sitting on the banks of Chebar River in Babylon when suddenly his attention was aroused by a sound like a rushing whirlwind. Looking to the north, he sighted what he first thought was a bright fiery cloud approaching. As it came closer he could see the color of amber (glowing metal) through the surrounding "fire infolding itself" (i.e., fire flashing continually) and then, down out of the sky came four objects. Each was described as a "wheel within a wheel," i.e., with an inner and outer circumference, which were in turn connected by a "ring" that was "full of eyes." Out of the landed objects came living creatures which "had the likeness of a man." Each creature had a "firmament" upon his head the color of a "crystal." The whole episode was so utterly foreign to Ezekiel that he found it extremely hard to describe.

A modern man describing this account might very well report that a bright glowing, pulsating, cylindrical-shaped cloud appeared that ejected four oval objects. The objects landed. Each looked like two saucers, one inverted upon another and connected by a surrounding rim or rim full of vents. Out of the landed objects came manlike beings dressed in metallic suits ("they sparkled like the color of burnished brass") with transparent helmets. ("And the likeness of the firmament upon the heads . . . was as the color of the terrible crystal, stretched forth over their heads above.") This account sounds uncannily familiar to modern sightings of the Type IIB and Type IB vintage.

Throughout Scripture there are similar accounts of strange objects and beings from the sky. If such were extraterrestrial craft, descriptions of them would necessarily be limited by the inability of the viewers to describe them except through the limited, non-technical language of a primitive culture. They would quite naturally describe such flying and landed objects in terms of familiar objects commonly found in the air and on the ground. A geologist once told me how African Bantu natives described his light aircraft as a giant bird with the roar of a thousand lions!

If other intelligent beings do exist in the universe, whether *fallen* or *unfallen,* the Christian would deduce that God has revealed Himself to them in some way and that presumably He has created them for a specific purpose. If some races are thousands of years in advance of us in a technical sense, they could very well be just as much or more in advance of us spiritually.

If mankind on earth has been given the privilege by the Creator to be His messengers to others on this planet, then it is highly probable that other beings in the universe have been given the same privilege. Grant such a race or races interplanetary or interstellar capability, and one could assume that such being would be used by God in His overall plan of revelation. This might be in much the same sense that Christian missionaries are used on this planet. Indeed, God may have used such beings to bring knowledge of Himself and His will to our own planet, as humbling as it may seem at first.

Whether or not Scripture does contain such records is obviously pure, unadulterated speculation. However, the Bible is quite clear on the fact that there are orders of rational creation in the universe other than man as he exists on this planet. Indeed, the book of Hebrews in the Bible tells us that man was made "a little lower than the angels."

Usually, the word translated angel in the Bible means "messenger." Since these powerful beings came from the sky and brought messages from and about God, they were acknowledged as messengers of God. It can be deduced from Scripture that such angels or messengers were made up of various orders and ranks. They were described as "gods," "sons of God" and "hosts of heaven." The prophet Daniel refers to them as "watchers." In practically every instance angels are described as appearing manlike. The popular idea of angels having beautiful effeminate faces and feathery wings is misleading and was partially derived from the false rendering of the Vulgate Bible version of Daniel 9:21.

Not only did angels have the physical appearance of men but they also had the physical characteristics of men. We read in Genesis 6:2-4 that the "sons of God" were able to intermarry with the daughters of men although such a union resulted in abnormal progeny. In Genesis 18:8 angels are seen eating physical food with Abraham, and in Genesis 19:13,24 we see them bombarding and destroying Sodom and Gomorrah in much the same way that man conducts modern warfare.

We have already seen from the account in Ezekiel that angels may have some relationship to cloudlike and oval aerial objects. There are other accounts in both the Old and New Testaments involving aerial objects and angels. In Exodus 14:19 we have the amazing account of a huge airborne object shaped like a pillar or cylinder. It was a cloudlike color in the daytime and glowed during the night. The description fits the modern portrayal of a Type II UFO. We are told that God or the Angel of the Lord controlled the movements of this object and communicated with Moses from it. This flying pillar not only guided Israel through the wilderness but also protected and fed them. The psalmist states that the manna "rained down upon them" and "man did eat angels' food" (Psalm 78:24, 25). Curiously, the two UFO configurations most observed today are oval and cylindrical. Thus the "wheels" in Ezekiel and the "pillar" in Exodus appear to bear a striking similarity to these configurations.

Moreover, in II Kings 2:3 we read of the account of Elijah being taken up in a vehicle described as a fiery chariot.

Moving into the New Testament, we have both angels and aerial objects directly associated with the advent of Christ. The glowing pillar of fire that was alluded to by Biblical writers as "the glory of the Lord," swooped low over a field outside the walls of Bethlehem, lighting up the hillside where shepherds tended their sheep. Voices from this glowing mass proclaimed the birth of Christ to the trembling shepherds. A few years later, a bright object that behaved neither like a star nor any other celestial body deliberately guided astrologers to the city of Bethlehem where the Christ child dwelt.

The mysterious pillar-shaped object referred to as *the cloud* or the *Glory of the Lord* makes other dramatic appearances within the Biblical accounts. Tradition and the Bible instruct us that both Moses and Elijah were taken directly into the heavens bodily. It may be significant that the next time we see them it is concurrent with the appearing of a bright glowing "cloud" that consorted with Jesus on the Mount of Transfiguration.

Was this the same type of pillar-shaped object that Moses had met on Mount Sinai? It is extremely interesting to note that both Moses and Jesus "glowed" after making contact with the "cloud." On Mount Sinai, angels gave Moses the Ten Commandments in the name of God Himself. On the Mount of Transfiguration, Jesus met with Moses and Elijah for a special conference. Even St. Paul's conversion and ministerial training were replete with a "glowing" light in the sky (Acts 9:3-5) from which Jesus spoke. The last time men had seen Jesus was on Ascension Day, when he was seen going to heaven in a "cloud." Shortly after this experience, St. Paul was taken to a place that he described as the "third heaven," where he heard things that he could not repeat (II Corinthians 12:1-5). It is no wonder that Paul did not need instructions from the Apostles. He may have received instructions directly from the "angels" that we see assisting the early apostolic church in the book of Acts!

These things are a matter for speculation and research. Too often we study the Bible with preconceived pre-twentieth century concepts and reasoning. It is quite possible that Christians today are as far off in imagining what Christ's Second Coming will be like as the Pharisees and Scribes were about His First Coming. The Bible says, "Eye hath not seen, nor ear heard, neither have entered into the heart of man, the things which God hath prepared for them that love Him" (I Corinthians 2:9); Jesus told His disciples, "If I have told you earthly things, and yet believe not, how shall ye believe, if I tell you of heavenly things?" (John 3:12)

These are just a few examples from the Bible of aerial objects and messengers reportedly used by God to carry out His unsearchable purposes. Since the Second Coming of Christ involves fearful sights and signs in the sky, including His coming with "clouds" and "angels," surely Christians should ponder the UFO phenomena in the light of this great event.

However, it is more probable that the Bible has no more to say about the UFO phenomena than it has to say about our own space program's efforts. Nevertheless, this entire subject has theological implications and requires serious attention on the part of the Christian church.

In conclusion, I would like to leave the following challenge to Christian theologian and layman alike: It is imperative that the whole question of our own space efforts and the probable existence of extraterrestrial life be examined fully in the light of the impact that both could have upon contemporary theology and a traditional interpretation of Scripture. Geocentric theological concepts of the Resurrection and the Second Coming of Christ might have to be expanded to include other parts of our solar system or wherever man might colonize. The discovery or awareness of intelligent extraterrestrials would imply that the Incarnation may not have been an event unique to just this planet. Even the doctrine of Creation may be profoundly affected. How far will man himself spread life as he begins to visit other planets? It is interesting to note that a literal rendering of the Genesis account would have man not created in the image of God (singular) but created in the image of the Elohim (gods)! It could very well be that the Creator has so ordered things that He employs perfect unfallen beings to spread and care for various forms of fallen and unfallen life throughout His creation.

In order to better appreciate and prepare for any such theological impact caused by revolutionary discoveries as discussed above, it would be good to study in depth the Church's reaction to a similar situation in the past, namely, the Copernican revolution.

Prior to the discoveries of men like Copernicus and Galileo, theology and scriptural interpretation were firmly wedded to an Aristotelian concept of the universe—that the earth held a privileged central position in the universe; for the moon, planets, sun and stars supposedly moved around it in perfect circles. The outmoding of this erroneous concept revealed the need for vast and sweeping changes in both science and Christian theology. At first the Church fought these new concepts. Even Martin Luther called the Copernican system anti-scriptural, and yet today Christians the world over accept such a system as common everyday knowledge.

The important thing to remember is that throughout the history of the Church, theology and scriptural interpretation has had to be *expanded* again and again in the light of new knowledge. Although such changes were distasteful and alarming to the generation in which they occurred, they in no way changed the basic message of the Christian Gospel.

As Christians face the serious implications posed by the ushering in of the space age and the UFO problem, they should not lose sight of the fact that the foundational truths of the Bible have always triumphed in the face of new knowledge. Christians and adherents of all faiths should come to this realization: Increased knowledge of the universe, coupled with a possible contact with intelligent beings from outer space, may well enrich man's understanding of his particular place and purpose in the universe as related to God and His unfathomable creation.

NOTES

    1. Edward J. Ruppelt, *The Report on Unidentified Flying Objects,* p. 200.
    2. *Ibid.,* pp. 1-5.
    3. Leonard H. Stringfield, *Inside Saucer Post . . . 3-0 Blue,* p. 91.
    4. *Ibid.,* p. 92.
    5. Midwest UFO Network (MUFON), 40 Christopher Court, Quincy, Illinois, 62301.

6. *Skylook,* February 1973, pp. 4, 5.
7. NICAP, *The UFO Evidence,* pp. 114-115.
8. *Ibid.,* 115.
9. *Idem.*
10. Donald E. Keyhoe, *The Flying Saucer Conspiracy,* pp. 16, 17.
11. *UFO Evidence, op. cit.,* p. 115.
12. Edward U. Condon, *Scientific Study of Unidentified Flying Objects,* p. 161.
13. Personal correspondence on file, dated May 22, 1967.
14. Keyhoe, *op. cit.,* p. 176.
15. J. Allen Hynek, "Are Flying Saucers Real?" *Saturday Evening Post,* December 17, 1966.
16. NICAP, *Strange Effects from UFOs,* pp. 3, 4.
17. *New York Times,* October 9, 1955.
18. House Report No. 242, *Proposed Studies on the Implications of Peaceful Space Activities for Human Affairs,* 1961, p. 215.
19. *Idem.*
20. House Report, *op. cit.,* pp. 216, 226.
21. *Ibid.,* pp. 216, 217
22. *Ibid.,* p. 226.
23. *Ibid.,* p. 225.
24. Personal Files and John G. Fuller, "Flying Saucer Fiasco," *Look,* May 14, 1968.
25. House Report, *op. cit.,* p. 225.
26. Walter Sullivan, *We Are Not Alone,* p. 283.
27. Earl L. Douglass, "Are We Being Watched?" *Christian Herald,* August 1959.
28. House Report, *op. cit.,* p. 225.
29. Raymond E. Fowler, "The Bible and the UFO," November 1966, and "Whatever Happened to UFOs?" July 1972. (Reprinted by permission from Copyright Christian Life Publications, Incorporated, Gundersen Drive & Schmale Road, Wheaton, Illinois, 60187.)
30. *House Report, op. cit.,* p. 240.
31. *Ibid.,* p. 241.

16

1973—YEAR OF
THE HUMANOIDS

There was definitely something here that was not terrestrial.
Where they came from and why they were here is a matter
of conjecture but the fact that they are here (on this planet)
is true beyond a reasonable doubt.

DR. JAMES A. HARDER[1]
APRO Consultant

As this book goes to press, UFO reports are again streaming in from all over North America! The first huge wave since 1967 has resurrected UFOs as a national controversy! The most recent Gallup Poll indicates that fifty-one percent of the people in the country believe in the validity of UFOs, and over fifteen million have been convinced they have seen them. The lead-in quotation for this chapter concerns the reported abduction of two highly reliable witnesses by occupants of an unidentified flying object during this recent outburst of sightings. This incredible case and many others will be discussed in some detail within this concluding chapter, *1973—Year of the Humanoids!*

What started as a local spurt of sightings in Georgia during the summer of 1973 soon escalated into the first massive UFO wave in North America since 1967. I received over ninety *local* reports in 1973! NICAP's records[2] indicate that the onslaught began in late September as UFO sightings spread like brushfire throughout the Southeast. Observations were being reported faster than police and other authorities could follow them up, some involving dozens or hundreds of witnesses in a single community. As recently as November, cases have been flowing steadily into NICAP headquarters from overworked NICAP investigators and busy

NICAP members who have been clipping news articles and relaying other information.

Few areas of the country have been spared by this wave, which spilled over into Canada at the same time it was spreading to western and northern parts of the United States. Sightings have been especially heavy in New England, the Great Lakes states, parts of the Midwest, and the West Coast. For reasons that are still not apparent, Ohio has been the source of many reports, including at least three involving photographs.

The reports span a broad range of events, from alleged encounters with humanoid creatures to unknown objects spotted by pilots and tracked on radar. Some of the best publicized cases are as follows:

Abduction at Pascagoula

One of the most provocative UFO experiences ever reported—the alleged *abduction* of two shipyard workers—continues to baffle investigators. Hypnosis, polygraphy, and other newer techniques have been employed in an attempt to verify or discredit the incident.

The unearthly report came to light late Thursday night, October 11, when two men, Charles Hickson and Calvin Parker, appeared at the Jackson County sheriff's office in Pascagoula, Mississippi. They excitedly told deputies that they had been seized by three misshapen creatures who emerged from a flying object near the pier where the men were fishing. According to their account, Hickson was grabbed by two of the creature and "floated" into the spacecraft while the third creature transported Parker. Parker "went limp" and fainted before reaching the object. Once inside, Hickson said, he was subjected to some form of physical examination by a football-sized device that reminded him of a "big eye." After the examination was completed, both men were returned to the river bank and left uninjured. The following day, they both were taken to Keesler Air Force Base, where they were checked for radiation. Fortunately, none was found.

On Saturday, October 13, both men were interviewed by APRO consultant Dr. James Harder, engineering professor at the

UFOs: Interplanetary Visitors

University of California, and Dr. J. Allen Hynek. Others involved in the interrogation were a psychiatrist, Dr. Bridges, and Dr. Julius Bosco. APRO reported the findings of its consultant, Dr. James Harder, in its excellent bimonthly bulletin.[3] The object had descended only forty feet behind the witnesses. It appeared to be about eighteen feet long with a hatch at its rear, out of which the three strange beings emerged. They were described as about five feet tall with a gray, wrinkled skin or covering. No neck was noticed and their arms ended in lobster-claw-like appendages. They either stood upon a pedestal or had "fused" legs, because they remained rigid and "floated," not walked, in their every movement. The creatures, or robots, had slits for eyes, small conelike appendages in place of ears, a tiny pointed nose with a hole under it.

On October 26, Parker was hospitalized in his hometown of Laurel, Mississippi, for a "nervous condition." On the basis of available information, NICAP reported that one of four possible explanations appears most likely for this case: (1) the events occurred as reported; (2) the witnesses are lying but are able to do so without detection by polygraph; (3) the witnesses were the victim of a hoax; or (4) the witnesses experienced some form of hallucination or dream that was extremely real to them. I phoned Dr. Hynek shortly after his return from Pascagoula and asked him for his evaluation of the event. He told me that he was convinced that both men had undergone a "terrifying experience." Hickson appeared with Dr. Hynek on the Dick Cavett Show. I must say that his story sounded very convincing, incredible as it might seem.

Burned by a UFO

Ohio Governor John Gilligan and his wife spotted a UFO from their car for over a half hour on October 15. Earlier, on October 3, a truckdriver and his wife in Missouri also sighted a UFO while driving, but this man did not get off as lightly as the governor. When he put his head out of the truck window to get a better look, a "large ball of fire" struck him in the face, knocking his glasses off. Temporarily blinded, he managed to bring the tractor-trailer to a stop but was unable to regain the use of his eyes for several hours. His wife drove him to a nearby hospital, where he was treated for burns and released. Examination of the glasses by a qualified physicist indicated that the frames had been subjected to heat, causing one of the lenses to fall out.

James Thornhill, a civil defense radar operator in Columbia, Mississippi, tracked a strange target on his radar set on October 14. Apparently the object reacted, because as it moved within three miles of the station it abruptly stopped in mid-flight and the radar set suddenly became "jammed." After trying for fifteen minutes to determine the cause for what had occurred, Thornhill said the equipment corrected itself and worked normally. By that time that UFO had disappeared.

UFO Tows Army Copter!

Captain Lawrence Coyne has been flying for a decade as an army and civilian pilot. Currently he serves as commander of an Army Reserve helicopter unit, the 316th Medical Detachment stationed at the Hopkins Airport in Cleveland, Ohio. When Captain Coyne and three crewmen left Columbus, Ohio, at 10:30 P.M. October 18, they had no forewarning that their helicopter trip to Cleveland that night would be one of the most unusual flights they had ever made in their lives.

Forty minutes after take-off, they were traveling at 2500 feet on a northeast course in the vicinity of Mansfield. Suddenly, one of the crew, Staff Sergeant Robert Yanacsek, spotted a red light to the east that was heading toward their helicopter at an estimated 600 mph. Captain Coyne put the copter into a dive in what seemed now to be a futile attempt to avoid a midair collision. He stated that: "At 1700 feet, I braced myself for the impact with the other craft. It was approaching from our right side. I was scared. There had been so little time to respond."

Just as a collision seemed imminent, the object abruptly halted about five hundred feet above them. Coyne and his crew gaped up at the strange object in utter amazement. "It had a big, gray, metallic looking hull about sixty feet long. It was shaped like an airfoil or a streamlined fat cigar." The craft also carried unconventional lights. Coyne stated that: "There was a red light in front. The leading edge glowed red a short distance back from the nose. There was a center *dome*. A green light at the rear reflected on the hull." All of a sudden this green light turned, as if on a swivel. It shined like a spotlight through the canopy of the helicopter "completely flooding out our red instrument lights and turning everything inside green."

The captain immediately got on the radio and tried to contact Mansfield Airport. The radio was functioning but would neither transmit nor receive. "I couldn't get the keying sound and there was no reception," said Coyne. Suddenly he stared in utter disbelief at his instruments. He was amazed to see the needle of the altimeter rising! "I could hardly believe it was reading 3500 feet, climbing to 3800. I had made no attempt to pull up. All controls were set for a twenty-degree dive. Yet, we had climbed from 1700 to 3500 feet with no power in a couple of seconds with no G-forces or other noticeable strains. There was no noise or turbulence either."

Somehow, the UFO had the copter in tow! This eerie ascent lasted only seconds and then, to put it in the captain's own words, "we felt a bounce and the other craft took off to the northeast." After seven or eight minutes, the copter's radio inexplicably began working normally and radio contact was established with the Akron-Canton Airport.

Silver-Suited "Somethings"

"Howdy, Stranger!"

On the night of October 17, 23-year-old Jeff Greenhaw, the one-man police force of Falkville, Alabama, responded to a call from a woman who claimed a "spaceship" had landed in the field behind her house. When he arrived, he found nothing but decided to inspect further. As he drove down a side road, he was startled by a figure in a silvery suit, whom he assumed was a prankster. Deciding to go along with the gag, he halted the cruiser and called out to the figure, "Howdy, stranger." The figure said nothing but began walking toward Greenhaw. The officer grabbed his Polaroid camera and began taking pictures. The figure approached to within about ten feet, then stopped. At this point, Greenhaw concluded that this was no gag and jumped in the police cruiser and turned on its flashing light. At the sign of the light, the strange creature started running down the road, with Greenhaw in pursuit. In his excitement, he accelerated too hard, causing the tires to spin on the road's loose gravel, sending the car off the edge of the road. When the dust cleared and he got back on the road, the figure had gone. "It scared me to death," said the young police officer.

UFO Roadblocks

On the very same night, Paul Brown of Athens, Georgia, reported that he had encountered a cone-shaped object and its occupants while driving along U.S. 29 at Danielsville, Georgia. His first sensation of the UFO was a bright light passing over the car with a "swishing sound." Panic-stricken, he jammed on his brakes as the object settled on or near the road a bare three hundred feet in front of his on-coming car! Terrified, he watched two small silver-suited creatures emerge from the object. Brown hurriedly grabbed a pistol out of the glove compartment and stepped halfway out of the car to challenge the oncoming figures. The beings according to Brown, went back into the object, which shut off its lights and rose into the air with a whooshing noise. Brown fired several shots at the retreating UFO but with no apparent effect. Investigating police found only the tire marks on the road made by Brown's braking automobile.

A similar case took place on October 22 at 9:45 P.M. at Hartford City, Indiana, along State Road 26. Mr. and Mrs. De Wayne Donathan stopped their car to avoid striking two four-foot, silver-suited creatures moving in the road. She managed to bring the car to a stop a bare thirty feet away from the strange looking creatures. When she saw what they were, she started the car off with a lurch and sped around them as they began moving off the road in a slow clumsy manner.

Deputy Sheriff Ed Townsend, a state policeman, and the sheriff's friend, Gary Flatter, responded to the Donathan's report. Mrs. Donathan was in a near state of shock and for awhile it seemed as if she might require a doctor's aid, but she gradually recovered. Although the investigation trio found nothing during an initial investigation, they did hear a strange, high-frequency sound in the area. Flatter decided to investigate further after the sheriff and state policeman left the area. While driving near the sighting area, he was astonished to see a menagerie of animals cross the road in front of him. He jammed on his brakes as seven rabbits, a possum, a raccoon and some cats darted across the road concurrent with a weird, high-pitched noise such as he and his companions had heard earlier. He sat in the cab of his truck and strained his eyes as he tried to see where the sound might be coming from. Then he saw them—two small figures standing in a plowed field just off the road. He turned his truck's (a wrecker) spotlight on them and gaped in amazement at two silver-suited *somethings* looking at him. They stood about four feet tall and had egg-shaped heads that appeared to be covered by something like a gas mask. As he observed them, they began jumping and rose into the air and floated down to the ground several times. Then they flew off, in a feet-down position, and disappeared into the darkness. A few red streaks in the air were left behind in their wake. On the following day, Deputy Sheriff Townsend and others found strange heel prints in the area. A complete description of this event may be found in the September-October 1973 *APRO Bulletin*. The report was investigated by APRO field investigator Donald Worley of Connorsville, Indiana.

The silver-suited *somethings* did not bypass New England. The town of Goffstown, New Hampshire, was the scene of some very strange happenings. The first indication of such occurred during the early morning hours of November 2.

"I THOUGHT IT WOULD TAKE ME"

Mrs. Lyndia Morel of Park Road, New Boston, New Hampshire, finished work at about 2:45 A.M. and went for a cup of coffee before driving home from Manchester, New Hampshire. Later,

as she drove along Route 114 towards the little village of Goffstown, she noticed something like a bright yellow star to her left but
didn't think too much of it. This was probably the planet Mars setting. However, after passing through the village, she took a left at
the "popcorn stand," a familiar Goffstown landmark. At this point,
the unbelievable happened! Descending directly in front of her was
a bright orange glowing aerial object. Simultaneously she heard a
high-pitched buzzing sound and experienced a tingling as if her
body was falling asleep. A strange pulling force took over her
body as the object drew closer. Then she saw *it*. Let's listen to
her own description of what happened from a transcript of the
taped interview conducted by NICAP assistant investigator John
P. Oswald.

> I was really scared because I was all alone and it was late.
> It was like—Do you know when your foot fall asleep or some-
> thing? That tingling feeling? Well it was kinda like that and
> yet it wasn't. There was a high-pitched frequency that I could
> feel.[5]

As the object drew closer, Lyndia saw a figure staring at her from
a transparent section. She told investigator Oswald:

> I can remember seeing a pair of eyes staring at me and saying,
> "Don't be afraid [not audibly but in her head]. I covered my
> eyes and yanked the wheel. I was petrified . . . and didn't care
> what I hit."[6]

Lyndia swerved across the road and onto the lawn of a Mr.
and Mrs. Beaudoin. Fighting her way past a growling German
shepherd, she screamed and pounded on their door. The Beau-
doins took her into the house and called the police. When officer Jubinville arrived, the object was gone. Only the setting
planet Mars could be seen, which was initially thought to have
been the departing UFO. "I really thought it intended to take me
away," said Mrs. Morel.

SMALL SILVER SUBJECTS

Assistant investigator John Oswald and myself read and photo-

graphed the police file card on one of the most fascinating reports
we had ever investigated. It read in part:

> Subject called this H.Q. and reported that there were small
> *silver subjects* running about his yard. (subjects were described
> as being 4.5 to 5.0 feet in height, no mouths, pointed noses,
> black eye dots, and . . . silver suits). . . . Patrolman Wike
> advised that Mr. Snow had seen *something* and that this was
> not a figment of his imagination.[7]

This unworldly incident had also taken place in Goffstown, just a
few days after Lyndia Morel's terrifying experience.

Shortly after midnight, on November 4, Rex and Theresa
Snow were startled by a brushing sound against their house. Rex
got up and looked out the bedroom window. Seeing nothing, he
dismissed the noises as having been caused by the wind and got
back into bed.

A few minutes later, Rex decided to get up again and let the
dog out, as it was making whining sounds in the kitchen. As he
walked toward the nearly shut bedroom door, he was surprised
to see light shining under the door from the corridor outside.
Opening the door, he found the corridor, which led to the kitchen,
illuminated with a diffuse glow. Walking to the kitchen, he saw
light streaming in under the window shades and through the cloth
curtain on the back door window. Their German shepherd, Miko,
was crouched on the floor near the door emitting a low growl.
Her teeth were bared and the hair on her back bristled.

Rex told me that his first thought was that there was a fire
burning outside. He went up to the back door, parted the curtains
and peered out. What he saw so amazed him that he just backed
away from the door. He could not believe what he had seen.
Looking out again, he saw that the diffuse white glow was emanating from two self-luminous, silver-suited creatures! They had
over-sized pointed ears, dark egg-shaped holes for eyes, and a
large nose covered by the same silver material that covered their
heads like "Ku-Klux-Klan" hoods. He could not remember how
many fingers each had, but their hands were covered as if with
silver gloves. Everything but the creatures' boots seemed to be

a seamless silver garment like a "wet-suit" coverall. A trial-and-error sketch of the creatures was prepared and drawn up by professional illustrator Rubin Silver. (See figure 8.)

FIGURE 8

Mr. Snow yelled for his wife, but she thought he was just kidding and was too tired to get out of bed. However, her joviality turned to fear when Rex reentered the bedroom and began loading his 38-caliber automatic handgun and returned to the kitchen. The dog Miko was now frantic and jumping against the backdoor. Rex opened the door and ordered it to attack the creatures, who were a bare sixty feet away! The dog, trained to attack upon his command, bounded across the back yard toward the weird beings. When she was about thirty feet from them, the figures stopped what they were doing and just stared at the oncoming dog. Abruptly, at this very point, the dog stopped in its tracks, made a few short lunges toward them, and then just walked right back to the door. Rex told me that she walked by him and into the kitchen, where she lay down on the floor and whined. The hair stood straight up her back.

Rex quickly closed the door. He said that a sudden fear took hold of him. His hands began shaking so badly that he could not even hold the gun steady. The figures continued to pick up things from the ground and put them in a silver bag. Their movements were slow but deliberate, somewhat like a slow-motion camera scene. Dumbfounded, Snow watched them turn and walk into the woods. His wife would not budge from the bedroom until they had gone. When she arrived, Rex was calling the police. Glancing out fearfully, she saw the whole woods lit up with an eerie glow, which slowly diminished to nothing. By the time the police arrived, the creatures were gone, but the police were convinced that Mr. Snow had seen something terrifying and said he was still shaking like a leaf and pale when they arrived.

I launched a thorough investigation into the incident. Other than a few broken twigs, no markings were found. The rocky wooded area dropped off into a twenty-foot deep gully and railroad bed. It is assumed that the creatures approached the Snows' backyard by climbing one of the paths from the gully. A thorough character check and analysis was performed. Taped interviews with both of the Snows were examined for internal inconsistencies. Our investigation ruled out the possibility of a hoax by or played upon the Snows. A shared hallucination under the circumstances seemed quite unlikely. The incident was evaluated as *an actual inexplicable event,* and a sixty-page report was mailed to NICAP for research purposes.

In chapter fourteen, I applied Chamberlain's method of multiple *hypotheses* to both the local and global UFO report baselines. The most logical hypothesis, the one that best accounts for all the reported facts about UFOs, is that they are manned and unmanned vehicles from another planet or planets!

It would appear that a superintelligent alien species is indeed becoming a more intimate part of our earth's environment and that mankind apparently has no control over the situation. As a nation and as a planet, we had better begin trying to peacefully adapt ourselves to its presence!

Remember—understanding and progress do not come by ignoring or ridiculing the inexplicable. Rather, they come by facing the problem squarely through investigation, acknowledgment and study.

"He who has ears to hear, let him hear."

NOTES

1. APRO, *APRO Bulletin,* September-October 1973.
2. NICAP, *UFO Investigator,* November 1973.
3. *APRO Bulletin, op. cit.*
4. *UFO Investigator, op. cit.*
5. Personal Files, UFO Report No. 73-61A.
6. *Ibid.*
7. Personal Files, UFO Report No. 73-62A/B.

APPENDIX I
SUMMARY DESCRIPTIONS
OF THE LOCAL SAMPLE

(Compare with witnesses' sketches in chapter twelve.)

Legend

EST—Eastern Standard Time
EDT—Eastern Daylight Time
(2+3)—Separate groups of witnesses

Number Date Time	City/Town State Locale	Type Shape Effect	Number of witnesses Description
63-1 23 June 0100 EDT	E. Weymouth Mass. City Power lines Field	IA Elliptical Sound Buzzing Roaring	(2 visual + 2 audio) An object about 30 feet in diameter and shaped like two bowls, one inverted upon the other and connected by a rim. It was observed hovering above some power lines 300 feet from the witnesses for 3 minutes.
64-4 18 May 2215 EDT	Lawrence Mass. City Airport	IIIE Light None	(1 + others) An Army pilot observed a high intensity yellow-white light approach the airport at about 300 mph. It turned 360 degrees and sped off at an estimated speed of 1000 mph without causing a sonic boom.
64-6 15 June 2310 EDT	Lynn Mass. City Courtyard	IA Elliptical Sound Whining Paralysis Vapor Television	(1 visual + 2 audio) An object about 25 feet in diameter shaped like a dark inverted dish with a central dome on top. It hovered 12 feet above the yard at a distance of 20 feet from the observer before ascending and moving off at high speed.
64-10A 25 Aug. 2130 EDT	Littleton Mass. Country Church Field	IA Elliptical Sound Soft roar	(3 + 1) A silvery object with a central dome on top and red and white lights on its rim. It hovered with a fluttering motion near the ground before moving off at high speed. The witnesses approached within 500 feet of the object.
64-10B 25 Aug. 2230 EDT	Lynn Mass. City Power Sub- station Rest home	IA Elliptical Sound Whining	(1 visual + 1 audio) A silvery object about 20 feet in diameter with a central dome on top and a glowing white rim. It descended to below treetop level about 300 feet from the observer.

Number / Date / Time	City/Town / State / Locale	Type / Shape / Effect	Number of witnesses / Description
64-11 26 Aug. 2120 EDT	Melrose Mass. City	IVA Elliptical None	(2) A glowing object like a big red star. It was about ⅓ of a degree in diameter when seen through a 2.4-inch telescope at 35-power and looked like a red pulsating ellipsoid wtih an orange-red halo.
64-12 28 Aug. 2205 EDT	Littleton Mass. Country	IIIA Light Exhaust	(1) A bright yellow glowing ball, seemingly 10 feet in diameter, crossed the highway in front of the observer's car. It was traveling in a horizontal trajectory and rose slightly to clear the top of a hill.
64-13 6 Sept. 2345 EDT	Medford Mass. Country Golf course	IIIA Light None	(2) A bright royal blue glowing object seemingly 25 feet in diameter moved horizontally with a bouncing up-and-down motion. A red light revolved around its perimeter.
64-15 1 Oct. 1250 EDT	Danvers Mass. City	IVA Elliptical None	(1) A dark disc-shaped object, calculated to be about 24 feet in diameter, passed over an industrial plant under a 2500-foot cloud. The object was moving at an estimated 300 mph at about a 2000-foot altitude.
64-16 6 Oct. 0030 EDT	Haverhill Mass. Country Cemeteries	IA Elliptical None	(2) A silver domed disc, about 30 feet in diameter and shaped like a half ball on an inverted plate which glowed around its bottom. It hovered about 30 feet above trees at a distance of 150 feet from the observers.
64-17 7 Oct. 1530 EDT	Waltham Mass. Country	IVA Cylindrical None	(1) A grayish black wingless object with two stubby fins at its rear which was following a C-119 Flying Boxcar aircraft.

Number Date Time	City/Town State Locale	Type Shape Effect	Number of witnesses Description
64-18 11 Oct. 1600 EDT	Brockton Mass. City	IVB Elliptical None	(3) A white round object that appeared to be about 50 feet in diameter chased 2 jet fighters traveling at supersonic speed. It descended from 30,000 feet to about 5000 feet before circling and accelerating upwards and out of sight at terrific speed.
64-19 29 Oct. 1810 EST	Arlington Mass. Residential Parsonage	IA Cylindrical None	(1) A yellow glowing cigar-shaped object, about 100 feet long and tilted 15 degrees upward, descended out of low heavy clouds to treetop level. A darkened area at one end and 2 vertical black stripes around its midsection was noticed.
64-20 13 Nov. 1800 EST	Shutesbury Mass. Country	IVA Light None	(1) A glowing red object that looked like a large "harvest moon" went from horizon to horizon in about a minute's time.
65-1 4 Jan. 1715 EST	Bethel Vt. Country	IVA Light Sparks	(2 + 4 + 1) The observers sighted 3 bright orange-red round objects pass before them at high speed and low altitude in rapid succession.
65-3 16 Feb. 2010 EST	Groveland Mass. Country	IVA Elliptical Sound Humming	(5 + 1) An object shaped like a dish inverted upon a dish with a top central dome. It carried a white light on its trailing edge and a blue light on its forward edge. It appeared to be 150 feet away at an altitude of 500 feet.
65-4 24 Feb. 1915 EST	Cambridge Mass. Residential	IIIB Triangular None	(1) A dull blue glowing object which rotated counterclockwise. It moved slowly in a long gradual descending flight path and then ascended at a 45-degree angle. It hovered about 20 seconds before moving out of sight.

Number Date Time	City/Town State Locale	Type Shape Effect	Number of witnesses Description
65-7 4 Apr. 1015 EST	Valley Falls N.Y. Country	IVB Elliptical None	(1) A white egg-shaped object was observed directly in front of 2 jet fighters. It rapidly ascended as if to avoid collision and moved rapidly away in the opposite direction.
65-10 14 May 1530 EDT	Bradford Mass. Country Golf course	IIIB Elliptical None	(2) A silver domed object like a cup inverted on a saucer that hovered and then shot away at terrific speed. Moments later it returned along the same path, hovered again, and then moved out of sight at high speed.
65-11A 22 May 1700 EDT	Salem Mass. Residential Harbor Power plant	IB Cylindrical None	(1) A gray object that looked like a blimp or dirigible was seen hovering low over the New England Power Plant.
65-14 16 July 0200 EDT	Sherborn Mass. Country	IIIA Oval None	(1) Airplane pilot made two observations from the ground of strange objects which carried yellow, green and red lights rotating around their circumferences. The objects moved with a distinct bouncing or up-and-down motion.
65-15 19 July 0400 EDT	Watertown Mass. Residential	IVA Elliptical None	(1) An airline stewardess observed a slow-moving silvery object from the ground. It changed color throughout the whole spectrum several times.
65-21 29 July 2110 EDT	Framingham Mass. Residential	IIIB Oval None	(2 + 1) A greenish white glowing object hovered over a house before accelerating away at a great speed. It suddenly reversed direction and returned along its previous flight path, changing to orange and then red before disappearing over horizon.

Number	*City/Town*	*Type*	*Number of witnesses*
Date	*State*	*Shape*	*Description*
Time	*Locale*	*Effect*	
65-22	N. Weymouth	IIIB	(1) The witness made two observations through 8x65 binoculars of an object shaped like a washtub which glowed orange, red and silver. It was performing irregular maneuvers. At one point, two smaller silver objects crisscrossed over it.
31 July	Mass.	Oval	
0420 EDT	Residential	None	
65-24	Lynn	IIIE	(2) Two bakers observed a slow-moving, glowing, red-tinged white globe glide noiselessly over a bakery and descend into an area of power cable towers about a mile away.
13 Aug.	Mass.	Oval	
1255 EDT	Residential	None	
	Power lines		
65-25	Salem	IB	(2) An object shaped like an inverted saucer on a saucer with a central dome was seen hovering 100 feet over a lake about 300 feet away. The dome had a central mast-like protrusion and its rim glowed red and yellow.
15 Aug.	N.H.	Elliptical	
2300 EDT	Country	Sound	
	Lake	Humming	
65-26	Haverhill	IIIB	(1) A former Navy aircraft spotter sighted a grayish silver object like two saucers facing each other hovering over the city as he approached along the crest of a high hill.
20 Aug.	Mass.	Oval	
1730 EDT	Residential	None	
65-29	Derry	IA	(3) Nine objects were seen flying at treetop level over a field just 400 feet away from observers. They flew in 3 sets of 3 and appeared to be black domes with a straight silvery fuselage and upright fin.
28 Aug.	N.H.	Other	
1840 EDT	Country	Sound	
		Buzzing	
		Sparked	

Number Date Time	City/Town State Locale	Type Shape Effect	Number of witnesses Description
65-30 3 Sept. 0130 EDT	Ipswich Mass. Country	IA Oval Physio- logical Hair rose	(1) A schoolteacher felt hairs on the back of his neck rise prior to sighting UFO hovering over golf course. It looked like an inverted saucer with whitish lights around its rim. The sight of it caused him to go off the road for a moment.
65-31 3 Sept. 0200 EDT	Exeter N.H. Country	IA Other Animals Horses **Dogs**	(1 + 1 + 3 + 1) This report involved several independent close encounters with a dark object carrying 5 bright red lights which flashed in sequence. Investigating police were approached by the object. It wobbled and descended like a falling leaf.
65-32 15 Sept. ? 2345 EDT	Sudbury Mass. Country	ID Elliptical Sound Whining Electrical Car	(1) When his car engine skipped and its lights dimmed, the witness stopped to check his engine in the midst of a rain storm. He got out of the car and saw a disc-shaped object with a glowing rim which sparked in sequence about 200 feet above him.
65-37 27 Sept. 1928 EDT	Andover Mass. Country	IVA Light None	(1) An Air Force-employed physicist sighted a sharply defined luminous ball of light, which he first thought to be a meteor. However, when it did not burn out he stopped to watch. It moved faster than a conventional aircraft.
65-39 2 Oct. 2020 EDT	Salem Mass. Residential Power plant	IA Cylindrical Sound Hissing	(1 + 1 + ?) The Coast Guard received many calls about an object which hovered over the N.E. Power Plant. It was cigar-shaped with an off-centered hump and a white light on each end. It swayed back and forth and was inclined 45 degrees.

Number Date Time	City/Town State Locale	Type Shape Effect	Number of witnesses Description
65-41 18 Oct. ? 2220 EDT	Sharon Mass. Residential	IA Elliptical None	(3 + ?) An oval object was observed which had a flashing red light on top and green, red and white lights around its circumference. It moved very slowly about 100 feet off the ground and an estimated 500 yards away from the witnesses.
65-41A 16 Nov. ? 1900 EST	Salem Mass. Residential Power plant	IIIB Light None	(4) A large red light and a smaller white light were seen hovering over the N.E. Power Plant during a rain storm. They sped off three times as fast as a jet aircraft.
66-2 21 Mar. 2200 EST	Exeter N.H. Country Power lines	IIIA Elliptical None	(5) A policeman investigated a vertically descending glowing object and came upon it moving up and down and back and forth over power lines. Other police arrived. It looked like a glowing egg with a dome, and red, white, blue and green lights flashed around its circumference.
66-2A 29 Mar. 2000 EST	Eliot Maine Country	IIIC Light Sound Pinging Animals Dogs barked	(6) The witnesses were attracted to the object by a pinging sound "like sonar" and many dogs barking. It was bright red with a halo and hovered and descended before moving out of sight.
66-2B 29 Mar. 1930 EST	Eliot Maine Country	IIIC Light None	(1) The witness observed a white glowing object moving as fast as a shooting star suddenly slow and stop before moving off again at high speed. A red light was seen on its top.

Number	City/Town	Type	Number of witnesses
Date	State	Shape	Description
Time	Locale	Effect	
66-2C	Hampton	ID	(1) Two objects with a red
29 Mar.	N.H.	Oval	light (or lights) revolving coun-
2000 EST	Country	None	terclockwise were observed. One descended to treetop level and paced the witness's car for about 1000 feet before accelerating up and out of sight.
66-3	Haverhill	IIIE	(3 + 1) A large bright light
29 Mar.	Mass.	Light	was sighted circling overhead and
2115 EST	Residential	Blue Vapor	changed colors from red to green to blue to white. It stopped and hovered before taking off at blurring speed from a standstill, leaving a rapidly dissipating blue vapor behind it.
66-3A	Confidential	IB	(1 + 2 audio) A brownish
29 Mar.	N.H.	Box	object with silvery tripod legs
1615 EST	Country	Sound	seen on the ground from a dis-
		Hum-	tance of 24 feet. It maneuvered
		ming	out from under trees before ac-
		Whining	celerating straight up and out of
		Physical	sight. Witness felt a blast of air
		Soil	from the object, which left de-
		Human	pressions in the soil.
66-4	Rehobeth	ID	(5 + 4 + 2) A dark object
30 Mar.	Mass.	Other	carrying very bright red flashing
2015 EST	Country	Sound	lights was seen by three independent groups in the area at different times. One group saw it hover over the road and then descend slowly into a wooded area.
66-9	Confidential	IIIB	(1) A police officer stopped
11 Apr.	N.H.	Elliptical	his patrol car to check on a build-
0230 EST	Country	None	ing and glanced up to see a glow-
	Residential		ing white elliptical object hovering overhead. He took a Polaroid photograph and when he was pulling film through the camera, the object moved off.

Number Date Time	City/Town State Locale	Type Shape Effect	Number of witnesses Description
66-10A 29 Mar. 1950 EST	East Eliot Maine Country Power lines	ID Elliptical None	(1) A silvery object shaped like a football was seen hovering over and almost touching power lines. It had 5-6 white glowing ports around its rim and a central dome situated on top.
66-11 12 Apr. 1945 EST	Dorchester Mass. City School Power lines	IA Oval Sound Humming Electrical Failure	(4 + 4) An oval-shaped object with a dome on top and colored lights around its perimeter was seen circling a school with an up-and-down motion. A power failure of undetermined cause occurred about a mile away from the sighting area.
66-12 12 Apr. 2010 EST	Brockton Mass. Country	IIIB Elliptical None	(1) The witness sighted an elongated elliptical object hovering off Route 24. It had a bright red-orange light affixed to each end.
66-13 16 Apr. 1955 EST	Sherborn Mass. Country	IIIB Elliptical None	(1) The witness sighted an elongated elliptical object hovering off Route 16. It had a bright red light on each end and blue lights along its perimeter.
66-14 16 Apr. 2244 EST	Weston Mass. Country Residential	IVA Cylindrical None	(2) Weston Police were called upon to investigate an object resembling a dirigible carrying bright lights.
66-16A 17 Apr. 1915 EST	Danvers Mass. Country Residential	IIIE Elliptical None	(3 + others) Several groups of people sighted an elongated oval object with rotating white lights along its perimeter. It appeared about the same size as a passenger train car. It circled slowly before entering a localized cloud.

Number Date Time	City/Town State Locale	Type Shape Effect	Number of witnesses Description
66-16B 17 Apr. 1930 EST	Peabody Mass. Country Residential	IIIA Light None	(4) A bright red glowing object was seen flying in circular and zigzag patterns. It suddenly darted away at an incredible speed faster than an aircraft.
66-16C 17 Apr. 1945 EST	Peabody Mass. City School	IIIA Oval None	(4) An oval object with a top central dome carrying red, green, white and blue flashing lights hovered over a school. It moved off rapidly with an up-and-down and back-and-forth motion before moving out of sight behind buildings.
66-16D 17 Apr. 2030 EST	Wakefield Mass. Country Lake	IB Oval Sound Humming	(4) An oval object was sighted that shot off beams of white then blue then red light. It moved rapidly with an up-and-down motion. At times a green light could be seen. It descended to about 50 feet above Lake Quannapowitt.
66-16E 17 Apr. 2100 EST	Abington Mass. City	IIIA Oval None	(3 + 3) An oval object with two bright white lights. A green light was also noticed when it was viewed through a telescope. It hovered, moved up and down and then back and forth.
66-17 18 Apr. 1915 EST	Peabody Mass Country	IIIE Oval None	(4) The witnesses sighted an elongated oval object carrying reddish green flashing lights on each end. It hovered for a moment and zipped back over the horizon faster than a jet plane. It repeated this maneuver three times. Its perimeter glowed blue.

Number Date Time	City/Town State Locale	Type Shape Effect	Number of witnesses Description
66-18 18 Apr. 2145 EST	Cohasset Mass. City	IIIA Oval None	(2) An oval object with 7 flashing red lights around its circumference was sighted. It also carried two smaller white lights. It zigzagged sharply when two searchlights swept toward it and accelerated straight up, shutting off its lights.
66-19 19 Apr. 2000 EST	Stoughton Mass. City	IVA Light Sound Humming	(1 + 1 audio) The object was described as a high-flying bright purple light which gave off a piercing humming sound.
66-20 19 Apr. 2011 EST	Hartford Conn. City	IIIB Oval None	(2) Two oval-shaped objects carrying red and green lights were seen hovering directly over the Rock Hill Veterans Home and Hospital.
66-21 19 Apr. 2200 EST	Bellingham Mass. Country Residential	IIIB Oval Sound Hissing	(2) The witnesses sighted an elongated oval craft with bright red lights on each end. It hovered before descending behind woods. Five aircraft and 1 helicopter flew over the area. Two of the aircraft circled the area.
66-22 19 Apr. 2400 EST	Peabody Mass. Country Residential	IIIA Oval None	(2 + 5) The object sighted was oval shaped and about the size of an automobile. It carried red, green and white lights. It moved with an up-and-down motion and appeared to land. Later, two witnesses approached field and saw lights rise from and leave the field.
66-23 19 Apr. 2345 EST	Quincy Mass. City	IIIA Oval None	(1 + 3) The witnesses sighted a large disc-shaped object which was accompanied by 2 smaller objects of the same shape. They flashed red and white lights, hovered and swung back and forth like a pendulum.

Number Date Time	City/Town State Locale	Type Shape Effect	Number of witnesses Description
66-24 19 Apr. 0015 EST	Sharon Mass. Country Residential	IIIE Oval None	(7 + 2 + 1) The police arrived in response to a report of a UFO. They described the object as being oval shaped with a glowing rim which looked like lighted windows. The object carried a steady red light on each end and was about the size of a car.
66-26A 22 Apr. 2100 EST	Beverly Mass. City School	IA Oval Sound Humming	(10) A total of 3 oval objects were sighted which flashed blue, green, red and white lights. One object hovered over a school and approached 3 observers at treetop level. Investigating police described this object as looking like a plate with colored lights.
66-26B 22 Apr. 2130 EST	Wenham Mass. Country School	IA Oval None	(3 + 1) Gordon College students and ground maintenance man saw an orange, roughly circular object approach within 600 feet of them at an apparent altitude of 100 feet. It executed a right-angle turn and moved off out of sight behind trees.
66-28 23 Apr. 2040 EDT	Randolph Mass. Country Lake	IB Elliptical None	(12) Police and others sighted an elongated egg-shaped object with white lights around its perimeter and colored flashing lights near its bottom.
66-29 24 Apr. 0500 EDT	Dorchester Mass. City Power lines	IA Oval Sound Humming Electrical Animal Physical	(5) An oval, domed object the size of a car encircled with red lights hit and shook a building. A concurrent power failure was traced to a burned cable near the object's flight path. Some above-normal radiation was noted. It was raining.

Number Date Time	City/Town State Locale	Type Shape Effect	Number of witnesses Description
66-30 1 May 2200 EDT	Watertown Mass. City Arsenal	IVA Oval None	(4) Witnesses sighted a low-flying oval object with bright rotating red, green and white lights pass over the Watertown Arsenal.
66-33 11 June 0345 EDT	Westport Mass. Highway	ID Oval None	(1) An object shaped like two plates placed one on top of the other buzzed an automobile and hovered ahead over the road. It had a top central dome and white, yellow, blue and green lights flashed around its circumference.
66-36 20 July 2230 EDT	Jaffrey N.H. Country	IVA Elliptical None	(3) An elongated object carrying parallel points of horizontal lights passed over the Mt. Monadnock Bible Conference Grounds. The lights changed from white to red to orange to yellow to green and back to white.
66-38 10 Aug. 0030 EDT	Moultonboro N.H. Country Inside a cabin	IA Light None	(1) A red-orange globe of light about 3 feet in diameter with a central black design skirted about the walls and ceiling. It gave off no noise, smell or heat. Although the weather was clear, it may have been ball lightning.
66-42 17 Sept. 0445 EDT	IPSWICH Mass. Beach	IIB Cylindrical None	(2) Witnesses sighted an elongated yellowish glowing cigar-shaped object hovering in a vertical position. It generated and absorbed smaller glowing objects which moved with an up-and-down skipping motion.
66-45 10 Oct. 2130 EDT	Medford Mass. Route 93	IVA Other None	(2) A former Air Force pilot and his wife sighted slow-moving lights like mirrors on a carousel with dark gaps between them. No navigation lights were seen. Witnesses sighted object from an automobile.

Number Date Time	City/Town State Locale	Type Shape Effect	Number of witnesses Description
66-45A 17 Oct. 2105 EDT	Chelmsford Mass. Country	IVA Other None	(2) The witnesses observed two extremely bright red lights with a string of dim bluish white lights in between them moving as if they were attached to an unseen object. The lights passed directly overhead.
66-46 28 Oct. 0100 EST	Lawrence Mass. City Water tower	IIB Cylindrical Telephones?	(1 + 1 + 3) A newspaper night editor responded to telephone reports of a UFO and sighted a white glowing cigar-shaped object hovering in a 45-degree position over water towers. A closer witness noticed bright white lights along its side.
66-48 15 Nov. 0715 EST	Beverly Mass. Country	IIB Cylindrical None	(2) Two hunters located in a boat off the coast observed 2 cigar-shaped objects hovering in a horizontal position over the Beverly Farms area.
66-49A 22 Nov. 1825 EST	Ocean N.H. Coast 10 Miles	ID Other Radar	(2) Two Coast Guard pilots on a training flight saw a white light like a rocket appear a mile away. It disappeared and then rose vertically in front of them, missing the aircraft by a hundred feet. Pease AFB confirmed the object on radar.
66-51 1 Dec. 1835 EST	Middleboro Mass. Route 25	ID Oval None	(1) An apparently oval object carrying 2 large bright red pulsating lights dived in front of the witness's car and stopped to hover over woods just off the road. A curved shape was seen behind the lights.

Number Date Time	City/Town State Locale	Type Shape Effect	Number of witnesses Description
66-52 13 Dec. 0100 EST	Rowley Mass. Country	IVA Oval None	(2) An orange-red glowing oval object with a halo of light around its perimeter descended and approached the witnesses before disappearing behind a road embankment, which obstructed their view.
66-53 22 Dec. 0045 EST	Cuttingsville Vermont Country	IIIA Light Sound Humming Electrical	(1 + 2 audible) The witness saw a frosty white ellipsoidal glow with a central bright spot. It hovered and then swung back and forth like a pendulum. Street lights went off and on three times during the sighting.
67-2 15 Jan. ? 0300 EST	Boxford Mass. Country Pond	IIIE Oval None	(1) A bright red oval object looking like an upside down saucer with a white glowing rim approached and circled the witness's home before moving away and disappearing from view.
67-4 18 Jan. 0015 EST	Williamstown Mass. Country Power lines	ID Oval Electrical	(4) The witnesses saw a flash in the sky just preceding area power failure. Soon after they sighted a lighted, domed object near the ground on the opposite bank of the Green River. When they drove away to find help, a red glowing object buzzed them.
67-5 20 Jan. 1845 EST	Methuen Mass. Country	ID Other Electrical Car engine Car lights Car radio	(3 + 3) A dark object with multicolored lights approached 3 witnesses in their automobile along a country road. After the object streaked off, 3 others in another car apparently observed it.

Number Date Time	City/Town State Locale	Type Shape Effect	Number of witnesses Description
67-7 10 Feb. 1745 EST	Woodstock Conn. Country	IIIB Other Sound Roaring Electrical Television	(4 + 3) A triangular-shaped object with its blunt end forward hovered over a farm. A white light was attached to each apex. It was silent when hovering but moved off with a rumbling or roaring sound.
67-8 12 Feb. 1800 EST	Kensington Conn. Route 15	IIIB Light None	(2 + ?) A bright white glowing object with a red light on each side hovered just off the road. The 2 known witnesses stopped to observe it with a number of other curious motorists.
67-9 16 Feb. 2215 EST	Amherst Mass. Country	IIIC Light Sound Swishing	(2 + 2 + 1) A glowing object like a bright white light bulb was seen hovering in the sky. It ejected a small red object and moved back and forth before suddenly accelerating out of sight over the horizon. Two policemen observed it.
67-11 17 Feb. 1855 EST	Andover Mass. Country Rts. 93/495	ID Other None	(1 + 2 + ?) A salesman for Flying Tiger Airlines saw cars ahead of him slow and stop to watch a silent object of unknown shape hovering low over the road. He passed directly under it and saw a rectangular pattern of floodlights on its underside.

67-12
17 Feb.
0105 EST
	Dorchester
	Mass.
	City
	Rest home
		IA
		Oval
		Sound
		  Whirring
		  Beeping
			(1 + 2 audible) An object was sighted which looked like a "cymbal" with a dome on top. It had 4-5 purplish lights around its perimeter. It hovered at treetop level over an elderly people's project before moving away and out of sight.

Appendix I **345**

Number Date Time	City/Town State Locale	Type Shape Effect	Number of witnesses Description
67-13 26 Feb. 0200 EST	Marlboro Mass. Residential	IIIE Oval Sound Roaring	(2) A former teacher and her husband were awakened by an intermittent sound like a car without a muffler. Upon investigation, they sighted a white glowing egg-shaped object with a red light on each side. It swung back and forth.
67-15 1 Mar. 1925 EST	Sharon Mass. Country	IIIE Oval None	(1 + 1) A noiseless white glowing oval which moved back and forth in the area of the witnesses' home. It left a white glowing fuzzy trail in its wake.
67-17 7 Mar. 2000 EST	Amherst Mass. Residential	VA Light None	(1) A bright white, slow-moving light source, which appeared to be twice the size and brightness of Venus. Binoculars did not reveal any structural details or identification lights. It changed to orange as it moved away.
67-18 8 Mar. 0105 EST	Leominster Mass. City Cemetery	IA Oval Sound Humming Electrical Car/Radio Paralysis	(2) A bluish white glowing object was seen hovering with a rocking motion over a cemetery. Its rim glowed as bright as an acetylene torch. A localized patch of fog was around it. The witness's car engine, lights and radio failed. Paralysis occurred.
67-19 9 Mar. 2025 EST	Andover Mass. Country	IIIB Other None	(2) The witness sighted a triangular cluster of 2 red and 1 white (at the apex) steady bright lights hovering about 1000 feet above the country club grounds.

Number *Date* *Time*	*City/Town* *State* *Locale*	*Type* *Shape* *Effect*	*Number of witnesses* *Description*
67-20 10 Mar. 0020 EST	Phillipston Mass. Country	IVA Oval None	(1) The object sighted looked like a half ball with its flat side down and glowed a bright orange-red all over. It was about ten times the apparent diameter of the moon, which was visible at the time of the sighting.
67-24 18 Mar. 1950 EST	Stow Mass. Country Power lines	IIIA Oval None	(3) The object was described as being oval with a dome and surrounded by a ring of vapor. It glowed violet when it was stationary but turned to a reddish orange when it moved away with a dancing motion.
67-25 24 Mar. 2100 EST	Georgetown Mass. Country Pond	IB Elliptical None	(3) The witnesses described the object as being shaped like a turtle-shell and flashing red and white lights. It hovered over Rock Pond before moving off faster than a jet aircraft.
67-28 11 Apr. 1850 EST	Royalston Mass. Country	IIIB Other None	(2) A mass of very bright lights was seen descending and hovering before moving slowly out of sight on an upward course. The lights were brighter than the moon, which was visible during the sighting.
67-29 11 Apr. 1845 EST	Orange Mass. Country Pond	IB Elliptical None	(3) A bright glowing object shaped like a squashed egg was seen hovering 100 feet over Tully Pond momentarily before moving off at great speed. A rotating red light was seen on the bottom of the object.

Number	City/Town	Type	Number of witnesses
Date	*State*	*Shape*	*Description*
Time	*Locale*	*Effect*	

67-30	Tully	IIIB	(4) A cream-colored object
19 Apr.	Mass.	Elliptical	about the size of a large car which
1930 EST	Country	Electrical	had a central dome. It flashed
	Near pond	Television	bright white lights which were replaced by red lights. It hovered, performed sharp turns and moved off slowly.

67-31	Orange	IIIB	(4) An object was sighted
20 Apr.	Mass.	Other	which carried 8 red blinking lights
1915 EST	Country	None	and two white lights. It hovered
	Near pond		and then moved away slowly out of sight.

67-32	Georgetown	IIIB	(6) Two dark objects carried
20 Apr.	Mass.	Other	2 brilliant flashing red lights and
2030 EST	Country	None	2 dimmer white lights as they pa-
	Pond		trolled in a sentry pattern over Rock Pond. They stopped and reversed direction several times.

67-33	Bolten	IIIB	(3) The witnesses sighted a
20 Apr.	Mass.	Oval	hovering mushroom-shaped object
2140 EST	Country	Sound	with a frosted white light on top
		Hum-	and a red light on the bottom.
		ming	Turquoise lights were located fore
		Vapor	and aft and 8 yellow glowing ports were located around its perimeter.

67-34	Georgetown	IIIE	(3) The witnesses sighted 2
21 Apr.	Mass.	Other	groups of 3 red and 1 white lights
1945 EST	Country	None	flashing in sequence. The object
	Pond		carried a large white light which appeared like rectangular windows through binoculars. The object moved into the overcast when several planes converged on the area.

Number Date Time	City/Town State Locale	Type Shape Effect	Number of witnesses Description
67-35 21 Apr. 2000 EST	Phillipston Mass. Country Pond	IVB Other None	(3 + 1) An unseen object carrying 2-3 bright red lights hovered and descended behind trees in the vicinity of Duck Pond. A conventional aircraft seemed to have been chasing the object.
67-35B Spring 67 0200 EST	Haverhill Mass. Country Pond River Airport	IB Oval Sound Whirring Smell Electrical Yard light	(1 + audible) An airport owner awoke to investigate a whirring sound and saw an object looking like two silver saucers placed rim-to-rim with a transparent dome. Two moving figures were seen inside the dome and ports glowed on its perimeter.
67-36 23 Apr. 2045 EDT	Orange Mass. Country Church	IIIB Other None	(1) The witness saw a circle of about 9 white lights that enclosed 2 red lights hovering about 100 yards from a church.
67-37 27 Apr. 2215 EDT	Salem/ Kingston N.H. Country	IA Oval Sound Beeping	(1 + 1 + 1) Three separate persons sighted an oval object with red lights around its perimeter and a central dome on top. Two protrusions were noticed on its underside. It hovered and shot away at high speed.
67-40 11 May 0205 EDT	Wareham Mass. Country	IIIA Oval None	(4) The witnesses observed 2 objects shaped like inverted dishes with red and white lights rotating around a rim. They hovered and descended behind trees in a cranberry bog and moved up and down like "yo-yos". Police spotlights caused them to zoom away.
67-41 29 May 0240 EDT	Saugus Mass. City	IA Oval None	(1) The observed object was shaped like a glowing red scallop with white flashing lights along its surface. It moved slowly with a rocking motion before darting upward and out of sight at high speed.

Number	City/Town	Type	Number of witnesses
Date	State	Shape	Description
Time	Locale	Effect	
67-42	Trenton	IB	(2) Two persons sighted a sil-
24 June	Maine	Oval	ver-gray, hat-shaped object hov-
1000 EDT	Country	Vapor	ering about 500 feet from the
	Ocean		shoreline. It emitted vapor at its
			base. The object ascended into a
			fog bank and descended again at
			a greater distance before moving
			away.
67-44A	Rowley	IVA	(1 + 4 audible) An orange
26 July	Mass.	Light	glowing object was seen moving
2315 EDT	Residential	Sound	over a set of power lines.
	Power lines	Whining	
67-44B	Newton	IIIE	(3) The witnesses sighted an
27 July	N.H.	Oval	elongated oval object carrying a
0100 EDT	Country	Signals	steady bright white light fore and
			aft. It also displayed a central red
			light and a string of smaller white
			lights flashing in sequence along
			its side. It flashed exact responses
			to sequenced flashlight signals and
			evaded a jet aircraft.
67-48	Newton	IIIE	(4) A circular-shaped object
8 Sept.	N.H.	Oval	with a central dome and red light
2230 EDT	Country	Signals?	circled the area. It also displayed
			3 pinkish lights along its rim and
			2 bright white lights on its lead-
			ing edge. It seemed to respond to
			flashlight signals after 20-second
			delays.
67-54	Amherst	IVA	(1) A geology professor and
23 Sept.	Mass.	Cylindrical	NICAP investigator sighted 2 sil-
1337 EDT	Country	None	ver cylinders without wings, rud-
			ders or stabilizers moving against
			a bright blue sky. They passed first
			in front of and then disappeared
			behind low cumulus clouds.

Number Date Time	City/Town State Locale	Type Shape Effect	Number of witnesses Description
67-55 2 Oct. 2030 EDT	Ipswich Mass. Country	IA Oval Animal Dogs barked	(4 + 1 + 1) The witnesses sighted an oval-shaped domed object which glowed yellow around its perimeter. It carried a red, greenish blue and a bright white light. At times it glowed red all over. It hovered, spun and moved up and down.
67-57 3 Oct. 2040 EDT	Cambridge Mass. Route 2 Pond	IIIB Oval None	(2) A glowing object shaped like the planet Saturn with a fuzzy amber center. White lights sparkled around its circumference. (It was not a barium cloud experiment, which they had seen earlier at 1918 EDT.)
67-61 26 Oct. 2130 EDT	Newton N.H. Country	IIIE Other Sound Hum- ming Animal Dogs barked	(4) An unseen object carrying two horizontal rows of 5-6 red lights and a green and white light. It circled and hovered momentarily and then reversed direction without turning. Dogs barked and whined in the area.
67-66B 28 Nov. 1715 EST	Danvers Mass. Residential	IIIB Light None	(2) A yellow glowing ball of light was sighted by a NICAP investigator. It alternately hovered, descended and hovered before moving out of sight.
67-66C 28 Nov. 1915 EST	Rockport Mass. Country	IVA Other None	(3) A lighted but unseen object passed over witnesses without a sound. It had one row of 8-10 revolving or blinking white lights and a parallel upper row of yellowish lights. The lights seemed to be attached to a curved surface.
68-2 17 Jan. 1830 EST	Ipswich Mass. Residential	IA Oval None	(1) The witness sighted an oval or fat cigar-shaped object with a horizontal row of many red and green flashing lights and an upper parallel row of 5 steady white lights. It descended and ascended rapidly.

Number Date Time	City/Town State Locale	Type Shape Effect	Number of witnesses Description
68-3 17 Jan. 2130 EST	Ipswich Mass. Country	ID Oval None	(3) A boomerang or oval-shaped object carrying 5 horizontal white lights approached a car and stopped in midair. It then moved slowly in front of the car before accelerating at great speed over the horizon.
68-8 11 Feb. 1900 EST	Johnston R.I. Country Pond	IB Oval None	(1) The witness reported seeing an oval domed object pass over his automobile at the edge of Hawkins Pond. It had pulsating white or pinkish lights around a rim which looked like a flashing theater marquee.
68-10A 10 Mar. 2100 EST	Pawtucket R.I. Residential Power station	IIIA Oval None	(1) A dark oval object with a small searchlight in front wobbled and moved with a motion like a "boat riding over the waves." It passed a power substation and followed power lines until it was out of sight.
68-11A Spring 68 1000 EST	Beverly Mass. Residential School	IIIB Oval None	(1 + 10) The witness was playing in the yard of the Centerville School when the sky got dark and a beige-colored oval object with pulsating yellow and green lights descended and hovered several minutes before moving away.
68-15 10 Apr. 2100 EST	Ipswich Mass. Country	IIIA Light None	(5 + 2 + 1) The first 2 groups sighted 3 bright white lights in a triangular formation swinging like a pendulum. The lead object suddenly shot away and others changed colors from red to blue to green to white. Nearby, 1 witness reported a glowing ring shining a light on houses.

Number *Date* *Time*	*City/Town* *State* *Locale*	*Type* *Shape* *Effect*	*Number of witnesses* *Description*
68-18 12 Apr. 2215 EST	Hamilton Mass. Country	VA Other None	(1) A student pilot was on Sagamore Hill (location of 2 radio telescopes) to watch a lunar eclipse. He sighted a cluster of bright lights which blinked from red to orange to bright blue. After hovering, they shot upwards out of sight.
68-21 14 Apr. 2100 EST	Beverly Mass. City Power plant	IIIB Other None	(3 + 2) Police investigated 2 phone calls about a string of white lights over the ocean and near the New England Power Plant. They saw these lights pulsating back and forth in sequence and a spotlight shoot down on the water before they streaked away.
68-23 17 Apr. 1945 EST	Hamilton Mass. Country Route 1-A	ID Oval None	(1) A dull, silver-gray, domed object hovered just off the road. It carried steady white and red lights. The Air Force Cambridge Laboratory Radio Telescope installation at Sagamore Hill is located nearby.
68-24 17 Apr. 2200 EST	Waltham Mass. City	IVC Other None	(2) A planetarium lecturer and his wife sighted what appeared to be a jet aircraft following a vee formation of 6 faint diffuse whitish lights arranged in 3 pairs. It appeared as if each pair was connected by a reddish tube of light.
68-25 19 Apr. 2100 EST	Ipswich Mass. Country	IIIC Elliptical None	(2) A teacher and her young daughter saw an elliptical mass of white light break into 2 white glowing masses, which ejected first one and then another smaller red light, which leveled out and moved away.

Number Date Time	City/Town State Locale	Type Shape Effect	Number of witnesses Description
68-26 19 Apr. 0230 EST	Malden Mass. City	IA Other Sound Pinging	(1) The witness was awakened by a sound like 2 steel knives being struck together. She glanced outside and saw a red glowing object with a point on top flying with a fluttering motion toward and then over a cemetery.
68-27 30 Apr. 0150 EDT	Ipswich Mass. Country	IIIA Oval None	(1) A round grayish object reflecting a flashing red light on its underside hovered low over trees. It dropped behind trees and then ascended straight up, hovered, and streaked away at a great speed.
68-32 28 May 2215 EDT	Roxbury Mass. City	IIIE Oval Sound Roaring Physiological Felt	(2) Communities in the area reported buzzing sounds. The witnesses saw 3 objects suddenly descend with an intermittent roar. The closest object was oval with a blue glowing square on its underside. The sound vibrated one witness's eardrums and stomach.
68-34 21 June 2100 EDT	Revere Mass. Residential	IA Light Animals Cat ran Dog howled Vapor	(3) An orange ball of fire slowly descended towards a maple tree and hovered. It wobbled and gave off a white trail of vapor before accelerating away and breaking up into many sparklike objects. (This may have been ball lightning.)
68-36 5 July 2230 EDT	N. Adams Mass. Country	IVB Light Vapor Reddish	(2) A green light larger than a star was seen moving slowly through the sky. Through binoculars it looked like a green ball with a reddish trail. When an aircraft approached it, the object "blinked out" and then reappeared after the plane went.

Number Date Time	City/Town State Locale	Type Shape Effect	Number of witnesses Description
68-41 29 July 0130 EDT	Barnstable Mass. Country Airport	IA Light Sound Humming	(2) The witnesses saw a snow-white glowing object seem to land near a deserted grass airport. When they passed the area, a sound like a large swarm of locusts was heard emanating from the field. The airfield had closed at sunset.
68-44 12 Aug. 2015 EDT	Gloucester Mass. Residential	IVA Oval None	(1) A whitish gold globe surrounded by a dark ring that looked like the planet Saturn overflew the witness's area.
68-48 16 Aug. 2200 EDT	Cambridge Mass. City	IA Light None	(1 + 1) A silent dazzling blood-red globe of light was seen hovering and pulsating at treetop level. It was the apparent size of a full moon.
68-54 23 Sept. 0230 EDT	Whitefield Maine Country River	IIIB Oval None	(1) A minister on vacation at a farm in the country awoke to see 2 pencil-shaped rays of light coming through the window. He looked out and saw an orange-red object shaped like "two saucers placed with their concave sections together" hovering in the sky.
68-55 29 Sept. 2011 EDT	Needham Mass. Residential	IIIB Other None	(1) An engineer who was familiar with astronomical phenomena and artificial satellites sighted a bright blue light source moving across the sky at 1-degree per second. It was about magnitude 2 brightness and pulsated 2 times per second.
68-57 19 Oct. 0130 EDT	W. Quincy Mass. Residential	IIA Cigar None	(1) A glowing white object was seen in the sky, which changed from an oval shape to that of a cigar standing on end. At times a smaller blue light appeared under it. It blinked out when approached by a conventional aircraft.

Number	City/Town	Type	Number of witnesses
Date	State	Shape	Description
Time	Locale	Effect	
68-62 25 Nov. 2230 EST	Dennis Mass. Ocean	IIA Cigar None	(3 + 2 + 2) A yellowish white glowing object looking like a cigar standing on end was seen hovering about one-quarter of a mile off shore and seemingly 200 feet above the water. An investigating policeman confirmed the sighting.
69-4 20 Jan. 2030 EST	Weymouth Mass. Country Abandoned ammunition depot	IA Oval None	(2) An object was sighted which looked like a white dish inverted upon a dish with a dark ring around its perimeter. It had a dome on top and 1 red and 2 amber lights on its leading edge. It moved up and down a few times before moving out of sight.
69-6 22 Jan. 2150 EST	Lexington Mass. Country Lake	IIIA Oval Sound Whirring	(2) An oval dark object with a central light on top and bottom and 4 white lights around its edge. It moved at times with a side-to-side swaying motion.
69-9 10 Feb. 2030 EST	Dartmouth Mass. Country	IA Light Physical Snow	(1) A truck driver left his vehicle to get a closer look at a ball of fire hovering low over snow-covered trees. When he approached within 200 feet of it with a flashlight, it accelerated away at a 45-degree angle, causing snow on the treetops to swirl.
69-17A 27 Apr. 1300 EDT	Unknown Conn. Airborne 25,000 feet	IVA Oval None	(1) Airline passenger saw a shiny, disc-shaped object, which was joined by 2 others that slowed to match its speed. They moved along with a rapid, rocking motion before accelerating upwards at an angle with a speed too fast for the eye to follow.

Number Date Time	City/Town State Locale	Type Shape Effect	Number of witnesses Description
69-18A 4 July 0700 EDT	Ossipee N.H. Country Pond	IB Oval Sound Hum- ming Physical? Water	(1 + 1 + ?) The prime witness was fishing in a boat and heard a splash behind him. As he swung around to investigate he looked up to see a silver object about 30 feet in diameter about 300 feet above him which rose to about 3000 feet and hovered.
69-27 14 Oct. 2040 EDT	Shirley Mass. Country	IVA Other Vapor	(1) The witness sighted a half circle of bright "sparks" which flashed at random on the leading edge of a dark object which passed about 3000 feet directly overhead. An infrequent spark and glowing vapor trail was seen to emanate from the rear of the object.
70-7 21 July 0745 EDT	Lynn Mass. City	IIIB Oval None	(1) An object described as appearing like a silver bowl inverted upon another silver bowl was sighted hovering in the sky. It was tipped slightly at an angle.
70-8 26 June 0100 EDT	Sharon Mass. Residential	IVA Oval None	(1) The witness sighted an oval object with rotating balls of white light around its perimeter. A bright yellow aura surrounded it. It descended slowly behind trees during a rain storm.
70-10 20 Sept. 1830 EDT	Beverly Mass. Country Golf course	IVA Oval None	(4) A bright red-orange ball with the apparent size of the full moon descended slowly behind trees near a golf course. It appeared to have spikes or rays sticking out at all angles which also glowed a red-orange color.

Number	City/Town	Type	Number of witnesses
Date	State	Shape	Description
Time	Locale	Effect	
70-12	Braintree	IVC	(1) The witness was observing a conjunction of planets when she sighted a vee formation of about 10 silver-gray circular objects. They appeared twice over the area within 5 minutes of each other.
25 Dec.	Mass.	Oval	
0400 EST	City	None	
71-1	Dennis	IB	(1 + 1 + 2 saw hole) A metallic-appearing cylindrical object was seen descending over a frozen lake. Its leading edge tipped forward and a trail of flame issued from its rear end. Investigating witnesses found elongated hole in ice and steam rising from agitated water.
7 Jan.	Mass.	Cylindrical	
0710 EST	Residential	Vapor	
	Lake	Flame	
		Physical	
		Ice	
71-8	Waltham	IIIB	(1) The witness observed a white glowing object which looked like a jellyfish or a mushroom. It hovered and then dimmed leaving just blinking white lights before it suddenly streaked away and out of sight in seconds.
27 Mar.	Mass.	Oval	
2220 EST	Industrial	None	
	Route 2		
71-10	Oxford	IB	(4) Some fishermen were approached twice at close range by a dark, domed oval object with a lighted windowlike rectangle. It flipped up on edge to reveal 8 glowing ports around its perimeter. It moved with an up-and-down and pendulum motion.
29 May	Mass.	Oval	
0400 EDT	Country	None	
	Pond		
71-11	Newmarket	IA	(2) The witnesses sighted a grayish white upright egg-shaped object with dark ports around its perimeter. It hovered a few feet above the ground in plain view in front of trees before ascending straight up and out of sight.
31 May	N.H.	Oval	
1310 EDT	Country	None	
	Field		
	Swamp		
	RR tracks		

Number	*City/Town*	*Type*	*Number of witnesses*
Date	*State*	*Shape*	*Description*
Time	*Locale*	*Effect*	
71-18	Cambridge	IIIB	(1) A silvery thin object
17 Nov.	Mass.	Rectangular	shaped like a rectangle was seen
1440 EST	City	None	rotating clockwise as it hovered over city. It ascended and disappeared into cloud cover.
72-2	E. Kingston	IA	(5) The witnesses came upon
5 Jan.	N.H.	Oval	the object while snowmobiling
2245 EST	Country	None	through a field which was inter-
	Swamp		sected by RR tracks. It glowed
	RR tracks		with a yellowish light and hovered about 10 feet above the tracks at a distance of 300 feet. It rose vertically and descended behind trees.
72-4	Scituate	IVA	(1) A policeman noticed a
20 Apr.	Mass.	Oval	light reflection moving along the
0245 EST	Industrial	Animals	ground and glanced up to see a
		Dogs	perfectly round white-glowing disc
		barked	move over him and descend into a marshy area behind trees.
72-5	Canterbury	IA	(3 + 2 + 1 + 2 audible) A
13 May	N.H.	Other	decahedron or top-shaped object
2150 EDT	Country	Sound	issuing a 10-foot colored vertical
	Power lines	Buzzing	exhaust and carrying a yellowish
		Animal	and a red-orange light descended
		Cat ran	with a falling-leaf motion to tree-top level and disappeared behind trees in a large swamp.
72-12	Beverly	IA	(1 + ?) The witness heard a
31 Aug.	Mass.	Oval	loud humming sound while cross-
1000 EDT	Highway	Sound	ing Route 128 on a bridge. He
	Woods	Hum-	glanced up and saw an oval ob-
		ming	ject with a central dome move over the highway with an up-and-down motion. Cars slowed and pulled over. It carried a reddish light.

Number *Date* *Time*	*City/Town* *State* *Locale*	*Type* *Shape* *Effect*	*Number of witnesses* *Description*
72-16 4 Dec. 0015 EST	Waltham Mass. City	IIIA Oval Sound Hum- ming	(2) A pilot and friend saw a starlike object which hovered and made rapid vee-shaped descents and ascents. It approached and passed over witnesses, who described it as pancake-shaped, covered with lights and having a central dome on its topside.

APPENDIX II
A UFO DETECTOR

(DESIGNED BY JOHN P. OSWALD)

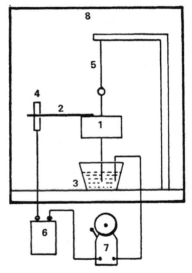

Simplified diagram of Oswald detector shows magnet structure and alarm system. Components include: (1) magnet, (2) needle, (3) reservoir of mercury, (4) loop, (5) suspension string, (6) battery, (7) bell, (8) glass enclosure. When magnetic fluctuations cause needle to touch loop, circuit is closed and alarm rings. To work properly, needle must be aligned with north and protected from outside disturbances.

CREDIT: NICAP

INDEX

361

CPSIA information can be obtained
at www.ICGtesting.com
Printed in the USA
LVOW11s0302120117
520665LV00001B/30/P